GREEN RUSH

Green Rush

The Rise of Medical Marijuana in the United States

Daniel J. Mallinson and A. Lee Hannah

NEW YORK UNIVERSITY PRESS
New York

NEW YORK UNIVERSITY PRESS
New York
www.nyupress.org

© 2024 by New York University
All rights reserved

Please contact the Library of Congress for Cataloging-in-Publication data.

ISBN: 9781479827923 (hardback)
ISBN: 9781479827930 (paperback)
ISBN: 9781479827954 (library ebook)
ISBN: 9781479827947 (consumer ebook)

This book is printed on acid-free paper, and its binding materials are chosen for strength and durability. We strive to use environmentally responsible suppliers and materials to the greatest extent possible in publishing our books.

Manufactured in the United States of America

10 9 8 7 6 5 4 3 2 1

Also available as an ebook

Dan dedicates this book to Rebecca for her constant support and love in this crazy life.

Lee dedicates this book to his love, Jillian, who has been by his side since his first days in Dayton and who has made every experience richer and warmer.

CONTENTS

Introduction: The States' Rush   1

1. Selling Pot: The Changing Narrative around Marijuana   17

2. Defiant Innovation: States, Federalism, and the Fight for Legalization   53

3. From the Statehouse to the Dispensary: Policy Design and Implementation   83

4. When Policy Creates Politics: States Learn as They Go   117

5. Laboratories in Limbo: The Future of Marijuana Policy   147

Acknowledgments   167

Appendix A: Full Models   171

Appendix B: Additional Information   175

Notes   177

Index   223

About the Authors   229

Introduction

The States' Rush

In 1996, voters in California and Arizona were considering a ballot initiative to legalize the use of marijuana for medical purposes.[1] The federal government's position was clear. President Bill Clinton's drug control policy director, Barry McCaffrey, stated, "This is not medicine, this is a Cheech and Chong show."[2] The Clinton administration declared medical marijuana a cynical hoax and former presidents Gerald Ford, Jimmy Carter, and George H. W. Bush cosigned a letter calling marijuana a threat to the public health of all Americans.[3] Republican presidential nominee Bob Dole went a step further, stating that "the marijuana leaf and the heroin needle have become the symbols of fashionable rebellion."[4] Yet these federal overtures did not stop Arizona and California voters from approving medical cannabis programs. The Arizona legislature would soon repeal the initiative passed by voters, and it would take fourteen more years for Arizona to adopt a true medical cannabis program. Meanwhile, California became the first adopter of a medical marijuana law—although implementation of the law was uneven and federal threats and raids kept patients and providers on the defensive.[5] Even though the federal government stood against medical marijuana, voters in Alaska, Oregon, and Washington approved their own measures two years later, and over the next twenty-five years, medical marijuana slowly spread throughout the country.

By 2023, the politics of marijuana have changed markedly. Thirty-eight states and the District of Columbia have adopted comprehensive medical marijuana programs, and another twenty-four states and D.C. have approved and implemented recreational or adult-use marijuana policies. While blue states such as California, Oregon, and Washington led the charge, conservative states like Arkansas, Oklahoma, and Missouri have now joined them to pass medical marijuana. Republicans remain more divided on cannabis than Democrats. Emblematic of both the shift and remaining divide, Republican President Donald Trump poked fun of his hardline prohibitionist Attorney General Jeff Sessions in 2018 by saying "This sounds like something my grandpa said in the 1950s."[6]

Myriad explanations have been offered for this sea change in policy: changing public opinion, shifting views of legislators, reassessments of the devastating drug war, states' desperate attempts to find new revenue streams, and so on.[7] But what has yet to be explored is the process that took medical cannabis from pariah to prevailing policy in a relatively short twenty-five years. Many have written about the federal government's fluctuating positions over the decades.[8] We argue, however, that it is impossible to understand the emergence and spread of cannabis liberalization in the United States without focusing substantial attention on the so-called laboratories of democracy: the states.

The term "laboratories of democracy" was coined by Supreme Court Associate Justice Louis Brandeis in a 1932 dissenting opinion. *New State Ice Co. v. Liebmann* was a rather forgettable case about the Corporation Commission of Oklahoma's process of licensing the sale of ice. The majority on the court struck down a 1925 Oklahoma law that made the manufacture, sale, and distribution of ice a public business. Brandeis, in his dissenting opinion, argued that the court was overstepping by limiting Oklahoma's ability to develop its own policies and solutions related to ice (which in turn significantly affects the state's food supply). Brandeis wrote:

> To stay experimentation in things social and economic is a grave responsibility. Denial of the right to experiment may be fraught with serious consequences to the Nation. It is one of the happy incidents of the federal system that a single courageous State may, if its citizens choose, serve as a laboratory; and try novel social and economic experiments without risk to the rest of the county.[9]

This turn of phrase has become a favorite among scholars of state politics, as well as anyone who finds themselves in the position of defending a state law. But rarely is the term more apt than the story of marijuana policy.

We have coined medical marijuana policy as a "defiant innovation."[10] Whereas the states are commonly viewed through Brandeis's lens of laboratories of policy experimentation, it is far less common that these innovations disregard national law. Of course, there is a constant tug of war between the states and the federal government over who has authority to do what.[11] However, most of the state policy innovations studied by political scientists and policy scholars occur under either ambivalence or encouragement by the federal government. Marijuana is different. States are innovating, as Brandeis and the large body of research on policy innovation and diffusion would recognize, but in doing so they are openly flouting federal marijuana prohibition. We argue in this book that such defiance of federal law did not originate with state governments themselves but through the specific institutional arrangement of the direct initiative in early-adopter states. We also argue that defiance is not a fixed concept. Most of the states that were early adopters of medical marijuana did so through ballot initiatives driven by issue advocates. Meanwhile, the federal government's enforcement of marijuana prohibition shifted, even though its official legal stance stayed the same. Combined, legitimizing actions at the federal level—fickle forbearance of prohibition enforcement and encouragement of "well regulated" state marijuana programs—and policy innovation among the states have propelled this defiant innovation forward. As both of these forces occurred and state-legal marijuana became the dominant policy regime, the magnitude of defiance weakened.

We can think of the federal government as having three stances toward emerging policy innovations: agreement with states on a policy, indifference toward the policy, or opposition to the policy. When the federal government is supportive of a policy and wants states to comply, it often uses incentives or sanctions to encourage states to adopt a policy. For example, when President Barack Obama signed into law the Affordable Care Act, the administration pushed hard to make Medicaid expansion an offer that states could not refuse. In another example, President Ronald Reagan's administration threatened to withhold lucrative federal highway funds if states did not raise the legal drinking age to twenty-one.[12]

For many policies, the federal position is indifferent to what the states do. For example, some issues are highly regionalized (e.g., state agreements about usage of the Great Lakes or the Colorado River). When the federal government is neutral, internal characteristics of the state and the makeup of the state government often drive change and innovation, as do the experiences of other states.

Finally, the federal government and states can be in conflict over specific policies. Typically, the most that the states will do is slow-walk policies, like the ongoing implementation of the REAL ID Act, or sue the federal government as an act of resistance, as occurred when states tried to block both President Donald Trump's travel ban and President Joseph Biden's vaccine mandate. But marijuana policy has been unique. Not only are states ignoring federal laws and guidance, but they are also providing an infrastructure for their residents to break federal law.

The national Controlled Substances Act of 1970 has classified marijuana as a Schedule I drug being "highly addictive and having no medicinal benefits," putting it in the same category as LSD and heroin. It also gives the federal government power to enforce prohibition of marijuana possession. And yet, thirty-eight states have created laws declaring that marijuana *does* have medicinal benefits and that people should be able to possess it for those ends. Even further, states have adopted numerous *innovations* to facilitate the production, testing, and distribution of medical marijuana. Unlike other federal issues, where states sue, slow-walk, or ignore certain policies, in the case of marijuana, states are being creative and openly contributing to the development of a new industry.

Leveraging rigorous social science methodology and theories of the policy process, we will explain why the defiant innovation of medical cannabis emerged, was legitimized, and spread to thirty-eight states and the District of Columbia. In this introduction, we lay the foundation for the rest of the book by describing the policy landscape on the eve of California and Arizona adopting the first comprehensive medical cannabis programs in 1996. To set this stage, we consider how there has been both consistency and upheaval in federal and state drug policy across the twentieth century. We then turn to providing an overview of how scholars have worked to describe and explain the policy process. Policy process theory provides the structure for how we organize our explanation of medical cannabis policy as defiant innovation. Then, we address how federal prohibition complicates state policies and frustrates regulators, law enforcement, businesses, and patients. Finally, we present an overview of the rest of this book. The story arc begins with California but extends to thirty-eight states and reaches into the early effort to adopt recreational cannabis.

But first, we must explain the political and social context for the rise of marijuana prohibition in the United States that culminated in the adoption of the Controlled Substances Act in 1970.

Marijuana Policy in the Twentieth Century

Historians have traced cannabis use back to the early European settlers to the United States, who used it mainly for fibers in linen, clothing, canvas, and rope. Cannabis as a flower was used for religious, medicinal, and psychoactive purposes.[13] By the middle of the nineteenth century, the scientific and medical field had begun to write about the therapeutic effects of the cannabis plant.[14] Of course, at that time, there were few regulations on drugs or substances of any kind. There was no government oversight of drug use, and addiction was considered to be a personal failing.[15] Problems began to emerge with this lax regulatory regime when morphine (a concentrated opiate) was introduced along with the use of hypodermic needles. The use of morphine during the American Civil War to treat soldiers on the battlefield led to the pervasiveness of opiate addiction, and opiate withdrawal came to be known as "army disease."[16] The lack of federal laws and inconsistent implementation of state and local laws regulating opiates led to a ballooning opiate addiction problem in the latter half of the nineteenth century.[17]

Not only was addiction ballooning, but so was xenophobia. Laborers migrated to the United States to work on large infrastructure projects. Chinese laborers on the West Coast largely built the transcontinental railroad. The Mexican Revolution, which lasted from 1910 to 1920, led to an influx of Mexican immigrants to the American Southwest to work in agriculture.[18] Laborers and refugees brought with them substances— namely, opium and marijuana—that were used in their home countries. As American policy took a nativistic turn, resulting in laws such as the Chinese Exclusion Act, the prohibition or heavy regulation of these specific drugs became one more means of control.[19] In fact, this prohibitionary regime for opium and marijuana marks the first wave of marijuana laws across the states.[20] A few states with port cities and larger foreign populations banned marijuana, including California in 1915, Texas in 1919, and Louisiana in 1924.[21]

The control of marijuana in the United States has always been associated with racial dynamics in the country.[22] The Latin name *cannabis* has been used in English since the sixteenth century, but Mexican immigrants called the substance *marijuana* or *marihuana*.[23] Early leaders in U.S. drug control popularized the name marijuana over cannabis or hemp as a way to make the drug sound foreign or alien. This was not a mistake, as the pejorative use of the term allowed for nativist attacks on the substance and its users. The distinction also confused some whites who did not know that the marijuana being smoked was just a weaker version "of the concentrated cannabis medicines that everyone had been taking since childhood."[24] And yet the federal government and most state laws continue to use *marijuana* over other terms, regardless of whether the laws are related to prohibiting or permitting marijuana use.[25]

Illicit drug control was nationalized through a series of congressional acts in the 1920s and 1930s. The most visible actor in this era was Harry Anslinger and his Federal Bureau of Narcotics (FBN). At the start of Anslinger's career in this role, he held moderate views on drugs. During a congressional hearing, he rebuked the gateway drug theory when asked a question about whether marijuana opened the door for users to try harder drugs.[26] But when Depression-era austerity led to budget cuts at the FBN, Anslinger pivoted. "One obvious solution to this bureaucratic crisis was to create a new scare to justify the bureau's existence."[27] Marijuana was being demonized—think *Reefer Madness*.[28] Anslinger used this demonization of marijuana, entrepreneurially, to amass power and to use that power largely against minoritized communities.

The history of law enforcement in the United States has been intertwined with race. While policing was informally started in the colonial period, the growth, organization, and professionalization of policing forces can be linked to slavery. After slavery's demise, police forces remained as a means of controlling African Americans in the South through Black codes and Jim Crow laws. As African Americans migrated to north and west, they faced de facto discrimination through policies like racial covenants that forced most African Americans into ghettos.[29] In this context, it is no surprise that othering marijuana use was an effective means to affect public opinion and pass legislation. In the ensuing decades, the War on Drugs would allow the government to use its police powers to further control and disempower African Americans through disenfranchisement and mass incarceration.[30]

Anslinger's most infamous quote captures how he attached marijuana use to Mexican immigrants and African Americans:

> Most marijuana smokers are Negroes, Hispanics, jazz musicians, and entertainers. Their satanic music is driven by marijuana, and marijuana smoking by white women makes them want to see sexual relations with Negroes, entertainers, and others. It is a drug that causes insanity, criminality, and death—the most violence-causing drug in the history of mankind.[31]

His efforts led to the passage of the 1937 Marihuana Tax Act, which regulated the importation, cultivation, possession, and distribution of marijuana. In function, the law prohibited the recreational use of marijuana through steep taxes on users ($100 per ounce, which is roughly $1,700 today). Importation and production of industrial hemp and medical research were also obstructed by the legislation. When Samuel R. Caldwell, a white man from Colorado, became the first person convicted of selling cannabis under the act, Harry Anslinger attended the trial in Denver.[32] Even though Anslinger is credited with the nationalization of marijuana policy, scholars note that "a restrictive public policy toward the drug was well rooted locally before that time."[33] From 1914 to 1931, twenty-nine states had adopted laws prohibiting cannabis use for nonmedical purposes.[34]

Anslinger remained in his position until 1962. His advocacy influenced the 1951 Boggs Act and the 1956 Narcotic Control Act, which established mandatory minimum sentences for drug-related offenses. Some states tacked on even harsher penalties.[35] But politically, there remained an appetite for prohibition. Even President Dwight Eisenhower called for "a new war on narcotic addiction at the local, national, and international level" in an article that ran on the front page of the *New York Times*; the story continued on page 72 under the headline, "President Opens War on Drugs."[36]

Concern over marijuana and broader drug control was not unique to the United States. Starting in 1912, the international community adopted a series of piecemeal drug control agreements through the League of Nations and, later, the United Nations. These agreements culminated in the 1961 Single Convention on Narcotic Drugs. The drug control system was guided by schedules based on perceptions of the addictive potential of a substance and its medical utility. Cannabis was placed in Schedule IV, the most restrictive category because of its "harmful characteristics, risk of abuse and extremely limited therapeutic value."[37] The United States signed on to the Single Convention on Narcotic Drugs in 1967, agreeing in principle to limit the production, trade, and possession of the listed drugs "except for amounts which may be necessary for medical or scientific research only."[38]

The next major milestone in American marijuana policy was the Controlled Substances Act of 1970 (CSA) and the initiation of President Richard Nixon's War on Drugs. The CSA established a schedule of federally regulated substances like that of the Single Convention, including placing marijuana in the strictest category: Schedule I. Drugs or substances listed as Schedule I "have *no currently accepted medical use in the United States*, a lack of accepted safety for use under medical supervision, and a high potential for abuse."[39] Marijuana is accompanied by heroin, lysergic acid diethylamide (LSD), peyote, methaqualone, and 3,4-methylenedioxymethamphetamine (MDMA or "Ecstasy"). As the federal government moved the CSA through the legislative process, a concurrent effort by the National Conference of Commissioners on Uniform State Laws developed the Uniform Controlled Substances Act of 1970 that was adopted by forty-eight states (Vermont and New Hampshire adopted their own laws).[40]

In less than a decade, the regulation of marijuana and other illicit drugs was agreed on at the international level and by the U.S. federal government and the states. For a short period, the scheduling of marijuana was consistent across the United States. But, as we discuss in chapter 1, the consensus would soften over the next two decades, ultimately leading to the dam breaking when Arizona and California citizens voted for medical marijuana laws in 1996. Moreover, twenty-five years after these states paved the way for medical marijuana, twenty-four states and the District of Columbia have now legalized adult-use recreational marijuana programs. Medical marijuana certainly paved the way for recreational, but the discourse surrounding the War on Drugs, the criminal justice system, and drug decriminalization has also evolved. The states are central to these evolutions.

In this book, we argue that is impossible to understand current American drug policy and the status of marijuana without understanding the policies developed and adopted by the states. In fact, changing federal marijuana policy has been so difficult that the states remain the locus of marijuana policy activity. Scholars tend to focus on federal policy when telling the story of marijuana reform in the United States, but there would be no talk of federal drug policy reform today without the work by elected officials, interest groups, and citizens in liberal and conservative states. This collection of actors used the complexity of the American federal system and its many different venues for policy change to advance marijuana policies as well as a new marijuana industry.

Policy Process Theory

Policy process researchers have been working for decades to conceptualize and understand the process of policymaking in governments across the globe.[41] There is no single grand theory of the policy process, but studies of the policy process are vibrant and diverse. A useful organizational framework is commonly taught to students of public policy and provides a mechanism for categorizing many specific process theories.[42] Figure 0.1 presents what can be referred to as the linear, sequential, or "policy cycle" model.[43] This version has four stages, although it is not the only conceptualization of the linear model that has been offered over time.[44] Most of the prevailing policy theories with active research programs today can be tied to specific stages in this model. We use this process model to organize the remainder of this book and draw from these theories to explain why states defied federal law and innovated to create comprehensive medical marijuana programs. Before addressing the specific outline of the book, let's first offer an overview of the four stages and the major theories that tend to be associated with each.

The first stage in the policy process considers how governments become aware of problems and decide to take up those problems. Public policy is often thought of as the avenue through which governments work to solve difficult public problems. There is a veritable ocean of potential problems that governments could consider addressing, but they

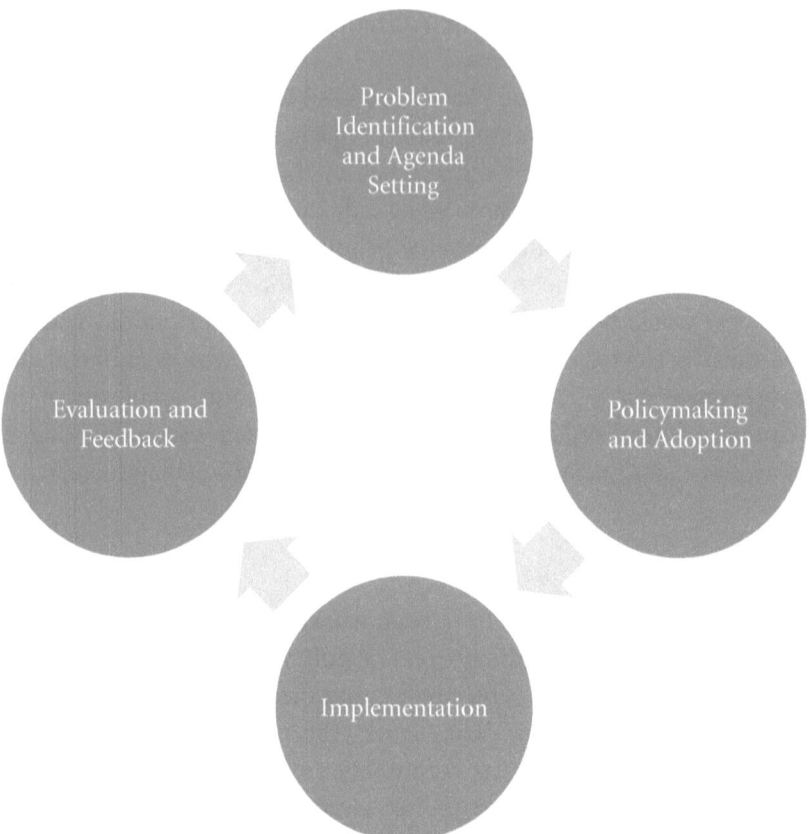

Figure 0.1. Four-stage policy process model.

are limited to the organizational and cognitive resources of their institutions and individual members.[45] Not all issues make the transition from a *private* or *social* problem to a *public issue*.[46] Agenda-setting theory, particularly John Kingdon's Multiple Streams Framework (MSF) and Bryan Jones and Frank Baumgartner's Punctuated Equilibrium Theory (PET), help to explain how governments identify problems and move them to their decision-making agendas.[47]

MSF considers how problems, politics, and solutions are often operating in parallel with each other, but their merger, through the work of policy entrepreneurs and strategic use of policy windows that open periodically, results in issues moving onto a government's agenda. PET is also about how governments set their agenda, but it is more about how individuals (i.e., legislators) and institutions process the vast amounts of information available to them. The design of institutions can introduce friction that slows policymaking, but institutional design also establishes processes that allow legislatures to handle large volumes of policy information simultaneously. Of course, the formal steps of the decision-making process still require organizations to make decisions on one policy at a time, which also contributes to relative stability in policies over time (i.e., the equilibrium). When stable policies are out of step with prevailing social problems and changes in society, pressure builds for major policy change (i.e., the punctuated aspect of the theory).

The second stage in the policy process is policymaking and adoption. Once an issue arises to a government's decision-making agenda, alternatives for adoption are considered and choices are made. Policy innovation and diffusion theory examines the macro-level factors that shape the decisions of governments to adopt a new policy.[48] It considers how the traits of governments, their resources, the attributes of the policy, and interdependencies among governments facilitate (or prevent) the spread of policy innovations. It is notable that not all policies are the same. While diffusion studies often treat policies as if they are the same, we will address the variation in state medical marijuana laws and how that variation relates to their adoption decisions.

Social construction theory is also particularly important for understanding how policies are designed, but it has applications across all the stages of the policy process. In policy design, the theory considers how the relative distribution of benefits and burdens in a policy are contingent on two factors: how the recipients are viewed (deserving or undeserving) and their level of political power.[49] Groups that are viewed positively (deserving) and have high political power, like the middle class and small businesses, tend to receive benefits from policy. However, groups that are viewed negatively (undeserving) and have low political power, like those with criminal records and unlawful welfare recipients, receive only (or largely) burdens. There are also groups, like families living in poverty and the unhoused, that have low power but are viewed as deserving. They tend to receive benefits, but such benefits come with their own burdens. For example, the Temporary Assistance for Needy Families (TANF) program that offers cash assistance has strict eligibility requirements, work requirements, and sanctions for failing to meet those requirements.⁵⁰ Finally, groups like big banks and corporations have high political power, but they are also commonly viewed as undeserving of government help. Nonetheless, because of their power, these groups do receive benefits from government. However, they also tend to receive some level of regulation. We will draw on examples of social construction theory throughout this book.

Politics and policymaking do not stop once a government adopts a new policy. The policy must be implemented effectively. Many circumstances, however, affect whether effective implementation occurs. A law can provide vague instructions. Additional politicking in the regulatory process can prevent or make effective implementation difficult. Further, effectiveness is not the only goal of a policy. Other goals include efficiency, justice, welfare, and liberty. It is difficult, if not impossible, for a policy to achieve all these goals.⁵¹ Governments rely on not only executive branch bureaucrats but often third parties such as other governments, nonprofits, and private companies to implement laws. Implementation theory tends to focus on how states implement federal policy, but its principles can be used to better understand implementation actions and their effects at any level of government.⁵² It also helps us consider the linkages between the politics of policy design, adoption, and ultimate implementation.

Finally, policies have feedback effects, and Policy Feedback Theory (PFT) helps us think about what they are. Foremost, the adoption and implementation of policies restructure the very politics of related future policy debates. This can lead to future iterations of the process building on the policy's success, reforming its failures, or even repealing it completely. Policy evaluation and political feedback can also help improve the implementation process. Policies also have feedback effects on citizens and groups. Policies, for instance, can either increase or erode feelings of citizenship, belonging, and personal agency. Feedback theory helps us think about all these potential effects.⁵³

Three other major policy theories warrant mention: the Advocacy Coalition Framework (ACF), the Institutional Analysis and Development Framework (IAD) and the Social-Ecological Framework (SES). IAD and SES are both rooted in the work of Nobel Prize–winning political scientist Eleanor Ostrom. These theories are helpful in understanding policies that relate to regulation of the economic commons, which tends to entail environmental and energy policies.[54] Ostrom's work has been instrumental in understanding self and collaborative regulation of environmental resources. Given the focus on the environment, however, we do not draw from this theory. ACF would be a better candidate theory for us because it seeks to understand the beliefs of coalitions that advocate on policies and how learning occurs across governments.[55] We will talk about policy learning while drawing from the ACF and other policy learning theory; however, we do not undertake a full analysis of the belief structures of marijuana policy advocates. This is no doubt a valuable exercise and a possibility for future research, but it is not part of this book.

The policy process model is a way to simplify and explain a very complex process. To add even more complexity, much of the policy innovation that we observe happens in the states. Thus, a policy that has been adopted and implemented in one state might have only been introduced in another. Throughout, we will help readers understand how the complexities of American federalism shape the defiant spread of medical marijuana policy in the United States. We will also consider how this specific policy helps policy scholars learn more about the policy process and federalism.

Book Outline

This introduction has set the stage for an in-depth examination of medical marijuana's rise and spread among the American states by telling the story of cannabis prohibition in the United States up to the adoption of the 1970 CSA. We have also set the stage for how the policy process structures the book and our understanding of how and why medical marijuana spread among the states.

Chapter 1 picks up the story of American marijuana policy just two short years after the CSA was adopted. Problems with marijuana prohibition emerged quickly and were reiterated for the nearly twenty-five years that passed between the passage of the CSA and California's adoption of the first comprehensive medical marijuana law in 1996. This chapter addresses how medical marijuana emerged on state agendas and how its framing evolved over time to facilitate the diffusion of the policy to increasingly conservative states (the problem identification and agenda-setting stage). There is a vast literature on policy framing, but it is less often the case that scholars examine how issue framing changes strategically during the diffusion process. But we know that groups will strategically choose what aspects of a policy they need to emphasize to gain support.[56] Much of this work is static—identifying the different frames used and which frames policymakers gravitated toward. Research on dynamic framing more often focuses on the role of the media in shaping opinion over time.[57] However, we will demonstrate how groups shape this narrative with their own strategic shift in focus as the political context evolves and a policy spreads.

Chapter 2 turns its attention to the adoption and diffusion of medical marijuana in the states (the policymaking and adoption stage). We review our concept of defiant innovation and update our earlier analysis by examining what factors cause states to adopt medical marijuana policies. Meanwhile, some of our conclusions from a previous examination of this question have changed, which shows that policy adoption is a dynamic process.[58] A finding that has not changed, however, is the centrality of the ballot initiative to the spread of medical marijuana policies. This process allowed citizens to put the issue of medical marijuana directly in front of voters, who were more receptive than legislators—many of whom feared being associated with a stigmatized policy. But other factors from our analysis have become less important over time. When we first analyzed the adoption of policies through 2014, a state's liberalism was a critical factor in whether a state had a policy. But revisiting this analysis just a few years later, we find that state liberalism no longer predicts whether a state has a policy. Since 2016, more conservative states have jumped onboard—thanks in part to the effective framing of medical marijuana that we describe in chapter 1 and revisions to the substance of medical marijuana laws adopted by those conservative states.

In chapter 3, we examine the implementation of medical marijuana policies. Using a comparative case study of Ohio, Pennsylvania, and West Virginia, we examine how the implementation process is shaped by a policy's design as well as the state's political context and resource constraints. The three states are useful case comparisons because they adopted medical marijuana policies in 2016 and 2017, but under differing political contexts. Republicans had single-party government in Ohio but were pushed to take control of medical marijuana legalization in the face of a serious ballot threat. Pennsylvania does not have the direct initiative, but it also had a divided government with a Democratic governor and Republican General Assembly and Republican buy-in. West Virginia had a much different experience; its single-party Republican government was out-of-step with public opinion on the issue, so an alliance of Democrats and libertarians got a bill through to a receptive governor. We argue that differing political environments, policy design, and resource constraints have shaped the differences in implementation outcomes in the three states. We also discuss how evaluations of implementation are challenging given normative differences in what defines a successful policy. Moreover, state differences in data collection and reporting make it difficult to draw comparisons—a challenge that is widespread in state politics research and further complicated by the federal government's ongoing stance of prohibition.

Chapter 4 then turns to addressing how policy learning and feedback occurred as states learned from early adopters and as the political dynamics of marijuana changed locally and nationally (the evaluation and feedback stage). Political lessons are just as important as practical policy lessons. Policy entrepreneurs and interest groups learn how to make a policy more politically palatable, and policymakers look for signals about the electoral risks of a policy innovation.[59] This is no less the case for marijuana policy.[60] In fact, marijuana laws were not only affected by policy lessons in early-adopter states but were also shaped by stipulations that the federal government placed on its forbearance in prosecuting marijuana dispensaries and growers and processors in "well regulated" medical and recreational marijuana systems.[61] The federal government has failed to pass concrete policy on medical marijuana—but presidential administrations have used the Department of Justice to set priorities and send messages to state governments about what is and what is not permitted. Furthermore, as policies are adopted, the politics of those adoptions and experiences with policy implementation set the stage for future policy debates in both positive and negative ways.[62]

Finally, chapter 5 discusses the feedback effects of medical marijuana policy on efforts to legalize adult-use recreational marijuana and expand medical marijuana programs to new states. We consider the myriad legal, political, and administrative challenges that arise from the fragile status quo of federal prohibition and state legalization.[63] And as policies expand, so do profits. Moreover, policymakers and interest groups must wrestle with the legacy of the War on Drugs and how to rein in inequities in the marijuana industry. Beyond mere speculation, in this concluding chapter, we draw from the experience of medical marijuana to highlight similarities and important differences in how recreational marijuana is progressing through the policy process in the United States.

1

Selling Pot

The Changing Narrative around Marijuana

> Marijuana came to be seen as not just something smoked by long-haired hippies to get high, but as a uniquely beneficial drug that could treat the debilitating effects of numerous diseases, from easing sixty-year-olds' pain and nausea from chemotherapy and preserving friendly professors' sight, to putting enough weight on dying young men so they could live a few more months before succumbing to AIDS.
> —Emily Dufton, *Grass Roots*, 208

In politics, problems in public life are debated and identified. This takes place in legislative bodies as well as through elections where political campaigns can be run on a candidate's or party's promise to solve a problem. Policies are often created to remedy problems that have been identified. Sometimes, though, problems are clearly partisan in nature, and there is no agreement on what the root problem even is. For example, Republicans lament that abortions are legal while Democrats lament that women do not have the right to choose. Related political debates tend to focus on first principles (i.e., fundamental beliefs and assumptions).[1] In other cases, there may be universal agreement on the problem but different explanations for why the problem exists and, consequently, different prescriptions for fixing it. Take school reform. Both political parties agree that public schools should be strengthened, but Democrats are more likely to support pouring more resources into the current system while Republicans are more likely to support "school choice" measures as a solution to the problem. Problems are also time-dependent. For example, they can arise from a technological disruption that takes time to understand and solve. Or shifts in sociocultural views and values can affect whether something is even conceptualized as a problem at all.

In the case of marijuana, there has been much disagreement about whether marijuana use is a problem—and under what contexts—and what should be done to fix it. Not to mention, the disagreement and terms of the debate have shifted over time. In the introduction, we provided a brief overview of how marijuana was demonized and criminalized in the early twentieth century. The Controlled Substances Act (CSA) can be viewed as a policy to fix a problem. That is, the federal government considered marijuana to be a dangerous drug that it needed to control. In the immediate aftermath of the passage of the CSA, however, the *criminalization of marijuana* quickly became viewed as a problem. In the 1970s, criminalizing marijuana fell out of favor with much of the public—and yet the opportunity to fix the CSA was missed. Instead, public opinion turned against marijuana again in the late 1970s after the emergence of a burgeoning and unregulated drug paraphernalia industry and some missteps by marijuana advocates and reformers. By 1980, *marijuana* was a problem again. Yet, by the 1990s, the *lack of access to medical marijuana* became a newly identified problem.

Criminalization Is the Problem

Even though President Richard Nixon's views on marijuana differed little from the anti-marijuana crusaders of the 1930s, 1940s, and 1950s, the perceptions of the American public shifted markedly in the 1960s. It was easier to sell Americans and lawmakers on the dangers of marijuana in the 1930s when its most prominent users were immigrants and those from the lower classes. By the 1960s, the groups that became the target of anti-marijuana efforts were counterculture activists and African Americans. To this day, it is impossible to separate public views on marijuana from views on its users.[2] As we noted in the introduction, fears over marijuana use by the "other" affecting dominant society (i.e., the counterculture and African Americans) culminated in its inclusion on Schedule I of the CSA, alongside harder drugs like heroin and LSD (also a drug associated with the counterculture). At the same time, however, marijuana use rose rapidly among all Americans in the 1960s and into the 1970s. It became especially prevalent in the suburbs and on college campuses.

Furthermore, marijuana use was a *political* act. Marijuana was tied to the broader countercultural movement in the United States that supported civil rights, protested the escalation of the Vietnam War, and critiqued the social mores and values of their parent's generation. As activist Jay Hansen told reporters in 1967:

> The reason we can no longer identify with the kinds of activities that the older generation are engaged in is because those activities are for us meaningless. They have led to a monstrous war in Vietnam, for example. And that's why it's all related—the psychedelics and the war, the protesting, the gap in the generations.[3]

Such thinking drew Nixon's ire and partially explains why another choice drug of the counterculture, LSD, was also included in Schedule I of the CSA.[4]

By the 1970s, political action also led to the formation of interest groups with the goal of protecting marijuana users and opposing harsh penalties for its use. In 1970, Keith Stroup formed the National Organization for the Reform of Marijuana Laws (NORML). Discussing the organization's name, Stroup would later say, "I appreciated the double entendre. We wanted to make a point that it was normal to smoke marijuana."[5] NORML quickly became a force on Capitol Hill—often buoyed by 1960s activists who, by the 1970s, started to have families and populate the suburbs.

The Nixon administration was out of step with culture, and it experienced another setback with the 1972 report from the National Commission on Marihuana and Drug Abuse. Marijuana was temporarily placed on Schedule I in the 1970 CSA, pending further review by a commission that was appointed by President Nixon. The commission is often referred to as the Shafer Commission, named after Raymond Shafer, the former Pennsylvania governor who chaired the commission. Shafer was also known as a staunch prohibitionist, and the other members of the panel were likely to support the president's anti-marijuana agenda.[6] In many ways, the Shafer Commission was expected to be a rubber stamp in support of prohibition. Nixon privately told Shafer, "I want a goddamn strong statement on marijuana ... one that just tears the ass out of them."[7]

The panel conducted a thorough analysis of marijuana that included sponsoring research projects, fielding public opinion polls, and taking testimony from experts. The final report, aptly titled *Marihuana: A Signal of Misunderstanding*, was 1,184 pages long and rebuked many of the efforts by the Bureau of Narcotics to spin information about marijuana. The report rejected the theory that marijuana use would lead to more dangerous drugs (i.e., the gateway theory) and rebuffed the assertion that marijuana use led to particularly violent or aggressive behavior.[8]

The report also criticized the prevailing enforcement efforts stating, "Criminal law is too harsh a tool to apply to personal possession [of marihuana] even in the effort to discourage use. . . . The actual and potential harm of use of the drug is not great enough to justify the intrusion by the criminal law with the greatest reluctance."[9] Furthermore, the report noted that "considering the range of social concerns in contemporary America, marihuana does not, in our considered judgment, rank very high. We would deemphasize marihuana as a problem."[10]

While the main question before the committee was related to the criminalization of marijuana, the committee also proposed increased support for research on the therapeutic value of cannabis:

> Historical references have been noted throughout the literature referring to the use of cannabis products as therapeutically useful agents. Of particular significance for current research with controlled quality, quantity and therapeutic settings, would be investigations into the treatment of glaucoma, migraine, alcoholism and terminal cancer.[11]

Even with the committee's thorough investigation and recommendations, Nixon had already stated his opposition to their conclusions, and marijuana remained on Schedule I.[12]

With the Nixon White House unmoved, the venue for pro-marijuana policy action moved to the states. In 1973, the National Conference on Uniform State Laws adopted amendments to the state-level Uniform Controlled Substances Act that were based on recommendations from the Shafer Commission. The removal of criminal penalties for possession was endorsed by several organizations including the American Bar Association, American Medical Association, National Council of Churches, and others.[13] Oregon was the first state to decriminalize

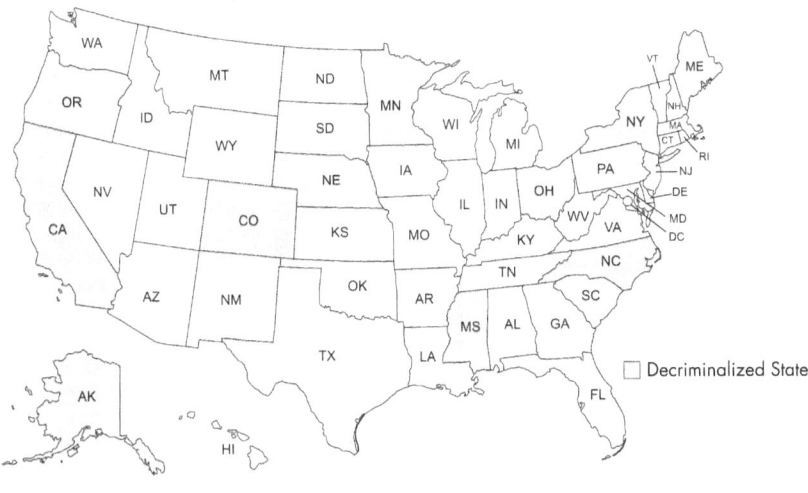

Created with mapchart.net

Figure 1.1. States that decriminalized marijuana, 1973–1978.

marijuana in 1973, but the move to decriminalize accelerated after Nixon's resignation in 1974.[14] By 1978, eleven states had decriminalized marijuana possession (see figure 1.1).

The greatest hopes for national marijuana reform came with the 1976 election of President Jimmy Carter. One of Carter's closest advisers was Dr. Peter Bourne, a physician who served as the head of the state of Georgia's narcotics treatment program. When Carter was elected, he invited Bourne to serve in the West Wing as Special Assistant to the President for Drug Abuse. Within two months of Carter's inauguration, the administration asked Congress to decriminalize marijuana nationally.[15] Bourne told a Senate committee that he had smoked marijuana and considered it safer than cigarettes.

The national media also predicted that marijuana's day as a criminalized drug was soon to be over. In 1977, a *New York Times* headline stated, "Marijuana Smoking Gains Wider Acceptance; Users' Freakish Image Fades." The text of the article notes that

> in just a dozen or so years, marijuana has graduated from a feared substance used mostly by ghetto youths and "long-haired freaks" to a mild "recreational" drug "toked" regularly in public and private by millions of

middle-class Americans, not excluding doctors, lawyers, policemen and newspaper reporters.[16]

Furthermore, a paraphernalia industry proliferated, taking advantage of the increasing number of wealthy marijuana consumers. Head shops had opened around the country selling rolling papers, bongs, and other drug paraphernalia. By 1977, sales generated $250 million in revenue.[17] But the next few months and years would radically alter the sunny assessment from activists.

No, Marijuana Is the Problem

The first major setback for marijuana reformers was the downfall of Peter Bourne. Bourne attended a 1977 Christmas party hosted by NORML. His presence alone was a significant statement—granting legitimacy to NORML and other drug reformers. Bourne made a fateful decision that night by going into a private room with NORML's leaders and snorting cocaine. The details of the story are contested, but Bourne's presence in a room with open drug use was not. A few months later, a story broke that Bourne had illegally prescribed quaaludes for a few of his White House colleagues. On the heels of this story, NORML's director, Keith Stroup, leaked the cocaine incident to the press to get back at Bourne over disagreements regarding the spreading of the pesticide paraquat on Mexican marijuana fields. Bourne resigned on July 20, 1978, leaving marijuana proponents without an advocate in the West Wing. The scandal also left enough of a stench around drug use that the Carter administration would never bring up decriminalization again.[18]

The other major setback to the decriminalization movement came from a powerful group of parent activists. The lax regulation of marijuana through states' decriminalization and the abundance of head shops drew the ire of parents as adolescent marijuana-use rates began to rise and head shops exposed young people to drug culture. Parents began to organize in several cities and took their issue to state and federal leaders, including Peter Bourne's successor—Lee Dogoloff—who was sympathetic to their cause. In 1979, parent activists were lecturing the U.S. Senate Subcommittee on Criminal Justice about the evils of the paraphernalia industry. By 1980, over 300 parent groups had formed across the country under the banner of organizations such as Families in Action (FIA), Parents' Resource Institute for Drug Education (PRIDE), and the National Federation of Parents for Drug-Free Youth (NFP).[19]

The parents' movement found an ally in the administration of President Ronald Reagan. First Lady Nancy Reagan embraced the movement, and by 1983, over 6,000 groups had formed. Later, the "Just Say No" campaign (borrowed from an Oakland activist) became ubiquitous in pop culture and a cornerstone of Nancy Reagan's legacy. While the Reagan administration was supportive of these antidrug programs, the lion's share of public money was spent on law enforcement and interdiction efforts.[20]

The backlash to the decriminalization movement in the early 1970s was swift. The parents' movement and the rise of Reagan presidency revived the War on Drugs. States retrenched on decriminalization quickly, and the inevitability of nationwide cannabis liberalization faded. While mandatory minimum sentences from the Boggs Act and Narcotics Control Act had been rolled back in the early 1970s, Reagan's Anti-Drug Abuse Act of 1986 reinstated many of the penalties. So how did we move from rigid criminalization in the 1980s and early 1990s to more than 70 percent of Americans living in states with legal medical marijuana today? To begin that story, we need to consider more formally how issues arrive on the government's decision-making agenda.

Agenda Setting: The Multiple Streams Framework

What is agenda setting? Since 1984, John Kingdon's Multiple Streams Framework (MSF) has been applied to hundreds of policies for the purpose of understanding how issues get on the government's decision-making agenda and ultimately receive enough attention to get a decision.[21] MSF offers a helpful structure for understanding how medical marijuana has advanced on the agendas of so many states. Kingdon argues that the agenda-setting process is fluid and that multiple participants affect whether and how a problem is defined, the possible solutions for the problem, and the political feasibility of possible solutions. Before using this framework to understand the emergence of medical

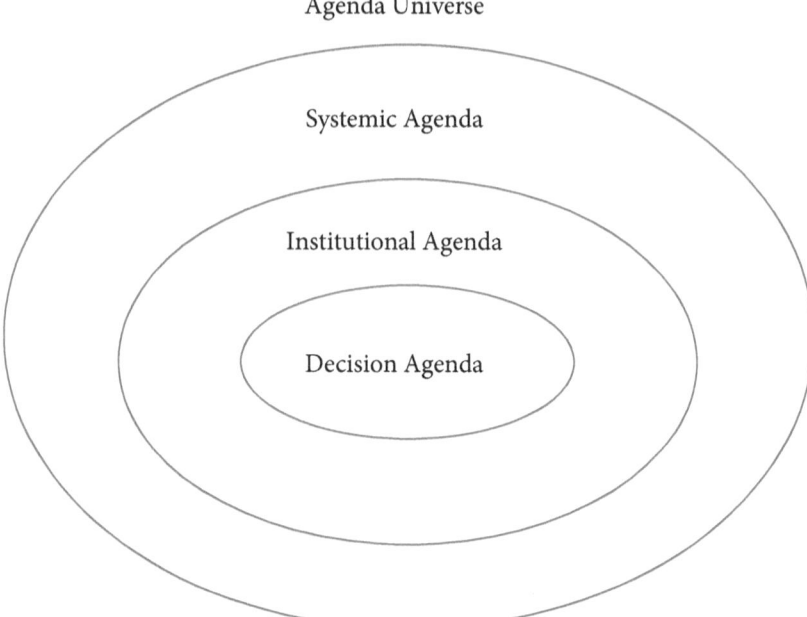

Figure 1.2. Nested agendas. Source: Adapted from Thomas Birkland.

marijuana on state decision agendas, we must first briefly explain the core concepts of MSF.

It is first necessary to understand that there are nested agendas in the policymaking space. Figure 1.2 displays one conceptualization of these agendas from Thomas Birkland.[22] The decision agenda is the goal of any policy proponent. That is our "School House Rock" image of how policymaking happens through the legislative process. But this is also the narrowest collection of policy ideas, because even governments must make decisions one at a time.[23] That said, governments can process many policy proposals in parallel before the final decision stage.[24] This is called the institutional agenda. For example, Congress has many topical committees that consider legislation. But each chamber can only vote on one piece of legislation at a time. Of course, it is not only the legislature that has an institutional agenda; so do the executive and the judiciary branches of government. Beyond the institutional agenda lies the systemic agenda. This is the "primeval soup" that contains all the possible policy ideas and proposals that exist within the boundaries of a political geography. The boundaries of the systemic agenda are shaped by the culture and norms of the political unit (i.e., the country, state, municipality). Finally, the agenda universe is the infinite set of policy ideas and proposals that exist. Agenda-setting scholars are not typically concerned with this amorphous agenda space, but they do care about explaining why, when, and how policies move from the systemic agenda to the institutional agenda and, finally, to the decision agenda.

It is important to recognize that what falls within each of these nested sets of agendas differs depending on political geography. In other words, what appears on the systemic, governmental, and decision agendas is different across countries and within countries. Within American federalism, states have very different agendas. Further, as states observe what their peers are doing and learn lessons from their successes and failures, they may see issues advance to deeper agenda levels than were possible before. Medical marijuana is an example. Before 1996, medical marijuana was on the agenda in few states. But as the policy spread and became more legitimate, and as advocates learned how to strategically alter their approach to agenda setting, medical marijuana moved from the agenda universe to the systemic agenda in every state, then to the governmental agenda in every state, and finally to the decision agenda in most states. MSF helps us think about how this process works.

Three Streams

MSF identifies three streams, or processes, that operate in policymaking: problem recognition, identification of policy proposals (i.e., solutions), and politics. A key assumption, one that is criticized, is that the three streams flow in parallel until they are brought together. It is within the problem stream where different conceptualizations of the problem compete. In the solutions stream, advocates and advocacy organizations have already prepared solutions to a problem or are looking for a problem to attach their preferred policies to. Kingdon calls this a policy "primeval soup" from which entrepreneurs draw policy solutions when the time is right.[25] Finally, within the politics stream resides political institutions (executive, legislative, and judicial), interest group campaigns, and the sense of the public mood. Successful policies must fit the prevailing ideological makeup of the government, and interest groups will work to link public opinion, elite preferences, and potential policies.[26] Policies advance to the government's decision agenda when these streams are coupled, meaning they are pulled together. Two things are required to make coupling happen—changes in the status quo of the streams, which is called ripening, and action by policy entrepreneurs.

Policy entrepreneurs are "advocates who are willing to invest their resources—time, energy, reputation, money—to promote a position in return for anticipated future gain in the form of material, purposive, or solidary benefits."[27] They help to pull the streams together by observing political trends, identifying attractive problem framings, and pairing those with feasible policy solutions. Policy windows are the typically brief periods of time when advocates can gain attention from governmental institutions and advance their agenda. Windows can open when unforeseen events happen (e.g., the attacks on 9/11 led to the formation of the Department of Homeland Security). Opportunities also arise with the swearing in of a new president or a change in which party controls Congress. Kingdon argues that the agenda-setting process is fluid and that several participants affect whether and how a problem is defined, the possible solutions of the defined problem, and the political feasibility of those solutions. Having briefly defined each of these components, we now turn to fleshing them out as a means to understand how medical marijuana advanced on the policymaking agenda in the United States.

Problem Stream

The problem stream is where policy problems are recognized and defined by different actors. In the world of politics and policymaking, *perception* of a problem is what really matters. Moreover, it is the perception of a problem by the public and political elites that helps get that problem on the government's agenda. Such perceptions are not fixed, and changes in problem indicators, issue framing, elite and media narratives, and public opinion can each help ripen the problem stream. We will address each of these in turn for medical marijuana.

Problem Indicators

Depending on the problem at hand, indicators can be wide ranging. For example, when a country's gross domestic product shrinks for two quarters in a row, this is an indicator of a recession. The size and duration of the recession indicate to government that there is an economic problem that needs to be solved. In the case of medical marijuana policy, in the story we have told so far, we left off with the resurgence of criminalization. In parallel with the reinvigorated War on Drugs in the 1980s and early 1990s, advocates began to focus on the potential medicinal benefits of the cannabis plant and how prohibition harmed potential patients. Several high-profile stories served as indicators of the narrower problem of prohibition's restriction of the medicinal benefits of marijuana.

Robert Randall was an aspiring speechwriter living in Washington, D.C. While searching for work, he also drove a taxicab and taught speech classes at a community college. After being diagnosed with a severe form of glaucoma, he searched for a remedy. In 1973, he discovered that his vision sharpened while smoking marijuana with a friend. He started to grow a few marijuana plants on his sunporch. His plants were discovered in 1975 by D.C. police when they raided a neighboring apartment.[28]

Randall fought the charges. He found research supporting the medicinal benefit of marijuana for glaucoma and subjected himself to medical research conducted at University of California, Los Angeles. In 1976, a D.C. Superior Court judge ruled that he "has established a defense of necessity. . . . The evil he sought to avert, blindness, is greater than that he performed" (growing marijuana illegally). Randall also successfully petitioned the Food and Drug Administration (FDA) to include him in a research program that allotted him ten marijuana joints a day.[29]

The executive director of NORML, Keith Stroup, claimed that "Bob was, in essence, the father of the medical marijuana movement." Randall was an ideal activist. His look and disposition went against stereotypes of marijuana smokers, and he traveled across the country sharing his story in both courthouses and statehouses representing the group he founded, the Alliance for Cannabis Therapeutics. In the 1990s, he started advocating for AIDS patients to apply for the FDA program in which he was enrolled. His activism laid the groundwork for the legal defense of medical marijuana, and his image gave credibility to the medical use of cannabis.

In the late 1970s, Mary Jane Rathbun befriended Denis Peron, a marijuana and gay rights activist. Peron ran the Big Top marijuana supermarket out of his home in San Francisco. Mary's marijuana brownies soon became a bestseller in the store and the surrounding Castro District. She built a lucrative business, but in 1981 she was arrested with twenty pounds of marijuana, fifty-four dozen brownies, and half an ounce of psychedelic mushrooms. She faced ten felonies, but like Randall, her image defied all stereotypes. Most of her charges were dismissed, but she was ordered to do community service.

Rathbun became dedicated to serving her community and continued to finance her charitable efforts by selling her brownies. When the AIDS epidemic hit, she focused on caring for the men that she called "her kids." She found that her brownies provided pain relief and helped provide energy and an appetite for those suffering. She was arrested again in 1992, when police raided a friend's home just as she was pouring two and a half pounds of marijuana into a batch of brownies. But this time, she was no longer profiting from her brownies. The marijuana was being donated to her, and she was donating her brownies to those in need. Her subsequent defense drew national attention, and she became the embodiment of a movement by appearing on national television shows. "In the face of rising death tolls," Emily Dufton wrote, "a matronly old woman giving brownies to the sick didn't seem like a terribly objectionable offense."[30]

Robert Randall and Brownie Mary added human and sympathetic cases to the medical marijuana movement. Beyond that, more people were being exposed to medical cannabis through personal interactions and media reports. Writing in 1997, less than a year after California adopted the first medical marijuana law, Michael Pollan wrote in the *New York Times*:

> Before the Prop 215 campaign, Americans had focused exclusively on the victims of drugs; now they were meeting victims of the war against drugs, and these people looked a lot like people they knew. The old stories of children with drug problems were suddenly displaced by stories of dying parents in need of pain relief. And these stories resonated with the experience of voters, a third of whom told pollsters they personally knew someone who used marijuana for medical reasons.[31]

Despite efforts by federal government officials to discredit marijuana for medical use, they could not control the narrative as more Americans gained access to medical cannabis. Stories like those of Randall and Rathburn raised the profile of the potential for medical marijuana and indicated the related problem of prohibition, at least for medicinal use. While broad decriminalization still seemed off the table, acceptance was growing in parts of the country for narrower liberalization of marijuana laws for the sake of those suffering from medical conditions like glaucoma, AIDS, and cancer.

Issue Framing

Language matters when defining policy problems. Further, shifts in how we speak about a policy problem and the target population affected also change how we think about the solutions.[32] Pot, reefer, weed, ganga, herb, chronic, dope, sticky icky, marijuana, cannabis (the product or plant). Toking, poking, blazing, Cheeching, smoking, consuming, taking (consumption). Hippie, stoner, burnout, pothead, connoisseur, user, patient (the consumer). In each of these lists of terms, there is a progression from one image to another. Words like pot, dope, reefer, and weed are highly stigmatized, whereas many professionals in the industry tend to use the more formal term cannabis when talking about the plant. Perhaps this explains why President Bill Clinton's drug czar, Barry McCaffrey, took much pleasure in drawing connections between marijuana laws and Cheech and Chong.[33]

In the 1998 stoner comedy *Half Baked*, Dave Chappelle's character describes different types of users: creatives, MacGyvers (handy), potheads (lacking motivation and forgetful), enhancement smokers, "after school special" smokers, scavengers, "you should have been there" smokers, and "I'm forty but I'm still cool" smokers. All of these are tropes and stand in juxtaposition to the fact that the marijuana sold in the movie is medicinal. There are no cancer patients, elderly glaucoma patients, or anyone suffering from AIDS in the film. But this was 1998. In 2024, the public perception of who consumes cannabis and why has become more complex. Ohio Democratic Senator Kenny Yuko provides an excellent example of how the frames have changed:

[For] a person my age, when you heard of marijuana back in those days, back in 2003, when I heard two words associated with marijuana, it wasn't "medical" and "marijuana." It was more like "Cheech" and "Chong," "Snoop" and "Dog," and "Willie" and "Nelson." . . . The reality of it is, once I did a little research, I found out how wrong I was. . . . This bill is not perfect folks, but it's what Ohio patient [sic] needs. It's not acceptable to make them wait any longer. If we can give just one veteran comfort, if we can ease one patient's horrible pain, if we can maybe improve or even save a child's life, this bill will be worth it.[34]

Yuko's statement, made during a 2016 Ohio legislative session, encapsulates how the images of medical marijuana have changed.

And yet, competing frames about medical marijuana laws are still widespread. In 2021, as the Nebraska legislature was considering a medical marijuana law, Republican Governor Pete Ricketts stated, "If you legalize marijuana, you're gonna kill your kids. That's what the data shows from around the country."[35] And when Mississippi's Republican Governor Tate Reeves begrudgingly signed a medical marijuana bill in 2022, he wrote in his signing statement: "There are also those who really want a recreational marijuana program that could lead to more people smoking and less people working, with all of the societal and family ills that that brings."[36] Such comments show that there remains plenty of skepticism around medical marijuana, especially from social conservatives.

What is framing? Essentially, framing is how we think about a topic. More importantly in politics, framing is how we communicate about a policy problem and thus shape how others think about that problem and its solution. Our thinking about a variety of topics is shaped by our backgrounds, education, and other considerations. Elites (e.g., politicians and the media) will strategically talk about topics in a way that makes us think narrowly about them. Further, elites and the media can explicitly prime audiences to think about a topic in a specific way. This is useful because people often think "off the top of their head" when communicating their political and policy preferences.[37]

Consider figure 1.3. The black frame around former British prime minister Boris Johnson's face and the word "disobey" immediately draws the eye to the center of the mural. Even when one tries to look at the

Figure 1.3. Example of framing. Source: Unsplash.

rest of the mural, that black framed image is distracting. This makes the frame powerful in how a viewer interprets and cognitively processes the whole mural. This is the same in policymaking. There are almost always multiple competing frames in political and policy debates, and the dominant frame that shapes public policy can change.[38]

The "M" Word

Another intriguing example of language and framing in cannabis policy is the slow shift away from using the word "marijuana" to using cannabis instead. Advocates have been very purposeful in shifting this language. Even though every state medical cannabis law has used the term marijuana, its usage has a racialized history.[39] Consequently, states have been updating their laws and forming new institutions like the "Cannabis Control Commission" (Massachusetts) and the "Department of Cannabis Control" (California).[40] Experimental evidence shows that the difference in terminology has no effect among the mass public, but the framing shift is ongoing, nonetheless.[41]

Media Narratives

Part of ripening the problem stream is changing the way that the public and policymakers talk about a problem and the populations connected with that problem. News "is a function, not of the nature of the world 'out there,' but of the work of those who must somehow bring into being some things which are more important than others."[42] The choices that news media make about how they cover an issue affects the way that consumers will understand the issue. Media will create "policy images" that shape how a policy is understood, and they "are always a mixture of empirical information and emotive appeals."[43] We conducted two types of analysis to better understand the media framing around medical marijuana. Because systematic gathering of state-level media is scant, we rely on two courses of national coverage to illustrate how media framing of medical marijuana evolved. First, we examined coverage of medical marijuana by national network news organizations and then in the *New York Times*.

NETWORK NEWS ANALYSIS

Using LexisNexis, we searched ABC News, CBS News, and NBC News for their news coverage of medical marijuana. We retrieved all articles from January 1, 1996, to December 31, 2020, that included cannabis or marijuana combined with medical in the headline.[44] This produced a sample of 161 transcripts from ABC ($N=26$), CBS ($N=75$), and NBC

($N = 60$). ABC coverage is lighter because LexisNexis includes only a random sample of stories. We pulled information from each story related to what types of individuals were quoted in the stories and the general sentiment of the article.

For example, in March 1999, *NBC News at Sunrise* ran a story that the nation's drug czar that said marijuana will stay on the government's list of illegal drugs. The story included a quote from a doctor stating "marijuana's potential as medicine is seriously undermined by the fact that people smoke it, thereby increasing their chance for cancer, lung damage." The segment then noted that marijuana may be helpful for people with terminal illnesses and cut to a short interview with a woman suffering with AIDS who uses marijuana to help with her appetite. The story allowed National Institute on Drug Abuse (NIDA) director Barry McCaffrey to have the final word stating that marijuana shows little promise as medicine and that it is harmful. In this NBC News segment, we note that a patient (positive), physician (negative), and politician (negative) were quoted and that the overall sentiment was negative.[45] The segment did not mention any specific policy venues like federalism or the Supreme Court. A second example comes from a *CBS Morning News* transcript about Hawaii adopting a medical marijuana law. The story led with a woman excitedly discussing how she tried medical marijuana to treat her pain from tumors on her foot. It followed with the reporter balancing the potential therapeutic benefits of the law with what critics are saying—that it violates federal law and that physicians could lose their licenses. The coverage then showed a state senator complaining that the bill is full of holes. Finally, the reporter noted that supporters of the bill "say the details can be worked out, pointing to other states that have launched successful medical marijuana programs without increased crime or drug abuse." In this example, we note that a patient (positive), advocates (positive), and politician (negative) were quoted and that the overall sentiment was positive. Furthermore, two policy venues are mentioned: federalism and state action on marijuana.[46] From this coding approach, we captured some impressions of the marijuana news coverage as well as changes in coverage in the ensuing years.

Table 1.1 provides information related to which sources were quoted in stories. These categories are not mutually exclusive; a single news

Table 1.1. Sources Quoted in Medical Marijuana Stories

	Number of Stories Quoted (%)	Positive (%)	Negative (%)
Patient	58 (36.0)	58 (100)	0 (0)
Politician	46 (28.6)	18 (39.1)	28 (60.1)
Doctor	41 (25.4)	26 (63.4)	15 (36.6)
Industry	23 (14.3)	23 (100)	0 (0)
Law enforcement	9 (5.6)	3 (33.3)	6 (66.7)
Policy expert	4 (2.5)	4 (100)	0 (0)
Total stories	181 (100)	132 (73)	49 (27)

segment can quote multiple sources. Patients were the most likely people to be quoted in these stories, followed by politicians. Notably, a significant number of politicians and physicians were quoted from both sides of the issue, and politicians were the only group more likely to be negative than positive. And surprisingly, few policy experts or law enforcement officials are quoted—although we should caution that we classified appointed leaders (e.g., the drug czar, attorney general) as politicians rather than law enforcement.

Figure 1.4 shows the information from table 1.1 in line graph form to compare the coverage over time. We use presidential administrations as time markers. Most politicians were quoted during the Clinton administration because it was the first administration to face the issue head on as states began adopting medical marijuana, and because the administration lobbied aggressively against these policies. However, each administration made significant policies related to medical marijuana. The decline of quotes from politicians is likely due to a mix of the novelty of the issue fading and the issue becoming less politically charged in subsequent administrations.[47] We also measured the tone of the coverage during each administration. Our analysis of newspaper coverage found predominantly negative coverage.[48] By comparison, coverage on network news was rarely negative (see figure 1.5). In each administration, the coverage is more positive than negative. Over time, there have been fewer stories that present medical marijuana as a debate between different interests or using a neutral (unclear) frame. This reflects growing certainty and positivity over marijuana in network news coverage

SELLING POT | 35

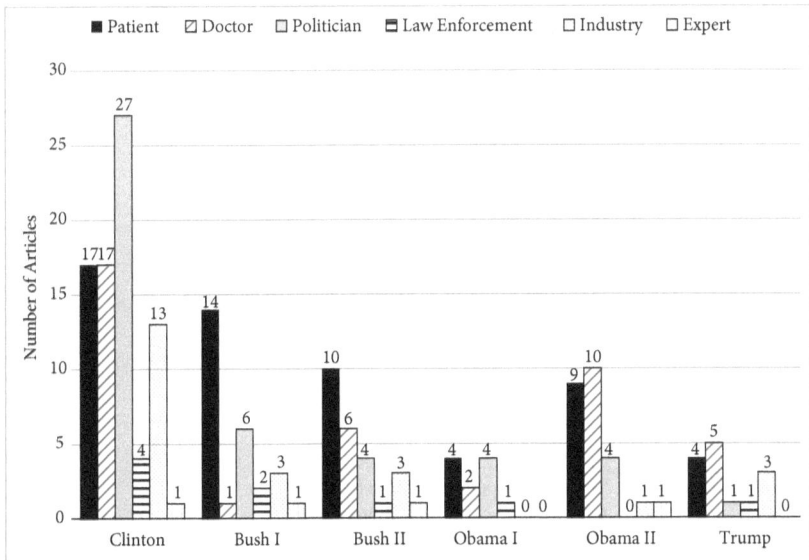

Figure 1.4. Sources quoted in medical marijuana news coverage by presidential administration.

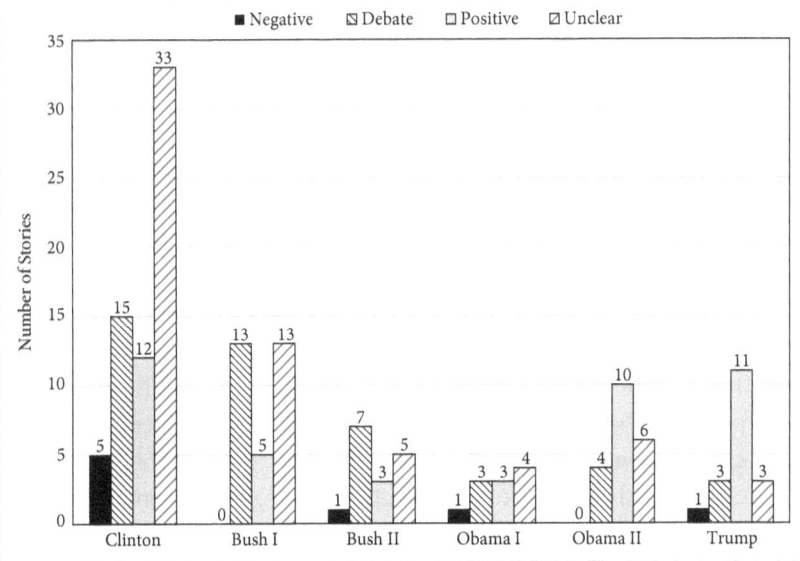

Figure 1.5. Tone of medical marijuana coverage on network news by presidential administration.

Table 1.2. Organizing Themes of Medical Marijuana Coverage on Network News, 1996–2020

Organizing Theme	Description	Percentage of Stories
State laws or state action on medical marijuana	The segment presents medical marijuana with a focus on state policy (e.g., the challenges facing the state or the legislative process behind the program).	65.8
Federalism	The segment presents the tension between federal and state policy on medical marijuana (e.g., coverage of Department of Justice statements about legality of medical marijuana).	55.9
Supreme Court	The segment highlights the role of the Supreme Court in ruling on the legality of state medical marijuana policies (e.g., coverage of *Cannabis Buys v. Oakland*, *Gonzales v. Raich* decisions).	25.5
Election or ballot initiative	The segment presents medical marijuana in relation to an election (e.g., coverage of a ballot initiative campaign).	9.3
Individual's legal issues with using medical marijuana	The segment presents medical marijuana and the legal issues facing individuals (e.g., families in need of medical marijuana to care for children with epilepsy).	7.5
Congressional action or position	The segment highlights congressional action or rhetoric related to medical marijuana (e.g., congressional reaction to *Gonzales v. Raich* decisions).	4.4

and society more broadly. As we discuss in chapter 4 on policy feedback, there is also more legitimacy as more states adopt medical, and eventually recreational, marijuana laws.

Finally, we analyzed the themes that were present in network news coverage of medical marijuana. Table 1.2 lists the major themes. We find that the most prominent theme is related to specific state laws (65.8 percent of stories), followed by federalism (55.9 percent). Notably, these categories are not mutually exclusive, meaning stories that cover both a state law and that state's tensions with federal government are double counted. In fact, 67 percent of stories with a state theme also have a federal theme. This tells us that reporters are typically linking state action regarding marijuana policy with federal prohibition. This is not unexpected but offers another means for observing the looming specter of federal policy over defiant state liberalization.

Figure 1.6 shows in multiple graphs how the themes from table 1.2 change over time. State policies and federalism themes are most prominent across time, with spikes in Supreme Court coverage that coincide with major hearings and decisions on medical marijuana (*Gonzales v. Raich*). Surprisingly, there are few segments that mention Congress, and when they do, they are quite tangential. For example, one story from 1997 is related to one of Clinton's nominees for an ambassadorship to Mexico who was facing scrutiny for his previous support of medical marijuana. Two of the seven segments aired after the 2005 *Gonzales v. Raich* decision, which held that Congress had authority under the Commerce Clause to prohibit state and local cultivation of medical marijuana. But there are not many stories about Congress's agenda or its ability to address the issue. We will discuss this in future chapters, but this lack of coverage makes sense when one considers the lack of congressional action on marijuana until very recently. In 2022, Congress passed the first piece of stand-alone legislation reforming marijuana laws to be signed into law. Before that, it had only passed a rider in the budget preventing the Department of Justice from going after state-legal marijuana companies.

In sum, the network news coverage of medical marijuana was much more positive than newspaper coverage during the same period.[49] The majority of articles focusing on state policy and federalism is consistent with research by Guy Golan that found newspaper editorials to be similarly centered on these issues (compared to op-eds that primarily focused on the medical benefits of marijuana).[50] While coverage was always disproportionately positive, it became *more* positive over time with fewer stories framing medical marijuana negatively or as a debate between groups. We also find that network news segments consistently included patients in their coverage—a group that shared positive experiences with medical cannabis and would garner the most sympathy.

THE *NEW YORK TIMES* ANALYSIS

The *New York Times* is considered the national newspaper of record, and it has a marked influence on the policy agenda and the rest of the media agenda.[51] We take a different approach with our analysis of its coverage of medical marijuana by examining which medical conditions were covered.[52] Why medical conditions? Medical marijuana is a policy that has beneficiaries—namely, patients with conditions approved by states

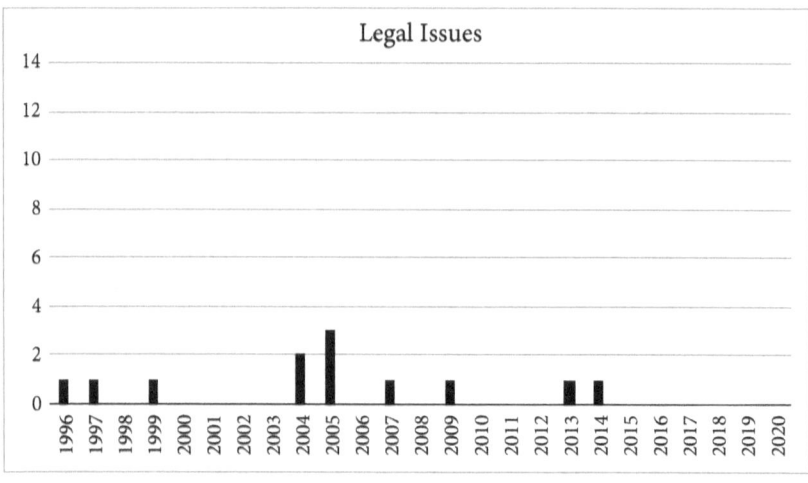

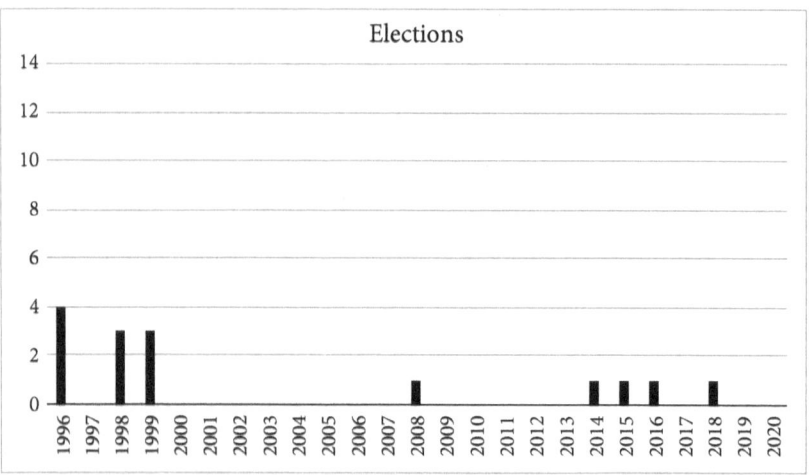

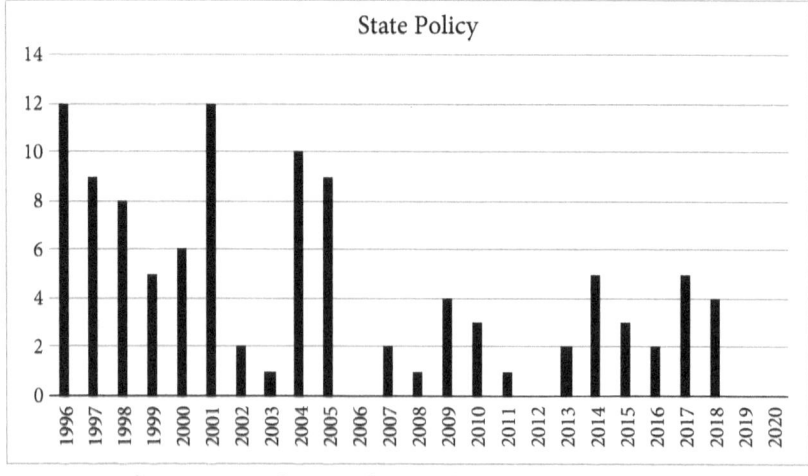

Figure 1.6a–f. Organizing themes of network news coverage of medical marijuana, 1996–2020.

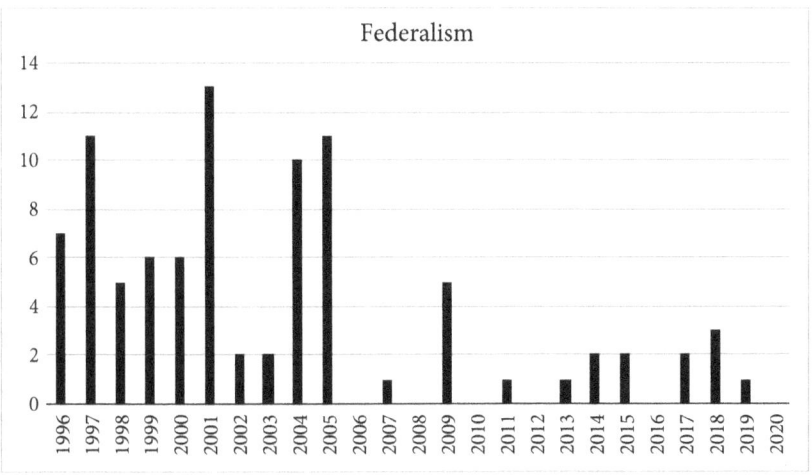

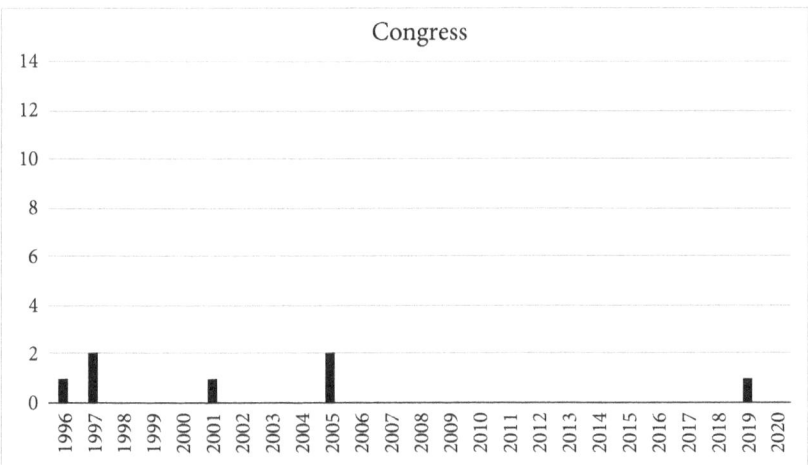

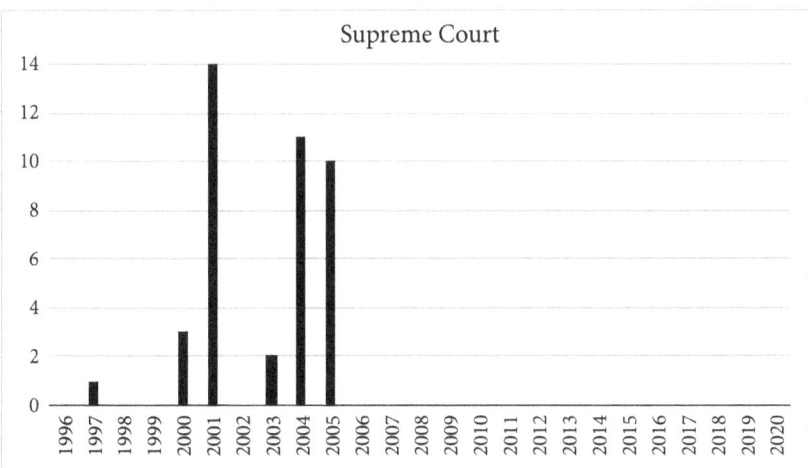

Figure 1.6a–f. (*continued*)

for access to cannabis. The way a policy's target groups are socially constructed affects the overall support for a policy and the distribution of benefits and burdens to those groups.[53] Moreover, self-stigma prevents some people from seeking treatment, while public stigma brings shame to those suffering from certain conditions.[54] For example, some individuals may view an AIDS diagnosis as a sign of moral turpitude[55] or be skeptical of mental health issues.[56] Other groups like children with epilepsy and veterans receive more positive social constructions and, accordingly, more benefits.[57] Importantly, perceptions of medical conditions can change and vary across subgroups. Thus, we examine how the media changed the frame of reference for medical marijuana patients in order to consider how the shifting patient frame also changes the debate over medical marijuana legalization.

To identify these groups, we searched for articles with "medical marijuana" in the headline or lede along with specific medication conditions: cancer, HIV/AIDS, epilepsy, post-traumatic stress disorder (PTSD), and opioids. Figure 1.7 shows in multiple graphs how *New York Times* coverage of the conditions associated with medical marijuana changed over twenty years. Initially, most of the coverage was paired with conditions like cancer and AIDS. But starting in the 2010s, new conditions become prominent in news coverage. The increasing attention to epilepsy is a product of the work of the "mommy lobby" that has drawn attention to the use of cannabidiol to mitigate seizures.[58]

There is also an increase in attention to PTSD. Many of these stories center on the potential of medical marijuana to treat veterans returning from the wars in Iraq and Afghanistan, which were part of the Global War on Terror, and suffering from PTSD.[59] And finally, coverage started to focus on medical marijuana's potential to mitigate the opioid epidemic. The opioid epidemic created pressures on lawmakers to respond. Meanwhile, a few studies showed that medical cannabis was associated with decreased overdose deaths, fewer prescription pain medication refills, and hospitalizations from opioids.[60] This drew attention to the claim that medical marijuana could be a substitute for more addictive and dangerous opioids. It is notable that this claim is not yet firmly supported by scientific evidence.[61] However, with overdose deaths reaching all-time highs during and after the COVID-19 pandemic, policymakers are looking for any options to stem the crisis.

In the analyses of news coverage by the networks and the *New York Times*, patients and medical marijuana are portrayed positively, highlighting the growing list of treatable conditions. As medical marijuana programs expanded to more states and other, larger social crises emerged—PTSD, pain, traumatic brain injury in Iraq and Afghanistan war veterans, and opioid overdose deaths—states also expanded their lists of approved conditions. This growing support for medical marijuana and the widening beneficiary view are the result of fresh insights from scientific research and the concerted effort of policy entrepreneurs and activists, who are using these points to make medical cannabis more accessible.[62]

Public Opinion

Shifts in public opinion can also help ripen the problem stream for policy action. There is no doubt that the United States has experienced a sea change in aggregate opinion on marijuana. Figure 1.8 plots the responses to a question asked by Gallup since 1969: "Do you think the use of marijuana should be made legal or not?" In 1969, only 12 percent of respondents answered "Yes, Legal." By 2020, this had increased to 68 percent. Of course, this opinion varies substantially across groups and by question wording (i.e., framing). For example, in Gallup's 2020 poll, 83 percent of self-identified Democrats answered yes to this same question, whereas only 48 percent of self-identified Republicans answered yes. Further, when legalization is defined as either medical or recreational, recreational only receives 60 percent support, but medical is supported by 91 percent of respondents.[63]

Breaking Free of the Morality Policy Frame

Another way to illustrate how marijuana's framing has changed over time is to think about how scholars discuss it. Policy typologies group like policies based on characteristics for the purpose of better understanding how policymaking differs across the types.[64] Perhaps the most well-known is Theodore Lowi's four-part typology: distributive, redistributive, regulatory, and constituent policies.[65] Scholars have pointed out, however, that morality issues like abortion, same-sex marriage, and the death penalty are their own separate type of policy and come with a

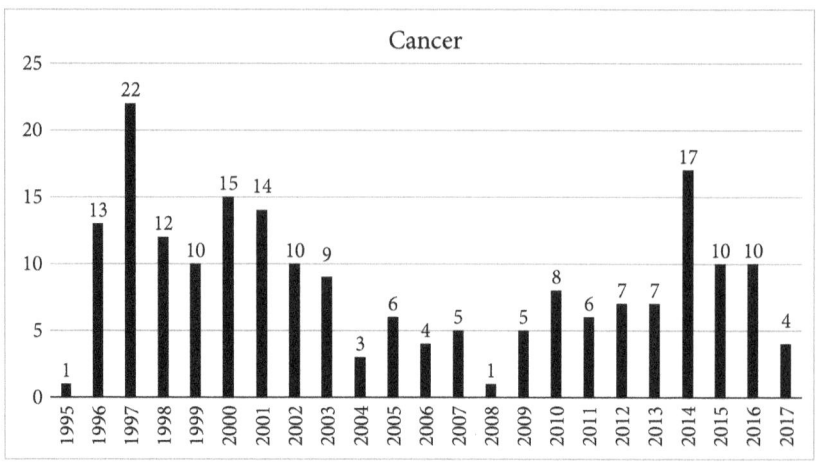

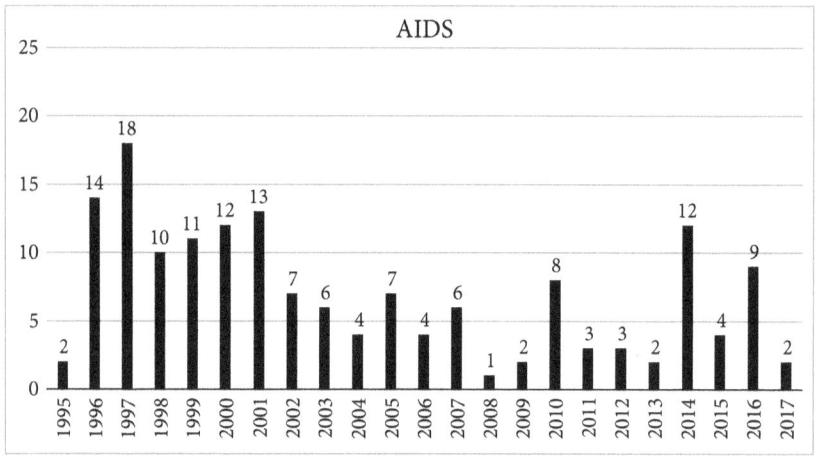

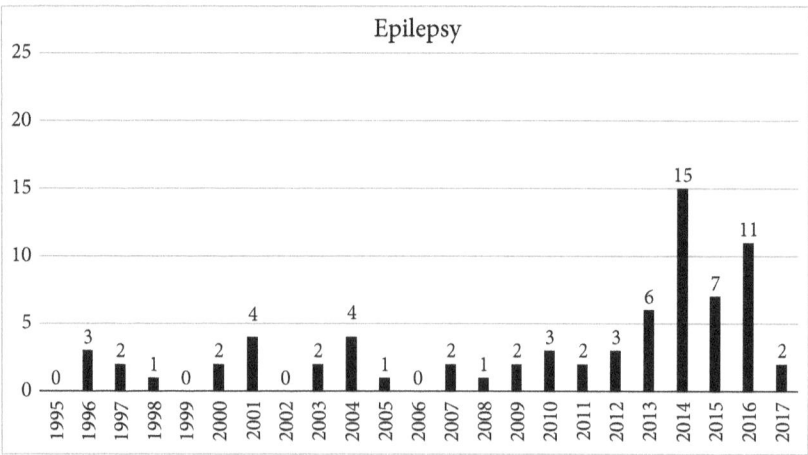

Figure 1.7a–e. Articles in the *New York Times* with specific mentions of the listed medical conditions, 1995–2017. Source: A. Lee Hannah, "The Politics of Passing and Implementing Medical Marijuana in Ohio," *Ohio Journal of Economics and Politics*, 24, no. 1 (2018), 43–70. Reprinted with permission.

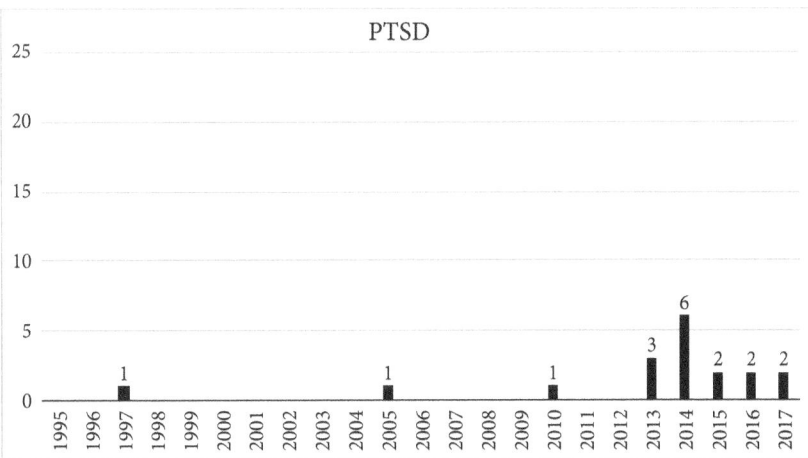

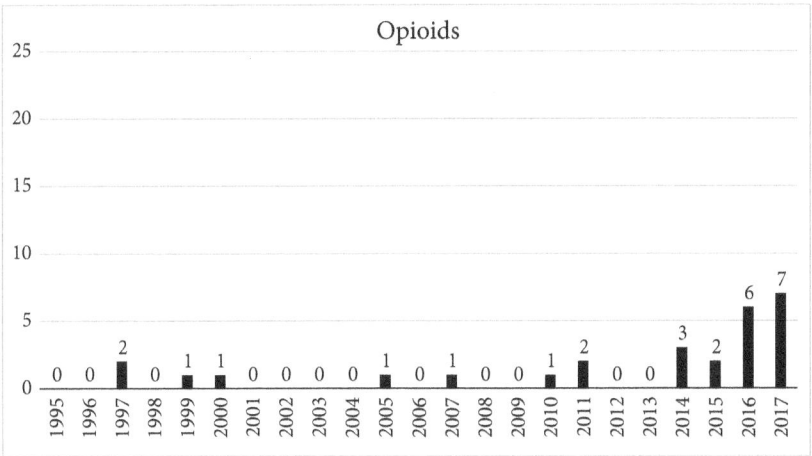

Figure 1.7a–e. (*continued*)

different politics.⁶⁶ In 2014, political scientist Kathleen Ferraiolo argued that marijuana policy is a morality policy. She notes that morality policies (1) involve debates "over first principles, or core values, rather than for example economic interests," (2) are "not amenable to compromise," (3) "involve conflicts over simple conceptions of right and wrong," and (4) are "often symbolic rather than instrumental."⁶⁷

Let's address each of the four types in turn. First, marijuana policy debates have become dominated by economic concerns rather than first principles (i.e., fundamental assumptions). At the state level, a common

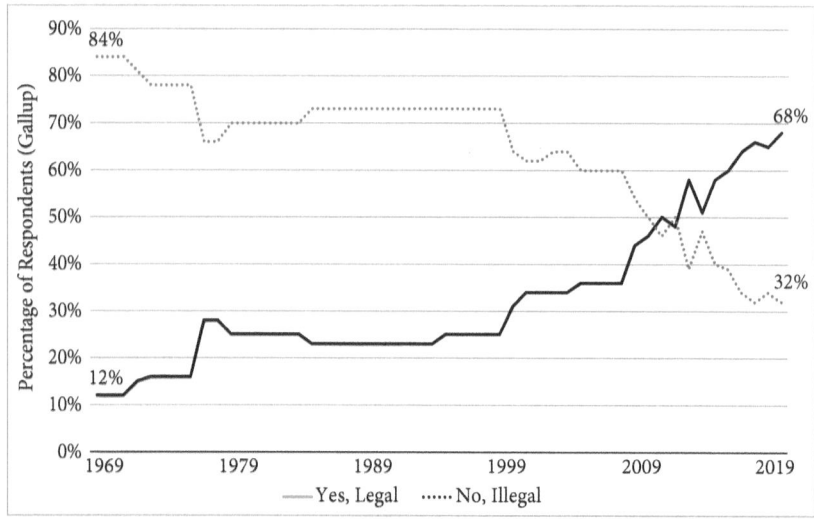

Figure 1.8. "Do you think the use of marijuana should be made legal, or not?" (1969–2020). Source: Megan Brenan, "Support for Legal Marijuana Inches Up to New High of 68%," *Gallup*, November 9, 2020.

argument for liberalizing marijuana, especially for recreational use, centers on the purported revenue that the state will raise post-adoption. Beyond that, debates in Congress about banking, in particular, have characterized marijuana as a major growth industry that needs to be supported to flourish. Cannabis is a multibillion-dollar industry that is expected to expand rapidly.[68] Political debates over marijuana policy, therefore, have become about far more than first principles.

Second, medical marijuana may not have been amendable to partisan compromise early on, but the debate has become more nuanced as medical marijuana has been shown not only to work but to be preferable to other treatments that society has collectively challenged (e.g., opioids). Our updated analysis in chapter 2 is compared with our 2018 study of medical marijuana diffusion.[69] The findings of our comparison indicate the declining ideological cleavage among the states over medical marijuana. Further, credible efforts are being made in highly conservative states that lack the ballot initiative (e.g., South Carolina) to legalize medical marijuana. We discuss later how compromise over the specifics of medical marijuana laws, notably increases in various restrictions, are precisely the compromises that have opened more conservative states to the policy.

Third, marijuana remains highly salient, but it is no longer a simple policy. State marijuana regulations are quite diverse and complex.[70] Further, states have been learning from each other in implementing the technical aspects of marijuana regulation and taxation.[71] It is also notable that simple conceptions of right and wrong have become more complicated as society questions the War on Drugs, racial disparities in policing, the costs of prohibition versus the costs of marijuana use, and the substantial shift in public opinion on marijuana use generally. Even in 1997, Michael Pollan of the *New York Times* wrote that California's adoption of medical marijuana "is rapidly transforming what has long been a simplistic monologue about drugs—Just say no—into a complex conversation between the people and their Government."[72]

Fourth, the notion of medical marijuana as symbolic instead of instrumental is nuanced. To be sure, most states have adopted medical programs that they want to work for patients. Accordingly, states have changed regulations and expanded qualifying condition lists. That said, some states are so focused on public safety or washing their hands of the issue that they do not write their policies in good faith. This has substantial impacts on (potential) patients. We discuss the practical effects of policy design on implementation in chapter 3 through the cases of Pennsylvania, Ohio, and West Virginia. Each state operated on a spectrum of good faith when writing their laws in 2016; for instance, Pennsylvania passed a program with bipartisan support, and West Virginia started opening dispensaries only in late 2021. We consider how the implementation differences across these states link back to the politics surrounding their adoption and design.

It is also notable that the moral dimension of marijuana has been changing among the public. In a May 2020 poll, Gallup found that 70 percent of Americans view "smoking marijuana" as morally acceptable. This was a higher percentage than stem cell research (66 percent), having a baby outside of marriage (66 percent), "gay or lesbian relations" (66 percent), and even buying and wearing clothes made of animal fur (54 percent).[73] Smoking marijuana was viewed as far more moral than viewing pornography (36 percent), even though pornography use is likely far more ubiquitous.[74] Even 51 percent of conservatives reported marijuana as being morally acceptable, just behind having a baby out of marriage (55 percent) and sex between an unmarried man and woman (55 percent). Of course, even as marijuana's stigma fades, it is not entirely gone.[75]

Policy Stream and Entrepreneurs

While problem identification is important for getting the attention of policymakers, advocates must also have some kind of policy to promote for solving that problem. The policy stream is the space where a variety of actors (i.e., a policy community) generate policy ideas. Kingdon referred to this as a "primeval soup," from which policy alternatives are drawn when a government is setting its decision agenda. Communities are loosely connected, and actors include government workers, interest groups, academics, researchers, and consultants.[76] Within the policy stream, policy entrepreneurs are active in both developing and promoting certain policy ideas and shaping the policy arena in such a way as to limit the politically viable options that can be considered.[77]

Agenda-setting power has two faces in policymaking.[78] One face is probably familiar: the ability to positively shape the agenda. Narrative control is one aspect of this power, and entrepreneurs and other actors use this power to advance their preferred policies. The other face, however, is negative agenda control. That is, the ability to prevent others from shaping the agenda and the prevailing narrative. This amounts to a blocking power, where entrepreneurs and other actors block non-preferred policy ideas. In short, if an individual or group can get the government to think about a policy problem in their preferred frame, and effectively block alternative conflicting frames, then they have significant power to set the agenda and the eventual policy choice. It is important to consider that Kingdon views each of the three streams as flowing separate from each other (i.e., in parallel).[79] This means that many policy ideas exist detached from a clear problem framing, or at least a commonly recognized problem. These policy ideas are simply waiting for their time to come, when entrepreneurs leverage events to tie them to emergent problems and frames.

A policy community includes both organizations and individuals. Each is key to the advancement of medical marijuana in the United States. NORML is one of the oldest advocates for cannabis liberalization; it was formed in 1970, the same year that Nixon signed the CSA. A second major policy advocate, the Marijuana Policy Project (MPP), was formed after a schism within NORML in 1995. MPP cut its teeth providing legal advice for the successful 1996 medical marijuana ballot initiative in California. Since then, MPP has engaged both in legal and policy development and lobbying efforts in multiple states and federally. One of its other early victories was influencing the legislative text of Hawaii's 2000 legalization of medical marijuana. This adoption was notable as the first instance of a legislature adopting the policy. In chapter 2, we will address the different manners of adoption. Like many advocacy organizations, MPP has developed model legislation that legislators and initiative campaigns can use when proposing a medical marijuana program.

Americans for Safe Access (ASA), formed in 2002, is also focused on providing model legislation for marijuana liberalization. That said, MPP and ASA differ in their recommended provisions, which creates competition for the attention of lawmakers. ASA is a membership organization that was founded by a patient and that advocates specifically for medical marijuana patients and physicians, whereas MPP is more broadly focused on liberalizing marijuana access. ASA also advocates for expanded research and sued the Drug Enforcement Administration (DEA) to force it to reschedule marijuana. In the end, state legislation has varied substantially in how it draws from either the MPP or ASA models.[80]

Individual advocates like Robert Randall and Mary Jane Rathbun (Brownie Mary) played important roles in humanizing the medical benefits of marijuana. The stories of their engagement also echo the results of our media coverage analysis. Media attention surrounding Brownie Mary's second arrest for marijuana distribution brought attention both to the AIDS crisis in California and the need for compassion toward patients.

As access to medical marijuana expanded through state adoptions, the profile of key advocates also began to shift. Whereas moms were a cornerstone of the antidrug parent's movement of the 1980s and joined forces with Nancy Reagan's "Just Say No" campaign, moms have more recently emerged as passionate advocates for medical marijuana, especially mothers of children with rare disorders that cause frequent, strong, and sometimes life-threatening seizures.[81] In some cases, these children experience *hundreds* of seizures a week. Pharmaceutical options for these disorders are largely nonexistent, and randomized controlled trials have shown evidence that cannabidiol specifically (a nonpsychoactive cannabinoid) can reduce seizure frequency.[82] Around the time that Colorado legalized recreational marijuana in 2012, these moms were increasingly connected on social media and eventually turned their attention to lobbying state legislatures.[83] Parents have also voted with their feet and moved their families to states with legalized marijuana. In one incident that gained national attention, Brian Wilson, father of a daughter with Dravet syndrome, pleaded with New Jersey Governor Chris Christie to not "let his daughter die." Christie had been stonewalling revisions to the state's then highly restrictive medical marijuana program.[84] Wilson's family ultimately moved to Colorado to seek treatment for their daughter. Parents were "the most potent force" there was for advocating for stricter drug laws in the 1980s.[85] Now, another group of parents has emerged as a potent force for pro-medical marijuana lobbying.

Similarly, veterans have become key advocates for medical marijuana and major players in state adoptions.[86] Veterans have mainly highlighted the benefits of cannabis for PTSD, traumatic brain injuries (TBI), and chronic pain.[87] In fact, former New York governor Andrew Cuomo symbolically signed a bill that added PTSD to the state's qualifying conditions on Veterans Day.[88] In 2018, Missourians approved an initiated constitutional amendment titled the "Medical Marijuana and Veteran Healthcare Services Initiative" that allocated all medical marijuana tax revenue toward healthcare services for veterans (see chapter 2).[89] In an effort to pass medical marijuana in North Carolina, Chayse Roth—a Marine veteran and advocate for NC Families for Medical Cannabis—told the state legislature, "If we really want to be the most veteran-friendly state in the union, this is just another thing we can do to solidify that statement."[90] Veterans have also organized to affect federal law by advocating for bills like the VA Medicinal Cannabis Research Act of 2021.[91]

Growing Calls for Social Equity and Justice

The emergence of adult-use recreational marijuana and the rapid growth of the marijuana industry in the United States has greatly increased the focus on social equity and justice concerns. Writing of the advocates behind the 1996 adoption of medical marijuana in California, Emily Dufton describes the "new face of pro-marijuana activism: white, middle-aged, and clearly sympathetic."[92] The same can easily be said of the mommy lobby advocating for the expansion of medical marijuana. Many of the most prominent advocates are white and middle class. This image stands in stark relief to the generations of Black and Hispanic Americans entangled in and harmed by the fifty-year War on Drugs. Social equity concerns emerged later in the spread of medical marijuana—the first social equity provision appeared in Maryland's statute in 2014.[93] New York and New Jersey, however, are prominent examples of the centrality of social equity in contemporary adult-use legalization debates. Both failed to adopt recreational marijuana in 2019 as it became apparent that the Black caucuses in both states were not satisfied with the attention paid to social justice. Many states now have tried to implement social equity provisions in their medical and/or recreational cannabis programs, but progress has been limited.[94] Additionally, government officials must often weigh competing goals—like economy, efficiency, effectiveness, and equity—when implementing these provisions.[95] We will discuss this issue further in chapter 4.

Thus, marijuana policies have been repackaged as advocates worked to expand the policy.[96] Significant to the story of medical marijuana is how policies are repackaged in order to gain acceptance in more conservative states. Early medical marijuana laws that were adopted by largely liberal states were often thin on regulations. As the policy spread and became legitimized, the laws began to incorporate more restrictions on packaging, personal cultivation of cannabis at home (home grow), advertising, and the number of dispensaries.[97] Such repackaging of the policy to suit different ideological demands is part of the ripening of the policy stream in different states. We now turn to directly discussing the role of state politics in medical marijuana agenda setting.

Political Stream

The political stream has three facets: the national mood, interest group advocacy, and government institutions. Mood is a general sense of how people in a state or nationally are feeling, rather than a specific opinion poll on a narrow topic.[98] Mood tends to operate like a thermostat: As policy shifts in one ideological direction in pursuit of the current mood (e.g., policy is becoming more liberal), the mood will shift back in the opposite ideological direction.[99] This is one of the stabilizing forces in American governance and policy. Periods of more liberal policy mood would help advance marijuana policy.

Interest advocacy groups operate within both the policy and political streams. In the political stream, they are engaged in identifying and advocating in venues that are receptive to their demands.[100] This is referred to as "venue shopping" and is quite common across all types of policies.[101] In the case of marijuana policy, the most prominent venue shopping occurred in decisions to advance policy through the direct initiative, where possible. We address this issue in chapter 2.

For the story of medical marijuana agenda setting, however, we would like to focus on political institutions and, particularly, the entrepreneurs who helped pave the way for medical marijuana. Political entrepreneurs are like policy entrepreneurs in that they use their resources—time, energy, money—to ripen the political stream, but they do so as members of political institutions. Party leaders play an important role in political entrepreneurship, but so do regular legislators who form a bridge between policy communities and political institutions.[102] When legislators are able to share stories of their personal experience with cannabis products, it can make a difference in their advocacy efforts.

One prominent example was state senator Mike Folmer from Pennsylvania. For several years, Democratic senator Daylin Leach had been introducing a bill to legalize medical marijuana in the commonwealth. It was not until Republican senator Folmer joined as a sponsor that the bill was able to gain enough Republican votes to pass the state Senate and House in 2016. When asked about whether he had ever used marijuana, Folmer admitted to traveling across state lines in 2012 and 2013 to obtain medical marijuana to treat the effects of chemotherapy for non-Hodgkin's lymphoma.[103] But Folmer pointed not to that personal experience, but to his engagement with moms of kids with epilepsy, as the factor that pushed him towards championing this issue.[104] Then there is Representative Nancy Mace (R-SC), who has used her personal experience of using cannabis to cope with PTSD from sexual assault to promote her States Reform Act that would remove cannabis as a Schedule I drug nationally. So, too, there was the groundbreaking political ad by Gary Chambers, Louisiana Democratic candidate for U.S. Senate in 2022. Chambers released an ad in which he smoked marijuana on screen (in decriminalized New Orleans) and discussed the disproportionate effect of nonviolent drug arrests on Black, Indigenous, (and) People of Color (BIPOC) communities. He said:

I've long felt that you're never going to destigmatize cannabis if all of the people that I know that smoke pot act like they don't smoke pot, so people don't criticize them. I don't think it's a bad thing that people smoke cannabis. I think the majority of people in America no longer think that. And so, the only way that you can destigmatize it is to just do it.[105]

While policy entrepreneurs have received a fair amount of scholarly attention, less is known about political entrepreneurs. Their role as brokers in the policymaking process is clear. Why individuals choose to champion the issues they do is less so. This is particularly the case for issues with high levels of stigma, like drugs. Folmer is again a good example. It was not until *after* medical cannabis was passed in Pennsylvania that he shared his own story with the public. However, by 2021, fellow Republican Nancy Mace used the power of her personal story to push marijuana liberalization. As stigma lessens, entrepreneurs are becoming more open to using their personal stories to push policies like cannabis liberalization. While complete normalization remains a distant goal, entrepreneurial political elites will continue to emerge to ripen the political stream for policies like medical and adult-use recreational marijuana.[106]

Getting on the Decision Agenda

For an issue to finally arrive on the government's decision agenda, two or more of the streams must "couple." Coupling simply means that the streams are brought together; they no longer operate in parallel. Both policy and political entrepreneurs can assist in stream coupling. Advocacy groups can help build pressure outside formal policymaking institutions, whereas political entrepreneurs build pressure from within. Windows of opportunity can also be opened for getting issues onto the government's agenda and moving a policy to adoption.[107] It is not necessary for all three streams—the problem stream, the policy stream, and the political one—to couple for an issue to arrive on the government's agenda. In democratic systems, there are regular windows of opportunity for coupling that occur when power changes hands between individuals and parties. Solutions that have been waiting for problems can have an easier time being picked up once a supportive party is in power. Or, activity in one venue, like the threat of a successful ballot initiative adopting medical marijuana, can force a legislature to pay attention and act. Through their committee structures, legislatures can process many different policies in parallel, but to pass a law, they are forced to serially process a single law at a time.[108] This means that while many policies make it onto the government's institutional agenda, very few issues ever make it to the decision-making agenda and receive a decision.

The Multiple Streams Framework helps us better understand the major factors that propelled medical marijuana onto the decision agendas in the states. While we have told a story of broad strokes, and the particulars differ to an extent within each state, we have found ripening in all three of the streams. Over time, political elites, the mass public, and the media changed their views on marijuana. Medical marijuana enjoyed a particular framing as a medicine that pulled it away from the image of hippies and substance abuse. The policy itself evolved so that more conservative states were more willing to compromise on the policy's goals. Advocates expanded the target beneficiaries of the policies in ways that also expanded the scope of conflict, drawing in more positively constructed groups like moms, children, and veterans. Political entrepreneurs became less afraid of using their own personal experiences with marijuana use to push for liberalization.

As we next turn to considering the story of policy adoption, it is important to recognize that while much of this discussion of agenda setting lends itself to considering legislatures as the venue for policy action, much of the early success in passing medical marijuana laws was due to the direct initiative. But not all states have the direct initiative, and twenty-two states have adopted medical marijuana through a legislature. Granted, most legislatures did not begin to adopt medical or, later, adult-use recreational marijuana laws until the policy started to spread to more states. The calculus on which states adopt policy innovations shifts as a policy spreads and gains legitimacy.[109] Early in the adoption of medical cannabis, the direct initiative was necessary to force the issue onto the government's decision agenda, albeit through an alternative institutional means. A combination of political entrepreneurs, shifting notions of who medical cannabis patients are, and emerging competitive pressures among the states helped to push medical cannabis onto the agendas of increasingly conservative states. We turn now to examining why states adopted medical marijuana laws in defiance of federal law and the centrality of the ballot initiative to that answer.

2

Defiant Innovation

States, Federalism, and the Fight for Legalization

I took a perverse joy—a pleasure in speaking the truth to legislative committees over the decades. But it's a good deal more fun when you actually have a chance of winning. And it's not in the General Assembly. It's at the ballot box. And we will win. We will prevail.
—Dan Viets, board president of New Approach Missouri,
St. Louis Post-Dispatch, 2018

On November 6, 2018, Missouri became the thirty-second state to adopt a comprehensive medical cannabis program when 65 percent of voters approved Amendment 2. Dan Viets—an advocate for marijuana reform in Missouri for forty years—led a campaign that raised more than $1.5 million and only faced a little more than $6,000 in opposition spending.[1] By the time medical marijuana arrived on the 2018 ballot, the only drama was related to ensuring that Amendment 2 passed instead of Amendment 3 or Proposition C—two other medical marijuana initiatives sponsored by other interest groups. The initiatives differed in some important ways. Amendment 2 imposed a 4 percent tax on sales and would direct those dollars toward veterans' services in the state. It was also the only plan that would allow medical patients to grow their own supply at home. Amendment 3 imposed a much higher 15 percent tax and would direct most of the revenue toward medical research. Proposition C would only tax at 2 percent, but the money would be distributed to veterans, drug treatment, early childhood education, and public safety. There were other nuances in each of the initiatives, but the fact that three initiatives qualified for the ballot in a conservative midwestern state was symbolic of how far advocates had come. The debate in

Missouri had advanced from whether the state should have medical marijuana to one over which policy was the best.

The victory of Amendment 2 was not a sign of a broader left turn in Missouri politics. Despite a strong national environment for Democrats, Missourians ousted their two-term Democratic Senator Claire McCaskill for Republican Attorney General Josh Hawley—a conservative firebrand. Moreover, Missouri's adoption of Amendment 2 on election night 2018 was not even the headliner in marijuana news. A medical marijuana initiative passed in Utah, one of the most socially conservative states, and Michigan voters approved an adult-use recreational program.

The example of Missouri is instructive. In a few years, marijuana activists like Viets went from fighting an uphill battle to easily passing an initiative. Amendment 2 was titled the "Medical Marijuana and Veteran Healthcare Services Initiative" and centered veterans as the core beneficiaries—both assuring veteran-specific conditions were covered for patients and by directing tax revenue toward veteran healthcare. The Veterans of Foreign Wars (VFW) of Missouri even made a rare endorsement of the initiative.[2] Furthermore, by 2018, three of Missouri's seven neighbors had passed medical marijuana laws—Illinois in 2013, Arkansas in 2016, and Oklahoma in the spring of 2018. Adoption by neighboring states sends a signal about a program's efficacy and popularity. States with more permissive policies will also attract the money and interest of their neighbor's citizens—whether that is to buy lottery tickets or to shop in a dispensary. Stopping the outflow of revenues then becomes one argument for adoption. And finally, advocates had access to the ballot initiative—a procedure for taking policies directly to voters that is available in just half the states. The Missouri example touches on several elements that are often present when states adopt a policy innovation, like medical marijuana.

Researchers of state politics pay substantial attention to the adoption and spread of public policies—a process called policy diffusion.[3] State policies are instructive for testing theories of policy adoption, design, and implementation and often become the foundation of federal law. Policymakers have used insights from state policies to encourage the spread of those policies across the states to address a myriad of concerns, from revenue generation to the protection (or restriction) of civil liberties. Popular policies will often diffuse to a plurality of states—and in some cases, the federal government might encourage such innovation. This is how policy diffusion is normally observed and described.

Yet, marijuana policy stands in stark contrast to most examples of policy diffusion. In this chapter, we explain how medical marijuana policies diffused incrementally, despite their explicit defiance of federal law—a process that differs from traditional studies of diffusion where the federal government is usually either supportive of or neutral toward a policy's spread. But it is also important to consider policy diffusion as a dynamic process. We contend that the factors that have encouraged the diffusion of medical marijuana policy have changed over time, as have the *costs of defiance*. We lead this chapter with a brief background in policy diffusion theory before diving into the case of medical marijuana adoption.

The Diffusion of Policy Innovations

Policy adoption in the American states is most often analyzed using the diffusion of innovations framework.[4] Frances Stokes Berry and William D. Berry have characterized a governmental unit's (i.e., a country, province, state) decision to adopt a policy innovation as a function of its internal motivations, internal resources, existing policies, and external influences.[5] Policy diffusion studies applying this theoretical model most often use internal and external characteristics of a state to statistically model the spread of policy innovations such as lotteries, smoking bans, and school curricula standards, as examples.[6] Factors internal to the states that shape their decisions to adopt policy innovations commonly include citizen and government liberalism, the state's economic strength (e.g., per capita income), the degree of professionalism in its legislature, and party control of government.[7] Depending on the policy context, researchers will also examine how the availability of the citizen initiative can push an innovation along, something to which we return in a moment in the context of medical marijuana. These variables are meant to capture the motivation and resources aspects of the theoretical model. Using larger datasets that include many policy innovations, diffusion researchers have tested how attributes of the innovations themselves, like complexity and salience, also shape the rate and extent of adoption.[8]

The most common external influences of adoption included in diffusion models are geographic proximity to past adopters and ideological distance from past adopters.⁹ Both are meant, to an extent, to capture the mechanism of diffusion that is occurring. In terms of interstate dynamics, diffusion researchers typically recognize five possible mechanisms within American federalism: learning, competition, social contagion, emulation/socialization, and federal coercion.¹⁰ If adoption by one's contiguous neighbors prompts a state to adopt that innovation, then it is often assumed that learning, competition, or even social contagion are the possible mechanisms driving diffusion.¹¹ States might also be more likely to adopt policies passed by states that are ideologically similar— viewing the policy as something to emulate.¹² Coercion by the federal government, be it directly through financial incentives or penalties or indirectly by paying attention to a particular issue, is another potential mechanism that drives diffusion in the states.¹³ Let us first discuss each of the four mechanisms of state-to-state—that is, horizontal—diffusion in turn before focusing on the federal government's coercive role (i.e., the fifth mechanism).

Learning captures either policy learning (i.e., understanding a policy and its direct and/or indirect effects) or ideological learning (i.e., understanding a policy's political effects).¹⁴ State renewable portfolio standards (RPS) offer a useful example of policy learning. One study found that state assessments of their abilities to implement an RPS were a factor in the decision to adopt.¹⁵ Specifically, a state would observe both the implementation environment in states that previously adopted the policy and the effectiveness of the policy. In other words, not only did lawmakers need to consider past effectiveness, but they needed to know that an RPS could be successfully implemented in their own state. In the case of ideological learning, policymakers are considering whether an innovation will be effective for them politically. They look to the electoral success of other liberals or conservatives in states that previously adopted the policy. In a survey experiment using zoning and home foreclosure policies, one study found that local officials with a strong ideological predisposition against a policy were unlikely to consider it in their city, but this resistance could be overcome if the policy's success could be persuasively presented.¹⁶

Competition-driven diffusion occurs when states adopt a policy to gain some competitive advantage over their peers.¹⁷ The classic example in the literature is the spread of state lotteries. States tend to enact policies like lotteries or gaming when they are seeking additional revenues but do not want to face the political heat of passing broad-based tax increases (e.g., income or sales).[18] They also do so when they are trying to gain a competitive advantage over neighbors, particularly when large populations of potential customers live close to their border.[19] Competition among neighboring states or within regions of the country tend to prompt a race to the bottom in areas like environmental regulations and welfare program generosity, but it can sometimes encourage a race to the top in areas like education and even welfare reform.[20]

Social contagion is more of a bottom-up diffusion mechanism, where interstate communications networks among citizens help increase the demand for a policy in a neighboring state.[21] While social contagion is among the least studied diffusion mechanisms, Julie Pacheco convincingly demonstrated that changes in public opinion among populations close to state borders helped to spread smoking bans.[22] In this case, instead of legislators responding directly to signals from neighboring states regarding the value of smoking bans, they were responding to the changing attitudes of their constituents who had observed that value for themselves.

Finally, emulation or socialization occurs when a state adopts a policy because of normative pressure.[23] The work of Joshua Jansa and colleagues has illustrated how such emulation occurs. State characteristics, particularly the professionalism of their legislature, plays some role in determining whether a state is likely to directly copy another state's law.[24] Still, states with less professional legislatures do reinvent complex policies when necessary.[25] Interestingly, copied legislation, at least in the areas of youth vaping and organ donation policies, tends to be less successful than when legislatures expend the resources to adapt a policy to their state.[26] Interest groups that produce model legislation, like the American Legislative Exchange Council, also help drive emulation behavior in diffusion networks.[27]

What about the Federal Government?

In the federal system in the United States, the national (federal) government certainly has a role to play in state policy innovations. Figure 2.1 depicts the different ways in which the federal government does (or does not) play a role in the diffusion of policy innovations within the U.S.

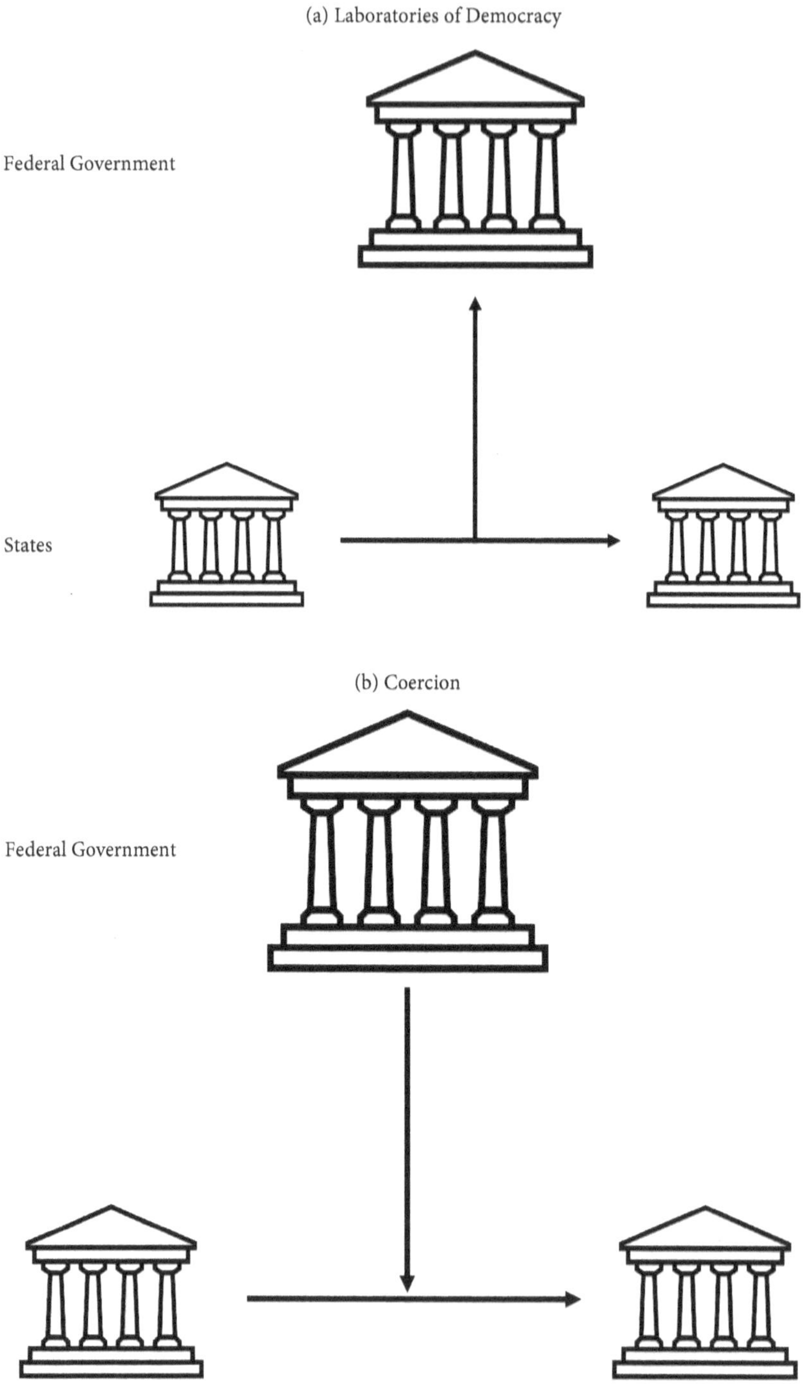

(a) Laboratories of Democracy

Federal Government

States

(b) Coercion

Federal Government

Figure 2.1a–d. The federal government and mechanisms of state policy diffusion.

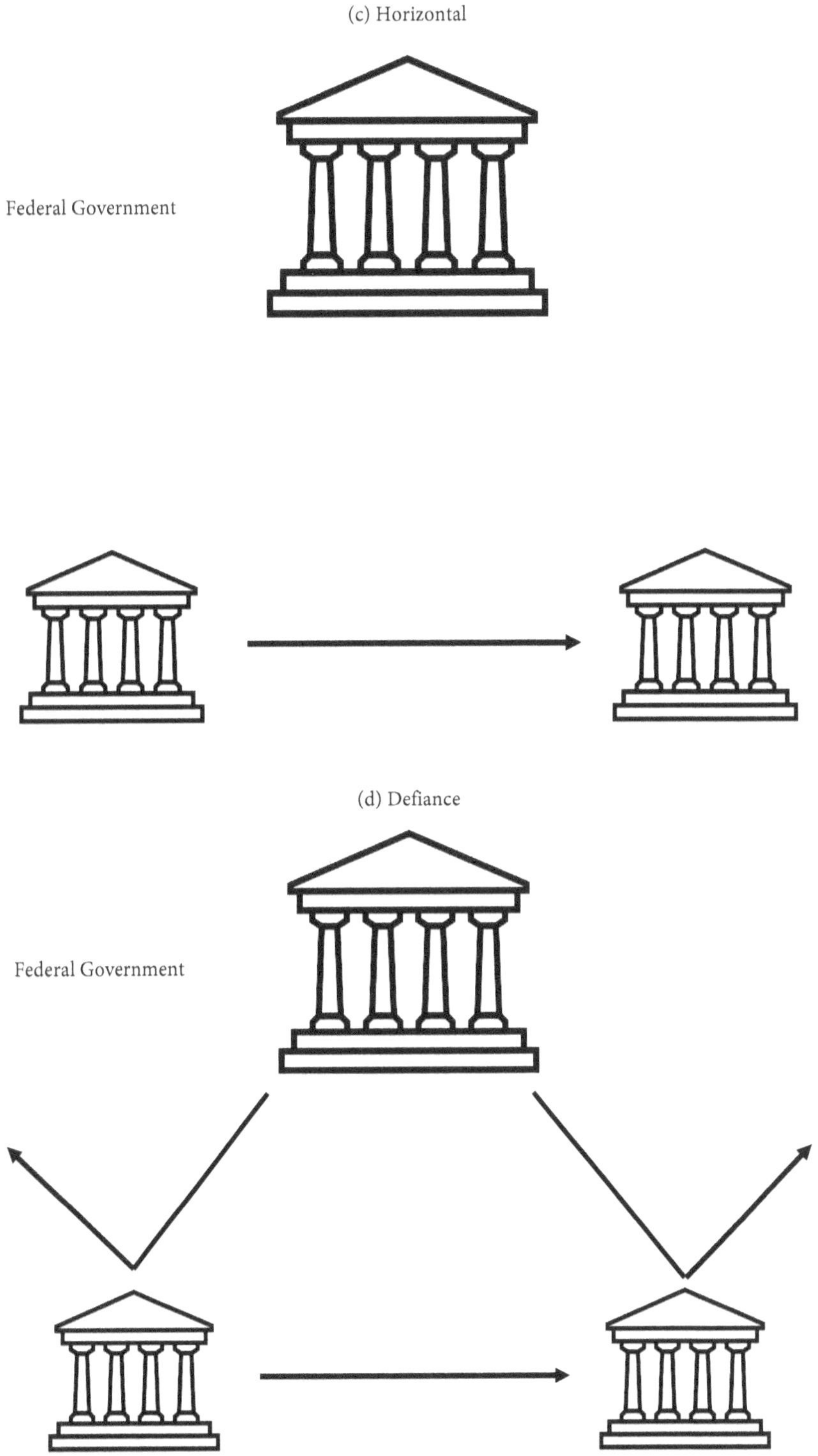

Figure 2.1a–d. (*continued*)

federal system. In this book's introduction, we discussed the traditional Brandeisian view of states as laboratories of democracy (see figure 2.1a). The states experiment with new ideas, and (we assume) the best ideas trickle up to the federal government. Diffusion scholars most often consider the federal government's coercive power, however (figure 2.1b). Through direct financial incentives and indirect crossover sanctions, and even by simply paying attention to a policy, the federal government can help push subnational policy diffusion along.[28] For many policies, the federal government takes a neutral position, meaning the mechanisms of horizontal (i.e., state-to-state) diffusion, as discussed above, are active (figure 2.1c).

We previously characterized medical marijuana as a "defiant innovation" (figure 2.1d).[29] By this, we mean it does not fit within the traditional view of the federal government acting as a coercive agent in prompting the states to adopt a policy innovation. Instead, the federal government has sent clear signals that it disapproves of a policy, but the states innovate anyway. In the case of medical marijuana (and adult recreational use, for that matter), states are acting in defiance of federal law to cultivate and diffuse a significant policy innovation. We have also argued that the extent to which marijuana policy can be called defiant fluctuates over time. The credibility of the federal government's commitment to prohibition has waxed and waned.[30] Of course, while signals from the executive branch and even Congress may have become more favorable to marijuana policy liberalization over the past three decades, the Controlled Substances Act (CSA) of 1970 is still the law of the land. Until marijuana's place as a Schedule I drug is reformed nationally, any state adopting a medical marijuana law is doing so in defiance of federal law. But it is not only the change in these federal signals that helps legitimize this policy. Each successive adoption by a state increases the legitimacy of the policy and makes it that much easier for additional states to follow. In sum, the costs—practical, political, reputational—of defying the federal government are not fixed over time and have in fact decreased.

Policy implementation research provides a foundation for understanding how states respond to federal signals and why they, at times, innovate in defiance of federal law. Malcolm Goggin and colleagues have sought to explain why states vary in their willingness to implement federal priorities and the subsequent success of federal programs.[31] As noted previously, the federal government can send signals in support of an innovation directly through incentives and mandates or indirectly through issue attention or congressional activity. However, the federal government not only provides inducements (i.e., positive signals) for state action but also utilizes constraints (i.e., negative signals). For either federal inducements or constraints to be implemented by the states, the signals sent to them must be credible, clear, consistent, repeated, and received.[32] When states respond positively to these signals, they are acting as agents of the federal government and are important to implementation of federal policy aims.[33]

However, states also resist federal mandates. For example, Congress passed the REAL ID Act (2005) in response to recommendations by the 9/11 Commission that the government establish standards for personal identification, including those issued by states (e.g., driver's licenses).[34] State leaders immediately pushed back on the law arguing that the federal government's position was an unconstitutional violation of privacy rights and that the "unfunded mandate" put the onus on states to pay for securing immense amounts of sensitive data and for acquiring new technologies.[35] Maine was the first state to adopt a law *opposing* the federal REAL ID requirements and, within eighteen months, twenty other states followed suit.[36] In this case, the federal government was trying to induce states to produce a desired policy outcome, but the states balked. The federal government's primary leverage in inducing at least minimal state compliance (i.e., offering a REAL ID option for residents) has been its regulation of air travel. Thus, even in the face of state resistance, the federal government has levers of coercion available to induce compliance. Of course, the final chapter of REAL ID implementation has not yet been written, as the Department of Homeland Security pushed back the final implementation deadline to May 7, 2025, a full twenty years after the law's passage.[37]

Federalism scholars have noted that such resistance to federal law increased across the states during the administrations of presidents Barack Obama, Donald Trump, and Joseph Biden.[38] While the federal government relies on a "cooperative" federalism for effective policy implementation, states have become increasingly "uncooperative," and even when implementing a policy, they do so at variable paces.[39] State attorneys general have been increasingly active in cross-partisan resistance to federal policy, as evidenced by Republican lawsuits under President Obama over the Affordable Care Act; Democratic lawsuits under President Trump over a range of policies, including the administration's immigration restrictions banning travel from several majority-Muslim countries and the ban of transgender individual's service in the military; and Republican challenges to Biden's COVID-19 vaccine mandate, among other policies.[40] State resistance to the expansion of Medicaid under the Affordable Care Act is likewise illustrative.[41] Medicaid expansion highlights how financial inducements can erode state resistance over time.[42]

Defiant innovation, however, occurs when the federal government *prohibits* an activity that states desire.[43] This is distinct from cases like REAL ID, where the states are refusing to implement a federal program. Granted, both are principal-agent problems, whereby the states as agents are not implementing the principal's (i.e., the federal government's) desires. In any case of implementation, agents—which may be states or street-level bureaucrats—have choices in whether they will comply with (work) the wishes of their principal, shirk their responsibilities, or actively sabotage the policy. The relevant distinction here is that mandate resistance is a case of agent shirking, whereas a defiant innovation, like medical marijuana, is sabotage.[44] In defiant innovation, states are not simply allowing a banned activity; rather, they *are actively promoting* the development of a *new* program, even when the federal government bans it.

States, of course, diverge in their willingness to engage in defiant innovation. A shrinking but still substantial minority is supportive of federal prohibition or is legitimately dissuaded from acting against federal interests and thus sees no reason to enact allowances for marijuana use. In fact, in 1994, California Governor Pete Wilson vetoed a medical marijuana bill because of concerns over federal law.[45] Even twenty-four years (and thirty-eight peer-state adoptions) later, Nebraska Republican Governor Eric Holcomb argued that he would refuse to look at marijuana reforms as long as it is federally illegal. Holcomb stated, "If the law changed, we would look at all the positive or adverse impacts it would have. I'm not convinced other states have made a wise decision."[46] Other states are sympathetic but lack the ecological capacity to enact defiant innovations and risk retribution (e.g., lawsuits) by the federal government or peer states.[47] As the plurality of states shifts from those opposed to the innovation to the neutral and the positive, the patterns of both adoption and enforcement change, just as the determinants of any policy tend to change throughout the stages of diffusion.⁴⁸ We now turn to delving deeper into how the cost of defying the federal government in adopting medical marijuana laws has changed since 1996.

The Costs of Defiance

To illustrate how the various costs of defying the federal government change as more states adopt and legitimize a defiant innovation, we will walk through five cases. The first two, California and Arizona, illustrate early adoption in two states with the ballot initiative. The next case, Vermont, captures early adoption by a state legislature. The final two cases, Ohio and Oklahoma, demonstrate how the costs of adopting changed later on in both legislative and ballot adoptions, respectively.

Early Adopters: California and Arizona

In 1996, Proposition 215, an initiative permitting the medical use of marijuana, was placed on the ballot in California. The initiative, originally conceived by activist Dennis Peron, was the first of its kind. Barry McCaffrey, President Bill Clinton's drug czar, and the entire Clinton administration put on a full-court press in opposition to the initiative. McCaffrey, along with Attorney General Janet Reno and Department of Health and Human Services Secretary Donna Shalala appeared on several television and radio programs warning about the negative consequences of the law. In an appearance on *Washington Watch*, McCaffrey stated that the government would subject physicians to prosecution under federal law "without question."⁴⁹ The administration also released a joint statement from former presidents Gerald Ford, Jimmy Carter, and George H. W. Bush arguing that Proposition 215 sends "the erroneous message that dangerous and addictive drugs such as heroin, LSD, marijuana, and methamphetamine are safe."

State and local officials in California were just as resistant. Attorney General Dan Lungren called Prop 215 "legal anarchy."⁵⁰ Orange County Sheriff Brad Gates argued the proposition was "not about medicine, it's about the legalization of marijuana."⁵¹ At the behest of Lungren, just a few months before Californians would vote on Proposition 215, 100 agents of the California Bureau of Narcotic Enforcement raided the Cannabis Buyers Club in San Francisco. Agents left with 150 pounds of marijuana, drug paraphernalia, tens of thousands of dollars in cash, and the records of 11,000 clients.[52] Of course, this did not stop the passage of Proposition 215. In the words of one anti-prohibition activist responding to the raid: "Passage of the medical marijuana initiative this November would clearly be a snub of [California] Gov. Wilson's policies. It is unclear at this time whether his jack-booted tactics will cause a backlash response on the part of the voting public."[53]

In Arizona, a more modest initiative drew less money and attention. Proposition 200 included provisions allowing physicians to prescribe Schedule I drugs for treatment of debilitating and terminal illness; it also advocated for criminal justice reform by requiring probation for nonviolent drug offenses instead of jail time. The law required that any prescription had to be endorsed by two physicians and paired with medical research supporting the treatment. It passed with 65 percent of Arizonans voting "yes"—a larger margin than in California, where 55 percent of voters supported the measure.[54]

Even though Californians and Arizonans approved measures to legalize medical marijuana, federal, state, and local officials took divergent approaches. With the support of the Clinton administration, the Arizona legislature and governor neutralized the ballot initiative by requiring any drug dispensed as medicine be approved by the Food and Drug Administration (FDA), making it impossible for physicians in the state to act without a significant change of course from the federal government. In California, physicians, patients, and activists faced legal uncertainty and challenges for well over a decade. While Proposition 215 encouraged state officials to "implement a plan to provide for the safe and affordable distribution of marijuana," the details were left to local lawmakers.[55] California Attorney General Lungren—who had supported earlier drug raids—deferred to localities. Localities against medical marijuana continued to enforce marijuana prohibition as if Proposition 215 did not exist. Meanwhile, local officials in supportive communities allowed cannabis clubs and dispensaries to form and operate.

The federal government's position remained vigilant. In 1998, the Clinton administration obtained preliminary injunctions on six northern California cannabis clubs. In 1998, with three more states poised to legalize medical marijuana, members of the U.S. House of Representatives passed a resolution (H.J.Res. 117) by a vote of 310 to 93 that stated:

> Congress continues to support the existing Federal legal process for determining the safety and efficacy of drugs and opposes efforts to circumvent this process by legalizing marijuana, and other Schedule I drugs, for medicinal use without valid scientific evidence and the approval of the Food and Drug Administration.[56]

Nearly all House Republicans voted in support of the measure, as did a slight majority of Democrats. The Senate never acted on the resolution but included language in the fiscal year 1999 omnibus budget package supporting the position of the resolution.[57]

Congress also acted to prevent the District of Columbia from going forward with a voter-approved medical marijuana program in 1998. After trying to stop the D.C. government from even counting the vote (ultimately losing in court), Congress blocked the implementation of the initiative with a rider known as the Barr Amendment.[58]

When George W. Bush entered office in 2001, his Department of Justice, led by Attorney General John Ashcroft, stepped up marijuana raids. In late September 2001, agents raided the rural home of Dr. Mollie Fry, a physician and medical marijuana supporter. In a drawn-out legal battle, Fry and her husband ultimately served five years in federal prison. And in 2002, the federal government shut down Scott Imler's West Hollywood dispensary, even though Imler was known for being diligent about complying with Proposition 215's guidance.[59] Even with aggressive legal maneuvering from the federal government and half-hearted implementation from state officials, a few states followed California's lead and adopted medical marijuana policies primarily through the popular initiative: Alaska, Oregon, and Washington in 1998, followed by Maine in 1999. Thus, by the end of the 1990s, it appeared that federal coercion was slowing the spread of medical marijuana, but that would not last.

Early Legislative Adopters: Vermont

In 2004, the Vermont General Assembly passed a medical marijuana measure through a Democratic-dominated Senate and Republican-dominated House. Republican Governor James Douglas faced tremendous pressure from the Bush administration and the White House Office of National Drug Control Policy and its director, John Walters. As the bill was moving through the Vermont legislature and ultimately to Governor Douglas's desk, Walters had already personally pressured Douglas at a summit in Oregon and called him twice to discourage allowing the law to go into effect. Walters also sent his deputy to Vermont's capital of Montpelier in efforts to get the legislature to drop the measure.[60]

Douglas ultimately decided to allow the measure to pass without his signature. His statement about the decision included both notes of sympathy for patients who found relief from marijuana as well as his personal reservations about the legality of the measure. Douglas stated, "I cannot actively support a measure that allows Vermonters to be subject to prosecution under federal law, increases the availability of a controlled substance, and sends a dangerous message to our children."[61]

There is no telling how much this decision may have affected Douglas's political future, but he certainly faced a difficult decision with immense pressure from his fellow partisans. Norman Runnion of the *Herald (of Randolf)* opined, "Now that's all well and good, but what Vermonters know, and President Bush knows . . . is that the Republican governor of Vermont 'aided and abetted,' to use a legal phrase, in making a very limited use of pot legal in this state."[62] The pressure campaign lodged against Governor Douglas illustrates the high stakes of adoption during this period.

Later Adopters: Ohio and Oklahoma

For decades, Ohio has been known as a national bellwether for public opinion.[63] However, the Ohio legislature lagged its constituents' opinion about medical marijuana. Two direct initiative campaigns forced their hand. First, in 2015, an initiative campaign poured over $20 million into Issue 3—an ambitious measure that would have simultaneously legalized medical and recreational marijuana.[64] The initiative was sloppily written and included what many feared was a monopoly for the ten growers specifically named in it. The initiative had enough red flags that the Drug Policy Alliance (DPA) and Marijuana Policy Project (MPP) withheld their endorsements.[65] The initiative was voted down by a 2 to 1 margin.[66]

However, the initiative put marijuana on the agenda and in the public mind, which forced legislators to address an issue that they had been successfully tabling for a decade. Polling revealed that medical marijuana was supported by 90 percent of Ohioans.[67] Armed with lessons learned from 2015 and a looming presidential election year, Ohioans for Medical Marijuana started moving on a 2016 ballot initiative with the support of MPP.[68]

Suddenly, Governor John Kasich and the Republican-dominated legislature had a choice: respond to public opinion and pass a medical marijuana law in a process that they could control or risk allowing a ballot initiative where they have no influence on the content of the law and that could potentially mobilize young voters in the 2016 general election, which included the high-stakes presidential race.[69] They chose the former and moved at breakneck speed to pass their own law.[70] But the legislature and governor were loath to celebrate their legislative achievement. Even though the bill passed with bipartisan support and some fanfare from activists, Governor Kasich decided to sign the bill along with several others in a muted ceremony.[71] The adoption process in Ohio reveals how the threat of a credible ballot initiative can push lawmakers to act, especially when their opinions and priorities are at odds with their constituents.

Oklahoma and Nebraska took a unique approach to their opposition to spreading marijuana liberalization. Fed up with neighboring Colorado's new adult-use recreational program (adopted in 2012), the states sued Colorado directly in the United States Supreme Court. States can sue each other in original jurisdiction cases before the court, but they must first obtain approval from the justices to do so. Oklahoma and Nebraska sought this approval in December 2014 but were ultimately denied in a 6–2 decision in 2016. The case would have addressed the open legal question of whether federal prohibition preempts state legalization, but even President Obama's Solicitor General Donald Verrilli filed in opposition of the complaint. He argued that Colorado was not harming its neighbors.[72] Ironically, just two short years after the decision came down, Oklahoma joined the movement of open defiance to federal marijuana prohibition in 2018 by adopting a medical marijuana law. In fact, the state adopted a program that has been called "the wild west of weed."[73] Moreover, it was one of the fastest states in implementing its new program and has the highest percentage of residents participating in the program (10 percent) of any state by 2022.[74] How did this happen?

Oklahoma may be one of the most conservative states in the nation, but its population has a decidedly libertarian streak.[75] This has led to one of the freest medical marijuana markets in the country. But, once again, the ballot initiative was a key institutional characteristic for opening up the state to medical marijuana. Oklahoma has historically been a highly punitive state in terms of regulating drug use, but polling revealed that this approach did not have the support of most Oklahomans.[76] Armed with this information, libertarian and liberal activists joined the cause to push for the legalization of medical marijuana.[77] A first attempt at getting medical marijuana on the ballot in 2014 failed to garner enough signatures. While successful in advance of the 2016 election, a dispute over the ballot measure language used by the secretary of state prevented the question from appearing on the ballot then. This dispute highlights the lingering institutional resistance to marijuana liberalization. When the measure was set to appear on the 2018 ballot, lawmakers again tried to resist. Governor Mary Fallin and nearly her entire cabinet opposed the measure, as did the state's members of Congress, law enforcement, major faith groups, the chamber of commerce, and the state's medical association.[78] Using her available power, Fallin put the question on the 2018 primary ballot in May instead of the general election ballot in November. The electorate tends to be smaller in primary elections with only the most reliable and partisan voters participating. Fallin anticipated an older and more conservative group of primary voters would vote the initiative down. As one proponent of the initiative put it, "She just did everything she could to wreck us."[79] It still passed with 57 percent approval.

Each of the aforementioned examples demonstrates how policy adoption is a dynamic process. The costs of adopting a defiant innovation like medical marijuana are not fixed over time. In fact, they decline as a policy is legitimized and as the federal government's increasingly mixed signals on prohibition open space for action. Early state adopters faced near-universal resistance—even within their own borders. Meanwhile, later adopters have the benefit of learning from the experience of other states and the security of knowing that a federal crackdown would need to be imposed on dozens of other states, too. In fact, it is common to see states include a list of other states that have passed medical marijuana bills in their laws to assuage worries of breaking federal law. MPP's Model State Medical Cannabis Bill recommends the following language: "Thirty-eight states and the District of Columbia have removed state-level criminal penalties from the medical use and cultivation of cannabis. [*Insert State Name*] joins in this effort for the health and welfare of its citizens."[80]

And several states have included language precisely like MPP's recommendation. Several state laws also attempt to minimize federal risks in their laws. For example, New Jersey's medical bill from 2010 states:

> According to the U.S. Sentencing Commission and the Federal Bureau of Investigation, 99 out of every 100 marijuana arrests in the country are made under state law, rather than under federal law. Consequently, changing state law will have the practical effect of protecting from arrest the vast majority of seriously ill people who have a medical need to use marijuana.[81]

MPP's model legislation recommends the following language: "States are not required to enforce federal law or prosecute people for engaging in activities prohibited by federal law. Therefore, compliance with this act does not put the state of _____ in violation of federal law."[82]

More recently, Supreme Court Justice Clarence Thomas criticized the federal government's lack of clarity on marijuana. In 2021, a Colorado dispensary named Standing Akimbo, LLC, appealed to the Supreme Court to block the Internal Revenue Service (IRS) from obtaining financial records about the business. While the Supreme Court ultimately deferred to the lower court decision, Justice Thomas used the case as an opportunity to sound off. "Once comprehensive, the Federal Government's current approach is a half-in, half-out regime that simultaneously tolerates and forbids local use of marijuana."[83] He elaborated on his point, noting the Supreme Court had asserted the federal government's supremacy over the states on marijuana policy in a 2005 decision in *Gonzales v. Raich*. However, the unwillingness of the federal government to resolve the matter over the succeeding sixteen years made the decision increasingly impractical and unjustifiable.

> Suffice it to say, the Federal Government's current approach to marijuana bears little resemblance to the watertight nationwide prohibition that a closely divided Court found necessary to justify the Government's blanket prohibition in *Raich*. If the Government is now content to allow States to act "as laboratories 'and try novel social and economic experiments,'" Raich, 545 U. S., at 42 (O'Connor, J., dissenting), then it might no longer have authority to intrude on "[t]he States' core police powers ... to define criminal law and to protect the health, safety, and welfare of their citizens." Ibid. A prohibition on intrastate use or cultivation of marijuana may no longer be necessary or proper to support the Federal Government's piecemeal approach.[84]

Having discussed the changing nature of the federal government's use of its coercive powers (or lack thereof) to prevent marijuana liberalization in the states, we can now delve deeper into the role of state institutional features—namely, the ballot initiative—in propelling the adoption of medical marijuana. We will then revisit our 2018 analysis of medical marijuana law adoption in the states to consider how significant additional expansion changes what we think about diffusion of this policy innovation.

The Ballot Initiative and Medical Marijuana Adoption

Citizen initiatives can serve as a legitimizer of innovative policies and set the agenda for other states, including legislatures in states that do not have the initiative.[85] It is always important to bear in mind that not all states have opportunities for direct democracy. Methods of direct democracy in the United States were modeled after European policies that allowed citizens to vote directly for specific policies. They caught on in the United States at the turn of the twentieth century when many newly established western states were beset by corruption—especially in the railroad and extractive industries. The adoption of direct democracy was also more common in states with large agrarian populations

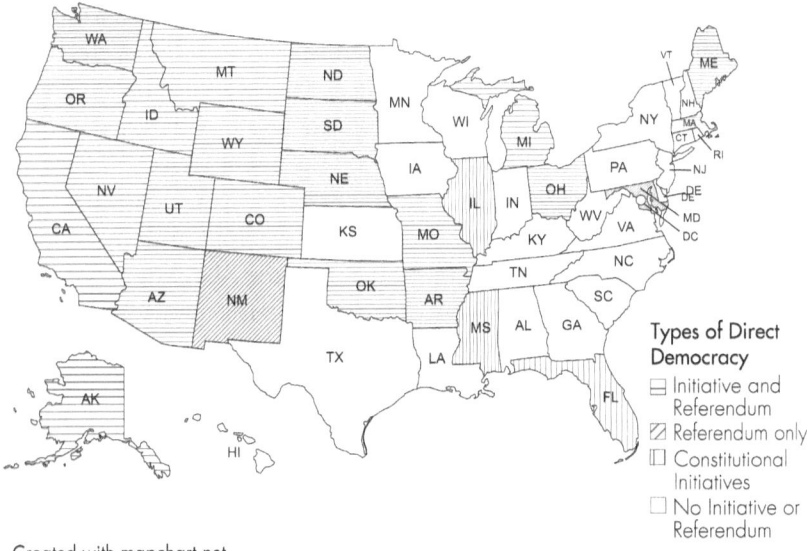

Created with mapchart.net
Figure 2.2. States with initiatives and referenda.

and small nonwhite and foreign-born populations. Both the agrarian populism of Democratic standard-bearer William Jennings Bryan and the pro-labor socialism of Eugene Debs embraced direct democracy as a means to empower the average citizen.[86] Between 1898 and 1918, twenty states adopted constitutional amendments that gave citizens the power to pass laws through the direct ballot initiative.[87]

Figure 2.2 shows the states that have at least one form of direct democracy: either the citizen initiative (direct or indirect) and legislative referenda, legislative referenda only, or constitutional referenda only.[88] Direct citizen initiatives are placed on the ballot by citizens and organized interests who complete signature campaigns to qualify, whereas indirect initiatives must be approved by the state's legislature before they appear on the ballot. The qualification process can be quite costly, and that is before factoring in the costs associated with running a successful campaign to attract voters.[89] Each state has different regulations and requirements for the number and nature of required signatures, the length of time that issues have to qualify for the ballot, and subject-matter restrictions. Each of these factors affect the cost and frequency of initiative campaigns.[90] A study by Ballotpedia found that

$118 million was spent on signature drives for the thirty statewide citizen initiatives that appeared on ballot in the 2022 midterm elections. That means the average petition drive in 2022 cost $4 million, and each signature cost $12.70, on average, to collect.[91] Referenda are measures first approved by legislatures to appear on the ballot for voter approval. Mississippi, Florida, and Illinois allow citizens to place constitutional amendments on the ballot, which is how Mississippi initially adopted a medical marijuana program in 2020 before the Mississippi Supreme Court struck down the law over broader concerns about flaws in the initiative process in the state writ large.[92]

Scholars have examined direct democracy from several angles, including how the institution affects voters and how initiatives affect the broader electoral environment—namely, how direct initiatives can mobilize voters and have downstream effects on other candidates' fortunes.[93] But initiatives can also have an impact on policy. Here, the scholarship has focused on policy congruence—a democratic principle that "public policies should reflect the majority will of the electorate."[94] While policy congruence is also achieved when elites and citizens have the same preferences, direct democracy provides an alternate way to achieve this goal. This can happen with citizens directly voting for a policy that political leaders are not addressing or through the initiative acting as a threat for legislators to act. Overall, the evidence is mixed on whether direct democracy leads to policy congruence.[95] In short, research has found that direct democracy enhances responsiveness for certain policy arenas, like the state minimum wage, electoral rules and institutions (e.g., term limits, redistricting reforms), abortion policy, and the death penalty.[96] Yet in other policy areas—gay rights and minority rights, more broadly—policy in states with direct democracy is no more congruent than in states without the institution.[97]

As for medical marijuana policy, while we do not have the public opinion data at the state level to measure preferences and policy congruence, evidence suggests that in many cases, direct democracy pushes medical marijuana onto the agenda.[98] Our analysis from 2018 and our updated analysis in this chapter shows that having direct democracy available increases the likelihood that a state adopts a comprehensive medical marijuana law. Furthermore, national public opinion data show that nearly 90 percent of Americans support medical access to marijuana—with the majority in support across races and ethnicities, age groups, ideology, and partisanship.[99] Thus, we can infer that the current states without medical cannabis do not have policy congruence. While they are more ideologically conservative and politically controlled by Republicans, even most Republicans support some form of *medical* marijuana, even if they do not support full legalization.[100] Importantly, however, only three of the states that have not adopted a comprehensive medical marijuana law provide citizens access to the ballot initiative. There is also an abundance of anecdotal evidence that the initiative has played into the calculus of legislators and governors. Not only have states like Ohio moved to cut off initiative campaigns, but other state legislatures (Utah and Mississippi) have acted quickly to amend or disrupt passed initiatives.[101]

In many ways, the map in figure 2.2 overlaps well with states that have medical marijuana laws. From 1996 to 2022, sixteen of the thirty-seven states that adopted medical marijuana policies did so through a direct initiative. Twenty-one of the twenty-five states with the direct initiative passed a comprehensive medical marijuana law. Importantly, not all direct initiatives are as easy for citizens to access. In Ohio, as we discussed, the initiative was the mechanism that pushed the legislature to act, whereas Illinois is a state where the law nominally grants the option of the initiative, but initiatives rarely qualify for the ballot.[102] Thus, while Illinois technically has direct democracy available, it is highly restrictive.

Figure 2.3 displays the cumulative total number of states that adopted medical marijuana laws between 1996 and 2022. The lines represent adoption by initiative and adoption by legislature, and the labeled years coincide with the first year of a presidential administration. Immediately evident is that many of the innovator and early adopter states took up medical marijuana laws through the initiative, as this method provided early cover for legislators who did not want to be identified with marijuana policy. Figure 2.3 also shows that the expansion of medical marijuana programs remained consistent after the initial period of rapid adoption and that many of these later adoptions were passed by legislatures. This was true regardless of who was in the White House, although the adoption slope steepened during the Obama administration. Initial ballot success

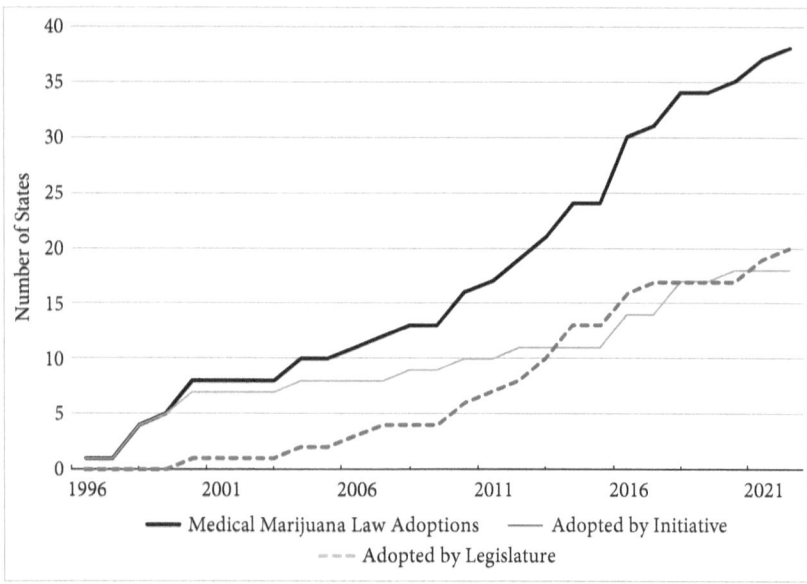

Figure 2.3. State adoptions of medical marijuana laws, 1996–2022.

and growing public support pushed legislatures to consider and adopt medical marijuana.[103]

Diffusion Analysis of Medical Marijuana Laws

Having established the importance of changing federal signals and the availability of the citizen initiative, we now turn to a more formal evaluation of the internal and external determinants of medical marijuana law adoptions by the states. Since the groundbreaking work of Berry and Berry on lotteries, hundreds of diffusion studies have used event history analysis as the method of choice to model the spread of individual and pooled sets of policies.[104] The advantage of an event history model is that it allows researchers to include both internal and external determinants of policy adoption into a single statistical model.[105]

As we have discussed so far, policy innovation diffusion is a dynamic process. Further, individual policy innovations do not diffuse in identical geographical or temporal patterns.[106] It is also notable that any given diffusion study is a snapshot in time. Studies rarely are observing a policy that has fully spread to all fifty states. While we should not expect innovations to be taken up by every state, there are many diffusion analyses that are conducted while an innovation is still spreading, and scholars have no clear definition for when a policy has fully diffused. Additionally, the internal and external predictors of diffusion change not only across policies but also over time and throughout the life of the diffusion.[107] Thus, depending on when a "snapshot" is taken, the evidence for or against different predictors of adoption can look very different. Our work on medical marijuana diffusion is a testament to these dynamics. We present updated results from our previous work that yield different yet enlightening results. The technical details of the modeling and full results can be found in appendix A, but here we will briefly review how the results changed and our argument for why.

Our earlier work analyzed medical marijuana law adoptions from 1996 to 2014.[108] Figure 2.4 shows the states that had adopted by 2014 in darker gray. We expected that the clarity of federal government signals regarding marijuana enforcement (marijuana seizures and other indicators for the Obama and Bush administrations), within-state demand for medical marijuana (cancer and glaucoma patients), ecological capacity (direct initiatives, legislative professionalism, citizen liberalism, size

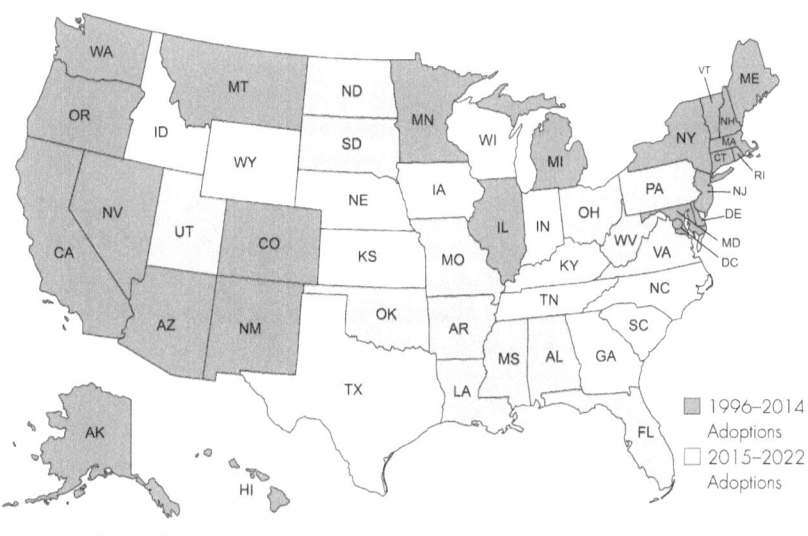

Figure 2.4. States with comprehensive medical marijuana programs, 1996–2022.

of the evangelical population, and state fiscal health), and state-to-state learning (regional and ideological) would shape the adoption of medical marijuana laws. We found, however, that federal enforcement signals and demand had little effect on adoption. Instead, implicit signals from different presidential administrations, a state's liberalism, and the availability of the direct initiative were important. In addition, we found that there was more evidence for an ideological pattern of adoption than a regional one. That is, political information appeared to be more important for the spread of this policy than states observing policy lessons from their geographic neighbors.

While our earlier analysis included twenty-three medical marijuana adoptions from 1996 to 2014, we updated the number to thirty-seven adoptions through 2022. Figure 2.4 shows the additional states that adopted between 2015 and 2022 in lighter gray. As with our earlier analysis, we examined implicit signals of federal prohibition enforcement (now including the Trump administration and the first two years of the Biden administration), the centrality of the citizen initiative to marijuana adoption, state ideology, and state-to-state diffusion. In terms of interstate dynamics, we examine both the effect of a state's neighbors on the likelihood of adopting marijuana and the effect of ideological "peers."

Updated Results

Table 2.1 provides the results of our updated analysis. It shows the effect direction (positive or negative) for the variables that have a statistically significant ($p < 0.05$) relationship with the likelihood of adopting a medical marijuana law. In terms of federal signals, we find that the likelihood of adopting a medical marijuana law declines in each successive presidential administration (when compared to the Clinton administration). This seems counterintuitive at first, given the steady increase in adoptions in figure 2.3. However, it represents the fact that there are fewer and fewer potential adopters among the states. The remaining laggard states will be harder to move toward adoption and are motivated by different reasoning than earlier adopters.[109] The citizen initiative remains a steadfast and strong predictor of medical marijuana adoption. There are, however, no longer any statistically significant state-to-state predictors of medical marijuana law adoption. Notably, in our

Table 2.1. Results of Updated Medical Marijuana Adoption Model from Hannah and Mallinson (2018)

Variable	Effect on Adoption
Bush administration	–
Obama administration	–
Trump administration	–
Biden administration	–
Initiative available	+
Evangelicals per 1,000 population	None
Citizen liberalism	+
Neighbor adoptions	None
Relative ideology	None
Time counter	+

Source: A. Lee Hannah and Daniel J. Mallinson, "Defiant Innovation: The Adoption of Medical Marijuana Laws in the American States," *Policy Studies Journal* 46, no. 2 (2018), 402–423.
Note: Effect only shown for statistically significant results ($p < 0.05$).

previous analysis through 2014, a state's ideology relative to other states that already adopted a policy was found to have an effect, but in our new analysis, it no longer does.[110] We will zero in on the importance of both the initiative and changing diffusion patterns in advancing the story of medical marijuana adoption.

The significance of the initiative stands out in figure 2.5. The y-axis comes from state ideology scores that range from most conservative (0) to most liberal (100).[111] The x-axis plots states that adopted early (1996–2009), late (2010–2022), or have not adopted (as of January 2023). Finally, black triangles represent states with the initiative and hollow circles represent states without the initiative. In the first wave of adoption of medical marijuana, the thirteen states that adopted are more liberal on average (mean = 58.8), especially those states that do not have the initiative and had to go through their legislature (mean = 74.9). In the later wave of adoptions, among the twenty-four adopter states, the average ideology score drops to 48.5, and more state legislatures acted. But the initiative did help to push some very conservative states (mean ideology of 41.8) to adopt. Finally, two patterns are evident among the thirteen nonadopting states—the states are more conservative (mean ideology of 38.2), and few of them have access to the initiative (only three of the thirteen).

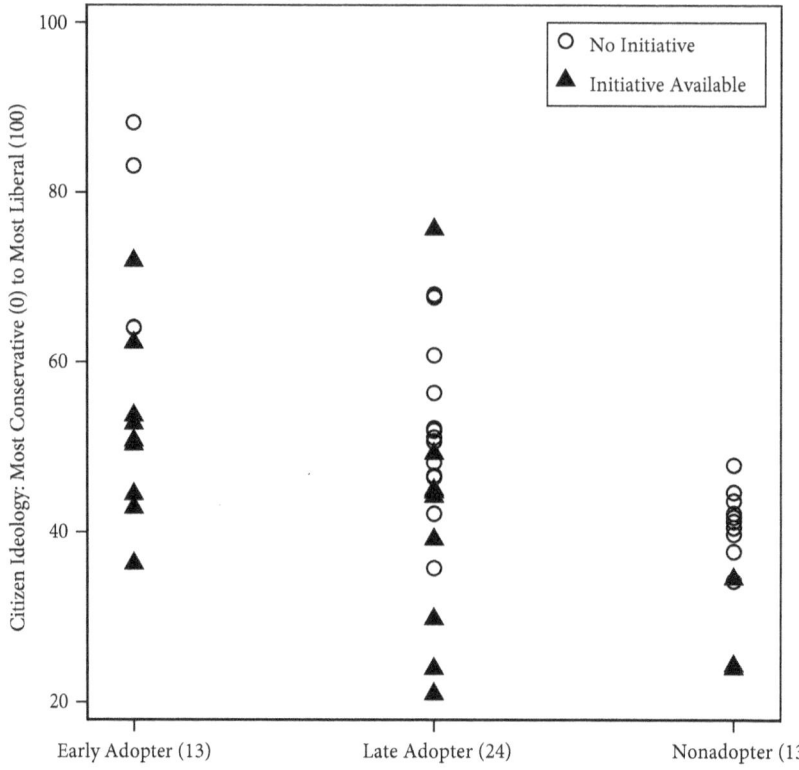

Figure 2.5. Adopter and nonadopter ideologies and access to ballot initiatives through 2022.

The most substantial change in the results across our two analyses comes with the diffusion variables. The updated model finds that medical marijuana appears to have not diffused through either a regional or ideological pathway. The ideological pathway was present in our earlier research, but updating the analysis through 2022 yields no effect. This illustrates that when a diffusion snapshot is taken can have substantial effects on the results received. Since predictors can change across the diffusion life course, expanding the set of adopters and modeling the overall likelihood of adoption can change the story.[112] Given that we are still observing the spread of this policy, it seems likely to us that the ideology of past adopters was a far more important signal earlier in medical marijuana's spread than now. Instead, there are fewer costs for defiance now, and as we showed with our stories about adoption in Missouri,

Oklahoma, and Ohio, changes to the substance of the policy have made it more palatable to more conservative states.

The lack of diffusion effects also suggests that medical marijuana adoption may be reaching a saturation point, whereby most of the states that have demand for a medical marijuana law already have it and those that support federal marijuana prohibition are less likely to consider adopting without fundamental changes in their internal political, economic, or social context. Thus, while thirteen states still had no medical marijuana statute when we conducted this analysis, the policy may have already saturated the states that are willing to act in defiance of federal law. After our analysis, Kentucky became the thirty-eighth state to adopt a comprehensive medical marijuana program, doing so in 2023. It was in fact an important change in political context that pushed the issue forward. Democratic governor Andy Beshear pushed the Republican-controlled legislature to adopt the law. His efforts included multiple direct appeals to citizens to pressure their representatives to pass the law and a November 2022 executive order that protected Kentuckians with certain conditions from prosecution for lawful purchase of medical cannabis outside of Kentucky. As for the other laggards, either proponents lack an institutional avenue to pass the law (i.e., the citizen initiative) or state leaders may be waiting for the federal government to clear the way through rescheduling marijuana or adopting reforms that will ease implementation.[113] Kentucky, however, demonstrates what we discussed in chapter 1, that changes in the formal political context can help push an issue onto a reluctant government's decision agenda.

Conclusion

What motivates states to innovate in defiance of federal law? Past research demonstrates that internal demand, institutional capacity, and financial constraints are associated with state decisions to shirk the implementation of federal policy.[114] However, we take this a step further to test whether these dynamics hold in the case of states sabotaging federal law by defiantly innovating new policy. We find that, in the case of medical marijuana policy, policy adoption was most clearly associated with components of a state's ecological capacity (the initiative and citizen liberalism). Early adoptions through the initiative gave way to a mix of legislative and initiative adoptions, thus corroborating the legitimizing effect of the popular initiative.[115] The story of how the federal government's position encourages or discourages adoption is less clear.

The dissonant relationship between time and presidential administrations complicates conclusions about the federal government's role. One way to view this circumstance is that the policy is becoming *less* defiant over time. That is, as medical marijuana laws have gained legitimacy with an increasing number of states adopting them, there is a decrease in defiance with each additional adoption. The tide of public opinion has shifted in support of loosening marijuana restrictions. Adoption by a majority of the states further legitimizes this defiant position while eroding the legitimacy of the federal government's position. In fact, legal cannabis has become in many ways the prevailing policy in the United States through substantial state policy innovation and even federal legalization of hemp cultivation in 2018. And it extends to the adoption of adult-use recreational marijuana policies that spread to twenty-three states between 2012 and 2023. As a comparison, only ten states had adopted a medical marijuana law a decade after the first adoption.

Even conservative Supreme Court Justice Clarence Thomas pointed out the eroding legitimacy of the federal position on marijuana in light of increasing state adoptions. As was noted earlier in this chapter, Thomas argued that the 2005 *Raich* decision assumed a consistent federal position on marijuana prohibition—but without that, the logic of prohibition fails. Federal prohibition still stands, but viewing state drug liberalization—even as it now extends to other substances like psychedelics—as defiant is becoming obsolete as the tide has shifted strongly and broadly *against* federal policy. In a sense, cannabis policy is a perfect illustration of Louis Brandeis's laboratories of democracy concept, as the states have experimented—granted, initially in defiance of federal law—and have now built pressure for the federal government to either take up the innovation itself or get out of the way.

The results of this analysis paint a picture of how defiant innovation progressed in the case of medical marijuana laws, but in a way that likely captures other acts of state statutory defiance in an era of congressional gridlock and polarization. The popular initiative and ideology were important driving forces of medical marijuana adoption in the states, regardless of mixed and varying implicit and explicit federal signals about prohibition enforcement. This is important for the broader study of policy diffusion, because there is limited attention to how and why policies do not fully diffuse and how the motivations for adopting a policy change as diffusion unfolds.[116] While ecological capacity is important for both mandate refusal and this case of defiant innovation, the ideological separation of adopters and nonadopters and the importance of citizen initiatives for spurring and legitimizing diffusion are key distinctions. Though, equally important is the fact that the early ideological split between liberal state adopters and conservative state nonadopters has broken down as the innovation was taken up in more conservative states. These findings provide an important starting point for differentiating types of state defiance and developing a fuller picture of how vertical diffusion operates in the United States.

American federalism is not neat and tidy. The federal government encourages innovation through issue attention and financial incentives while also taking up and nationalizing successful innovations from the states. But there is also an important element of struggle within federalism. There are costs for states and municipalities that defy the federal government. For example, cities and universities across the United States faced the possibility of federal sanctions during the Trump administration for refusing to report undocumented immigrants to U.S. Immigration and Customs Enforcement.[117] The federal government could conceivably do the same thing to states with recreational and medical marijuana provisions by withholding billions of dollars in federal money committed to the War on Drugs. Additionally, a presidential administration hostile to cannabis liberalization could take the states to court and test the Supreme Court's support for federal preemption.[118] But, of course, this has not happened yet. In 2022, President Biden further lowered the cost of state defiance by expunging criminal sentences for federal cannabis possession and directing the Department of Health and Human Services to review marijuana's status as a Schedule I controlled substance. This is why our merging of diffusion and implementation theory is important. States, particularly when choosing to defy federal law, must respond to changes not only in their ecological capacity to innovate but also in the overall federal ecosystem. If federal signals clarify and intensify in the next administration, states may make different choices in either (a) defying in the first place or (b) choosing how they defy.

Future work building on the theoretical foundation established here can help explain not only the *when* of defiance but also the *how*. State approaches to marijuana are not identical, and that variation can be used to understand the extent to which choices are dependent on internal capacities or external forces from peer states or the credibility and legitimacy of federal commitments. It is to this idea that we turn in chapter 3 as we consider variations in policy design and implementation. The study of policy diffusion can speak to the practical effects of this struggle in a powerful way by identifying how patterns of policy adoption change as the relationship between the federal government and the states varies across policies. State and local defiance in policy areas that are either expressly prohibited by the federal government or where the government has made unclear legal commitments is unlikely to subside, particularly in an era of fragmented federalism.[119]

3

From the Statehouse to the Dispensary

Policy Design and Implementation

This bill was passed with no allowances for that type of safety and security. Commissioner (Mary) O'Dowd and I had this dumped in our laps by the last administration at three o'clock in the morning when Gov. Corzine signed it and we're not going to permit a program like this to be started unless there's the appropriate safeguards available.
—Chris Christie, former Republican governor of New Jersey, *Observer*, 2012

Former New Jersey governor Chris Christie provides one of the best illustrations of how a medical marijuana policy can be snuffed out in the implementation process. Christie's predecessor, Democrat Jon Corzine, signed Senate Bill 119 on his last day in office.[1] Two years later, after only one company had been given a temporary permit to start growing medical marijuana, Christie complained:

> "What there is a huge demand for is marijuana, not medical marijuana," Christie snapped, his arms folded defensively. "This program and all these other programs are, in my mind, a front for legalization—unless you have a strong governor and a strong administration that says, 'Oh, medical marijuana? Absolutely, we're going to make it a medically-based program.'" His tone turned sarcastic and his eyebrows raised. "No demand there—very little."[2]

The safeguards that Governor Christie adopted limited the growth of the medical marijuana program. Four years later, in June 2014, only 2,342 patients had signed up. The few dispensaries that had opened at the time said they needed at least 2,000 regular patients to break even. The small numbers were due to several factors. For example, only 296 of the 21,000 licensed physicians in the state enrolled for fear of the legal and political backlash. Furthermore, patients had to see a physician four times a year to maintain eligibility.[3] Dispensary owners not only had to tackle administrative burdens unleashed by the state, but they also had to win local approval and be subject to municipal taxes.[4] By the time Christie left office in 2018, prices remained prohibitive, many forms of medical cannabis were prohibited, and only six dispensaries—1 for every 1.5 million people in the state—had opened.

Christie's successor, Democrat Phil Murphy emphasized cannabis liberalization in his campaign platform. In the first week of his administration, Murphy noted his approach would be a "very stark distinction" from Christie's "hostile administration tugging the strings of state bureaucracy" and that the program's failure was because "the law's spirit has been stifled."[5] Within months, reforms were passed that led to the opening of more dispensaries, home-delivery options, and lower prices. By mid-2019, participating physicians doubled and registered patients tripled.[6] The administration also developed the program with knowledge that an adult-use program was inevitable.[7] Now, over a decade since the state first adopted a medical marijuana policy, the program is thriving. Ironically, some of the most successful dispensaries are along the Pennsylvania border. Even though Pennsylvania's legislature adopted a medical bill in earnest two years before Murphy took over in New Jersey, prices were substantially lower in New Jersey. For many medical users, especially in Philadelphia, a drive to New Jersey was worth the time, fuel, and legal risks.[8] This cross-border flow of marijuana seekers has only increased with New Jersey's implementation of adult-use in 2022, putting pressure on Pennsylvania to liberalize.[9]

In chapter 2, we discussed how comprehensive medical marijuana policies have been adopted and diffused to the majority of states since 1996. But the story does not end once a policy is adopted by a state. In fact, circumstances present in the design and adoption process directly affect the implementation of a policy. As Malcolm Goggin and colleagues put it, implementation research moves "from how a bill becomes a law to how a law becomes a program."[10] As the example from New Jersey shows, state leaders have substantial influence over the relative effectiveness of medical marijuana laws. Furthermore, the surrounding political context, particularly within a federal system, shapes how states implement some policy innovations. In the case of medical marijuana, implementation during the early initiative-driven phase of adoption was slow because states still feared intervention by the federal government.

We begin this chapter with a brief overview of policy design and implementation theory. Before digging into case studies of implementation, we set the stage by discussing the broader implementation environment shaped by changes in the federal government's stance toward marijuana. As well-regulated medicalized marijuana programs were legitimized, particularly under guidance from the Department of Justice during President Barack Obama's administration, a clearer implementation strategy emerged in the states. We will discuss how the federal government has sent varying signals about the permissibility of state marijuana laws. And as the programs grew in complexity and expanded the availability of medical marijuana to a supermajority of Americans, demand for federal action has grown. Then, we will describe how design and implementation efforts vary across the states. This chapter will compare the cases of medical marijuana implementation in Pennsylvania, Ohio, and West Virginia. These neighboring states adopted medical marijuana under different circumstances between April 2016 and April 2017, and they are at dissimilar places in terms of how well their programs are functioning today. We argue that these differences are at least in part explained by political differences in the states—particularly in the governor's office, state legislature, agencies implementing the laws, and localities.

Implementation Theory and Policy Design

It is useful to think of each stage of the policy process as a particular phase in a policy's life that is shaped by the current context as well as those events that occurred before. Implementation is a vital stage where government and third-party partners produce the good or service called for by the people and their representatives. But it is important to recognize that implementation is often shaped by how the policy was designed in an earlier stage. Choices made during the design process can free or constrain those tasked with implementation.[11] Further, the vagueness of laws, whether they originated in the legislative process or the ballot initiative, offers discretion for implementers.[12]

The scholarly study of implementation is mature, with over fifty years of history.[13] Much of the attention, however, has been on state and local implementation of federal policy, including a substantial focus on fiscal federalism.[14] In the case of medical marijuana, we are seeking to understand how states backed away from the implementation of federal law and how their own efforts at implementing medical programs varied. Specifically, we seek to explain why, given the federal context left by the Obama administration, three states—Pennsylvania, Ohio, and West Virginia—have implemented their policies at such different paces. We argue that the implementation research can shed much light on this question and help us understand better how state capacity, politics, and policy design shape the implementation of medical marijuana.[15] We begin by briefly reviewing implementation theory.

Implementation Theory

Malcolm Goggin and colleagues provide a theoretical framework for understanding policy implementation.[16] Prior to their work, implementation research was either atheoretical and case-based or sought to develop theoretical frameworks without sufficient empirical testing. Goggin and colleagues sought to push implementation theory forward by firmly recognizing the role of the states in the implementation of federal policy and examining why there is often variation in how states implement policy. Though implementation research generally targets state-level implementation of federal policy initiatives, it is nonetheless also applicable to studying implementation of state policies within and across states.

This theoretical framework aims to explain the implementation process and its outputs and outcomes. Practically speaking, outputs can include administrative rules promulgated for implementation, further enabling legislation (particularly relevant for policies passed through the ballot initiative), the appropriation of resources, monitoring of bureaucrats implementing the program, enforcement efforts by the executive branch, and subsequent policy redesign. Herein, and in the case comparison of Pennsylvania, Ohio, and West Virginia that follows, we consider the importance of policy design, formal and informal actors, organizational capacity, and ecological capacity for effective policy implementation.

Policy Design

The first key factor expected to shape implementation is the policy's design—specifically, its content, clarity, consistency, and form. Content refers to specific commitments of resources, the policy's credibility to implementers, and the implementers' perceived certainty of the policy's effects. Clarity refers to whether both the means (desired policy tools) and ends (the policy's goals) are clear to implementers. For decades, policy researchers have worked to categorize and compare policy tools—the "techniques through which governments generate, evaluate, and implement policy options"—that are or are not employed by governments when designing and implementing public policy.[17] Tools are not used discretely, however. They appear in bundles or mixes that differ in systematic ways across government. The characteristics of marijuana policies across the states vary considerably.[18] Three specific types of policy bundles have been identified. First, the pharmaceutical bundle includes regulations on the use of cannabis as a recommended drug. Second, the permissive bundle includes rules that govern the personal use of cannabis. Third, the fiscal bundle includes those tools that relate to taxation and spending.[19] Scholars study why governments choose different bundles of tools and what impacts those choices have on implementation outcomes.[20]

Consistency is measured over time throughout the implementation process. It addresses whether each time an arm of the government issues a new and related policy; it is being consistent in its message content and approach. Otherwise, implementation will necessarily be delayed or deterred if messaging or the implementation approach continues to change. Granted, consistency is not always positive. When implementation does not change, even though the social or economic context is changing, this is called policy drift.[21] However, problems do occur when bureaucrats take it upon themselves to shirk or sabotage their implementation of the goals and priorities of a policy.[22] Thus, consistency in purpose and application of policy tools is important for good implementation.

Finally, the policy's form matters. This is evident in the realm of marijuana policies, given that some have been adopted through the traditional legislative process and others have been adopted through the ballot initiative. When policies are adopted through the initiative instead of through a more traditional legislative pathway, they may run into more resistance during implementation. First, the mere fact that activists used the initiative process suggests they do not have enough allies in the legislature to get a policy adopted. Furthermore, an initiative's sponsors and supporters do not have legal standing within the government. This means any ambiguity in the law is going to be interpreted in the best interests of the formal actors within government.[23] Meanwhile, a law passed by a legislature is more likely to have champions in the chamber or governor's office that want to see implementation through.

Particularly in the area of drug policy, concerns have been expressed about policies "crafted by non-scientific advocates and subjected to popular vote by an insufficiently informed public."[24] However, it is important to take each initiative and piece of legislation on its own merits in evaluating whether the form is affecting implementation and achievement of policy goals.[25] In the case of Pennsylvania, Ohio, and West Virginia, each state's policy was adopted in the legislative process, thus we cannot assess whether form influences implementation. However, we can consider how each policy's design affected implementation.

Formal and Informal Actors in Implementation

Formal and informal actors in the policymaking system have opportunities either to support or inhibit implementation of policy.[26] Formal actors are the legal institutions of government—the executive branch, the legislature, and the judiciary—whereas informal actors are individuals and groups that contribute to the policy process—interest groups, political parties, and policy entrepreneurs. Formal actors, like state legislators and governors, often have constitutional and legal powers to coerce or block the advancement of policies through the process.[27] If a legislature is begrudging in its acceptance of a policy, it can hamper the executive branch's plans to implement the policy. For instance, the legislature has the power of purse, so it can constrain funding necessary for effective implementation. Legislators also engage in oversight, which affects how policy gets carried out.[28] Legislative oversight can push the bureaucracy to enact implementation reforms when there are failures, though the success of this approach is conditional on the capacity of the executive agencies to enact those reforms.[29] Legislatures also structure a policy's design toward the attainment of certain goals, including goals that may not be shared by governors.[30] Both design and oversight can help move the policy's implementation toward the legislature's preference, even if the executive's preference differs. In this case, it is the legislature's capacity to pursue oversight and sanction the executive branch that plays a key role.[31] Certainly, governors and their administrations play a powerful role in shaping implementation. They can either make the policy path straight or hamper it with constraints. As the example of Governor Christie showed, a strong governor directing executive agencies can obstruct policies in the implementation phase.

Informal actors, like interest groups and policy entrepreneurs, who share core or peripheral beliefs regarding a policy will form advocacy coalitions to advance a policy.[32] Implementation is strengthened when a policy is also backed by a strong advocacy coalition.[33] Of course, coalitions can also work together to countermobilize against policies that they do not want to see enacted or implemented, particularly when there is popular support for such resistance.[34] Marijuana has long had vocal advocates for over a century, though its power as a movement has waxed and waned over the decades.[35] That said, the movement is arguably at its zenith in organizing power given the influence of organizations like the National Organization for the Reform of Marijuana Laws (NORML), Americans for Safe Access (ASA), and Marijuana Policy Project (MPP).

Organizational Capacity for Implementation

For policy to be effectively implemented, those doing the work must be properly resourced. Bureaucratic capacity varies greatly across public organizations, and capacity building can be part of the policy design process. In fact, policy innovations, like medical marijuana, often require the creation of brand-new capacity and reform in how bureaucracies are structured and operate.[36] For example, if regulatory authority is vested in a state department of health, that will require new stakeholders engaging with the department, alteration of the organizational structure, new offices, and new management. Such capacity building can include new funds for personnel, equipment, or space; further, it may require new authority and development of new competencies and capabilities among staff.[37] Bureaucracies use their capacity in terms of "expertise, personnel, and data" to shape how a policy is implemented; in fact, the stronger a bureaucracy's capacity for effective policy implementation, the more it can advance the policy in alignment with its preferences, even at the expense of a legislature that may have different preferences.[38] Florida provides an example here. In 2019, Governor Ron DeSantis (R) pushed the legislature to drop a ban on smokable medical marijuana and loosen requirements for licensing.[39] He threatened that if they did not change the law, he would order law enforcement to no longer enforce those parts of the law. The governor has both the political and institutional capacity to follow through on such threats and pull the policy's design and implementation toward his preferences.

Large but fragmented capacity also hinders implementation. While greater numbers of personnel and higher budgets provide resources necessary for effective and prompt implementation, the involvement of too many organizations can hinder it.[40] At times, governments restructure and consolidate agencies in response to governance failure. The intelligence community after September 11, 2001, is a good example. Before that day, the federal intelligence community had billions of dollars of resources—but intelligence operations were spread across sixteen different organizations. The breakdown in communication and intelligence sharing between these organizations was one of the factors blamed for the terrorist attacks on 9/11.[41] In response, Congress created the role of the director of national intelligence and restructured how the intelligence agencies work with each other. In general, having too many separate entities involved makes implementation more difficult.

Ecological Capacity for Implementation

Finally, states vary greatly in their ecological capacity, which can be thought of as the various external resources that are useful for policymakers in both doing their job and sustaining support for their work. Such capacities are fiscal, political, and situational. Fiscal capacity is perhaps the most obvious, because effective implementation requires adequate and dedicated funding.[42]

Political capacity can include things like the overall ideology (e.g., liberalness) of a state's citizens and government, how open the political system is, the state's general level of policy innovativeness, and its political culture.[43] Each of these factors relates to the maintenance of political support for a policy over time. If a state's overall level of liberalness or conservativeness matches well with a policy, then there will likely be continued public support for its maintenance or even expansion. However, if a policy becomes out of sync with the ideological preferences of a state's population and, in turn, its government, criticism of that policy will increase. Such criticism makes effective implementation increasingly difficult. Openness refers to the degree of citizen input that states allow.[44] If citizens are locked out of the implementation process, this can also erode public support for the policy. A state's policy innovativeness refers to the state's overall willingness to move quickly in taking up new policy innovations, like medical marijuana.[45] States that are generally more innovative have a political capacity to be nimbler in reforming policies to increase their effectiveness.

Finally, situational capacity refers to how much attention the public and the media are paying to a policy. Both public and media attention should result in more responsive policymaking and implementation.[46] Political scientists refer to this as a policy's salience.[47] The general expectation is that if an issue has high salience—that is, the public and media are paying attention and consider it important—then policymakers will also turn their attention to that policy.[48] Policies that are highly salient are taken up and adopted by the states more quickly than those that are less salient.[49] High salience among the public also results in swifter policy implementation.[50] Granted, this is what we should expect from democratic institutions, including the bureaucracy that is, to an extent, shielded from direct voter accountability.[51]

Having laid the theoretical groundwork for what factors shape effective implementation and how these factors vary across the states, we will now turn to considering the broader implementation environment for medical marijuana before examining these factors in our three state cases.

The Effect of Federal Prohibition on Marijuana Policy Implementation

The implementation of medical marijuana policies provides one of the best examples of states acting as laboratories. After states pass medical marijuana laws, they must establish a regulatory framework that considers several different actors, including patients, physicians, law enforcement, and providers. Operating with little guidance, states have by and large learned through trial and error and the experiences of other states. But even when states develop laws that properly balance the concerns of myriad stakeholders in the state, friction with federal prohibition is unavoidable.

States are not drug regulators. They regulate many aspects of the healthcare system, including research, development, and use of emerging treatments like biosimilars and stem cells, but they do not engage in testing and certifying the efficacy of pharmaceuticals. States do, however, reinforce federal drug scheduling, which has direct implications for healthcare. States can also impose additional regulations beyond the federal rules. One can look to the challenges surrounding medication-assisted treatment of opioid-use disorder to observe how federal and state policy affect healthcare. Depending on the specific formulation, opioids span all five schedules of the Controlled Substances Act (CSA), but doctors are largely free to prescribe them.[52] Opioid-use disorder treatments like methadone and buprenorphine, however, are on Schedule II and, until 2021, had strict restrictions on doctor prescribing.[53] The Department of Health and Human Services (DHHS) relaxed those restrictions, but states can still add their own stipulations on top of the federal policy floor in ways that restrict access to these highly effective treatments. Since marijuana is a Schedule I drug, it is considered to have no medicinal value and thus cannot be prescribed under federal law. This puts physicians in a tenuous position. The Drug Enforcement Agency (DEA) issues registration numbers to doctors who are permitted to dispense Schedule II through Schedule V drugs. Instead, physicians can recommend marijuana but not discuss specifics with patients, such as which product, type of product, or dosage amounts to try.[54] Of course, this limits the true medical care that physicians can provide a patient because they cannot monitor how the cannabis is (and is not) working for the patient.[55] It also leads patients to hide their medical marijuana use from their primary care physicians, which prevents important discussions about potential interactions with medications.[56]

While our research suggests that federal signals made little difference in *adoption* (see chapter 2), federal signals have affected *implementation*.

As states began to defy the federal government and, to an extent, legitimize the use of marijuana as a medicine, federal officials initially pushed back. For cannabis growers, producers, and distributors, there is no protection from the CSA under state medical marijuana laws).

The executive branch's commitment to enforcement of marijuana prohibition, however, has waxed and waned. President Bill Clinton's administration made clear that doctors were liable to forfeiture of their licenses if they recommended medical marijuana, but Clinton did not push to preempt California's law, and his Department of Justice allowed for a medical use exemption.[57] The George W. Bush administration did away with the exemption and not only went after growers, distributors, and users but also threatened the states themselves. The Bush administration tested the boundaries of the CSA in court in 2005 in the case of *Gonzales v. Raich*.

In August 2002, Diane Monson was visited by deputies from the Butte County (California) Sheriff's Department and agents from the DEA on suspicion of growing marijuana. Monson argued that her six plants were being grown for medical purposes. After a standoff between local and federal officials over the legality of her actions, the DEA destroyed her six plants. Monson and the caretakers of Angel Raich, another cannabis patient, sued the U.S. attorney general arguing that the CSA was unconstitutional to the extent that it prevents them from obtaining medical access to marijuana. The Ninth Circuit Court of Appeals ruled in favor of Monson and Raich, finding that state-sanctioned medical marijuana use was a "separate and distinct class of activities" outside of the purview of the CSA. In *Gonzales v. Raich*, the U.S. Supreme Court overturned the Ninth Circuit's ruling with a sweeping view of Congress's power under the Commerce Clause. Despite Monson and Raich's activity of growing marijuana being intrastate and in compliance with California's medical marijuana program, the court ruled that the Commerce Clause of the United States still allows Congress to enforce the CSA.

The controversial 6–3 ruling provided broad powers to the federal government to enforce prohibition in states with medical programs.[58] Just weeks after the *Gonzales v. Raich* decision, the Bush administration launched an operation that raided marijuana clubs in San Francisco, confiscating plants and records and arresting fifteen people on federal drug charges.[59] Further, Bush's drug czar, John Walters, firmly pushed the debunked "gateway" effect of marijuana to harder drugs and tied marijuana to the War on Terror by arguing that profits from its sale falls into the hand of Al-Qaeda.⁶⁰

The case of Washington State illustrates the effects of these federal changes on early medical marijuana law implementation. Washington's ballot measure I-692 passed in 1998 with 59 percent of the vote. It allowed individuals to possess marijuana and allowed for home cultivation, but it did not establish a framework for dispensaries or regulatory control for the drug supply chain (growing, processing, and dispensing). Governor Christine Gregoire vetoed efforts by the state legislature to exert greater control over the budding medical marijuana market and the "gray market" dispensaries that emerged.⁶¹ Threatening letters from two U.S. attorneys were blamed for the veto. Beyond threatening members of the industry, the attorneys threatened state employees. In a letter to Congress, Americans for Safe Access argued that "state employees who conducted activities mandated by Washington legislative proposals would not be immune from liability under the [Controlled Substances Act]."⁶² The statement continued, arguing that "the impact of threats made by U.S. Attorneys against public officials was the suspension or derailment of medical marijuana laws in the states of Arizona, California, Delaware, Hawaii, Montana, Rhode Island, and Washington, as well as municipalities across California."⁶³ Thus, the federal government was signaling that state employees were potentially liable as traffickers of illegal marijuana if they had to take a more active role in regulating the nascent industry. While no state officials have been prosecuted under this view of the law, the threat of federal legal action delayed officials in medical marijuana-legal states from developing best practices in policy implementation.

Acrimony with the federal government is apparent in other early state efforts at providing for medical marijuana. California's first program was called "the Wild West for weed: no state regulatory model, notoriously lax enforcement and an undefined set of prescription criteria that makes obtaining a medical marijuana card little more than a wink-wink formality."⁶⁴ California Senator Diane Feinstein claimed that "Proposition 215 was so poorly written that 'you'll be able to drive a truckload of marijuana through the holes in it. While it seems simple, the devil is in the details or, in this particular bill, the lack of details.'"⁶⁵ Because of continuous state court challenges and the specter of federal government intervention, California did not pass an implementation bill for Proposition 215 until 2013, *seventeen years* after medical marijuana was adopted.

Colorado tried moving toward and then away from regulating dispensaries before enacting what is considered the first comprehensive regulatory approach to medical marijuana in 2010. Since then, Colorado has emerged as a thought leader in both medicinal and recreational marijuana policy. It was not until later in the Obama administration, however, that the U.S. Department of Justice (DOJ) paved the way for protection of highly regulated marijuana programs.[66] Under the Ogden and Cole memorandums, DOJ gave deference to state law by vowing to not pursue legal members of the marijuana supply chain in states with well-regulated programs as long as they did not threaten federal priorities, like reducing violence and gang activity.[67] This clarification pushed states to increase their regulations, ushering in an era where states increasingly medicalized programs that were previously flimsy on details and state engagement. Even with this environment, however, states vary a great deal in how they design and implement their medical marijuana programs.[68]

While paving the way for more robustly regulated medical marijuana programs, the Obama administration's memos did not provide a permanent federal fix. States still operate in legal limbo. The federal government has held a position of forbearance by choosing not to enforce some marijuana laws. Nevertheless, the federal government through Congress or the president has not rewritten laws in a way to provide long-term protection to the burgeoning industry and the states. Thus, DOJ's guidance under Obama to not target marijuana markets in *well-regulated* programs encouraged states to improve regulations but did not provide a permanent remedy. Nor did the Rohrabacher–Farr amendment. The Rohrabacher–Farr amendment was passed by Congress in 2014 as a budget rider and prohibits DOJ from using funds to interfere with the implementation of state medical marijuana laws. While these policies bind federal law enforcement, they do not change the fundamentals of federal prohibition. The U.S. attorney general can still unilaterally change DOJ guidance and enforcement priorities, and the Rohrabacher–Farr amendment must be renewed by Congress on an annual basis.

The inability of the federal government to provide more substantial changes to federal law leads to fears of "whipsaw enforcement," a process where "conduct invited by one administration is singled out for retribution by the next."⁶⁹ This means that even if an administration changes its approach to enforcement of marijuana laws (as did Obama's DOJ), private parties will not have an effective defense against future prosecutions. This issue came to light when Donald Trump was elected president in 2016. While he was considered as having ambivalent views on issues such as marijuana and states' rights, his nomination of staunch prohibitionist Senator Jeff Sessions (R-AL) to attorney general had the potential to disrupt medical marijuana programs. Sessions was a dyed-in-the-wool drug warrior. In 2016, mere months before leaving the Senate to become attorney general, Sessions referred to cannabis as "dangerous" and argued that "good people don't smoke marijuana."⁷⁰

Rohrabacher–Farr was attached to the fiscal year 2017 budget.⁷¹ On this issue, Sessions wrote to Congress:

> I believe it would be unwise for Congress to restrict the discretion of the Department to fund particular prosecutions, particularly in the midst of an historic drug epidemic and potentially long-term uptick in violent crime. The Department must be in a position to use all laws available to combat the transnational drug organizations and dangerous drug traffickers who threaten American lives.⁷²

Illustrating just how far cannabis policy had progressed both at the state and national levels, Sessions's actions backfired. Senator Cory Gardner (R-CO) directly lobbied President Trump for a guarantee that the Justice Department would not go after state-legal operations in Colorado.⁷³ Senate Minority Leader Chuck Schumer (D-NY) got behind federal legalization and introduced his own bill into the mix.⁷⁴ Senator Mitch McConnell (R-KY) successfully pushed for legalizing hemp through the 2018 Farm Bill. That said, President Trump used a signing statement to express his reservations on the amendment, indicating he would "treat this provision consistently with my constitutional responsibility to take care that laws be faithfully executed."⁷⁵

Sessions's next action was to rescind and replace the Obama-era Cole memos. However, many federal attorneys, particularly those with portfolios covering marijuana states, were reluctant to overturn the spirit of the memos.⁷⁶ Even President Trump said of his attorney general's comments on rescinding the Cole memo: "This sounds like something my grandpa said in the 1950s."[77] The replacement memo written by Sessions gave U.S. attorneys investigative and prosecutorial discretion in the case of cannabis. U.S. attorneys, however, largely responded that the memo simply meant that they would continue approaching their priorities as they had been.[78] Sessions's efforts to undo federal forbearance on marijuana prohibition enforcement demonstrates both the precarity of marijuana laws, as more presidential support may have aided his efforts, and the counterpressures facing the federal government.

Attorney General Bill Barr, Sessions's successor at the DOJ under Trump, assured Congress during his confirmation that he would respect states' rights to regulate cannabis policy. He stated that he would not "go after companies that have relied on the Cole memorandum." However, in 2020, Barr was subject to an investigation after a whistleblower alleged that the DOJ had put cannabis companies through antitrust probes that many allege were unnecessarily arduous and inappropriate. And at one point, the majority of DOJ antitrust investigations under Barr were targeting cannabis companies.[79] Further illustrating the fickleness of federal forbearance on marijuana, Merrick Garland, President Joe Biden's first pick for attorney general, publicly stated that the DOJ would not prioritize marijuana enforcement. However, as of September 2023, he had not yet reinstated the Cole memo.[80]

While states have had varying levels of success with implementing medical marijuana, federal prohibition remains a consistent roadblock. Its effect on the rapidly growing cannabis industry is most stark. First, federal prohibition always holds the door open for a federal crackdown, which adds risk (and cost) to investment. Second, because prohibition limits the transport of medical marijuana across state lines, companies must build a foundation for a "seed-to-sale" enterprise in every state, which also raises costs and the inefficiencies of duplicative efforts in multiple states. Finally, as we discuss in chapter 4, federal and state business and tax regulations lead to several challenges related to banking and tax benefits. Marijuana businesses cannot take advantage of common business deductions through Section 280E of the Internal Revenue Service tax code.[81]

It would seem at first glance that marijuana policy runs counter to the era of coercive federalism, within which it flourished.[82] This is a period where the federal government used its coercive power to "bend subnational governments to its will" through policies like No Child Left Behind, among others.[83] However, Dale Krane argues that states responded to coercive federalism is two ways: resistance or "heightened independent policy activity."[84] Marijuana clearly fits into the latter category of heightened independent activity, though it can also be said that the Obama administration's DOJ policy was a successful use of coercive federalism. Instead of offering incentives, the administration clearly delineated through a series of memos that it would reduce enforcement in *well-regulated* medical and recreational states but would intensify efforts elsewhere. This approach led to the medicalization of state programs, serving to protect the industry, at least for as long as federal forbearance remained in effect. Forbearance continued as the Trump administration asserted itself in marijuana policy, despite Attorney General Jeff Sessions, a prohibitionist, revoking the Cole memos. Thus, over a decade of federal forbearance, state medical marijuana programs grew and thrived.

How Does a Fully Comprehensive Medical Marijuana Program Operate?

Before moving forward with a broader discussion of medical marijuana implementation in the states, it is important to sketch out what a comprehensive and fully operational program looks like. There are a few key components that must be worked out in unison. They include regulatory oversight, supply chain management, medical regulations, and legal regulations (figure 3.1).

Most states set up separate commissions to oversee and report on medical marijuana policy. Such offices often operate under one or multiple state departments. In Pennsylvania and West Virginia, the programs are housed under the Department of Health. In Ohio, oversight is provided by the State of Ohio Board of Pharmacy (dispensaries), the State Medical Board of Ohio (physicians and qualifying conditions), and the Department of Commerce (cultivation). These boards oversee the implementation of the policy and report on the programs according to their statutory obligations. These regulatory bodies set up rules and

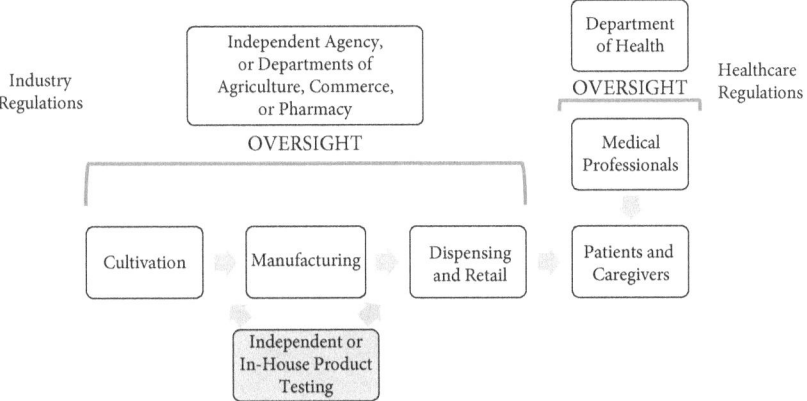

Figure 3.1. General organization of a medical marijuana program.

guidelines for the industry, and they also have the authority to inspect and audit businesses that produce and sell cannabis.

Industry Regulations

To provide medical cannabis, states must have a plan to establish a brand-new industry. This is even more complicated than other regulatory fields because the industry must be completely self-contained within the state. Federal law on cannabis prohibits interstate commerce, so all cannabis plants must go from seed-to-sale within the adopting state. Therefore, states must determine a way to support the entire supply chain of medical cannabis, from cultivation to dispensing. Once growers are established, the flower can be processed and manufactured. Depending on the state, growers or separate processing facilities convert some of the cannabis into tinctures, oils, edibles, or pills for consumption or use with vaporizers.

States with newer medical marijuana laws (i.e., most recently enacted laws) usually require that manufactured products go through an independent lab facility either after cultivation or production, or both (as is the case in some states). These labs test the potency of products and screen for pesticides and other contaminants so that the products comply with state regulations on levels of tetrahydrocannabinol (THC) and cannabidiol (CBD) as well as permissible formulations. Several programs still put the burden of testing and reporting on producers rather than independent laboratories.[85] A comprehensive study of state testing programs found that all states had implemented robust testing for pesticides, but few would meet Food and Drug Administration (FDA) standards suitable for clinical trials.[86] Finally, the product makes its way to the dispensary to be sold to patients.

At each of these points in the supply chain, states have regulatory discretion. In some states, businesses can apply for licenses that combine cultivation, production, and dispensing. This model, called vertical integration, can give organizations greater control over their supply and control costs.[87] Every aspect of the supply chain for cannabis products is heavily regulated. These regulations range from rules on employee qualifications to very specific details about how cannabis must be stored and labeled.[88]

States can also set regulations that affect the broader cannabis market. For example, Pennsylvania tried to incorporate social equity into its licensing decisions by including diversity plans and community impact plans. Such plans accounted for 20 percent of the potential points on the application. However, these plans had little impact on decisions in the first phase of licensing and a modest impact during the second phase.[89] Instead, the licensing board favored applicants that scored highly on measures of security, capital, and business history. Ohio also attempted to incorporate social equity in its 2016 law. The law required that 15 percent of licenses go to companies that are minority-owned.[90] However, the court struck down this provision in 2018 after businesses that had not been awarded licenses, despite having higher scores than minority-owned businesses, sued. The court agreed, finding that the quota was a significant and excessive burden for a new industry with limited participants.[91] In 2022, Ohio's pharmacy board voted to award an additional seventy-three dispensary licenses, more than doubling the number of dispensaries. The board also decided that rather than awarding dispensaries to the applications with the highest scores, they would instead implement a lottery for all applicants that surpass the minimum requirements. The hope was that this would put small and minority-owned businesses on equal footing with the larger multistate companies.[92] These changes illustrate Deborah Stone's argument that there are many ways to cut the cake when it comes to equity.[93]

West Virginia did not incorporate equity provisions into its program.[94] It is unclear whether that decision was driven by West Virginia's relative lack of diversity or if it was simply not in the political calculus for a state that is much more conservative than Ohio or Pennsylvania.

Medical Regulations

States also develop their own regulations related to qualifying conditions, patient and caregiver requirements, and necessary training for physicians to obtain a certificate to recommend cannabis.[95] States also establish the process for patients and caregivers to acquire medical cannabis. They often restrict the quantity of products allowed, which can pertain to either the number of plants permissible for home cultivation in certain states or the monthly purchase limit at a dispensary. States keep a list of qualifying conditions and have a process for evaluating and adding new conditions. States vary substantially on what conditions are included on these lists, although some states (e.g., California) have moved to allow any physician to recommend medical cannabis for any condition that they deem warranted. While not all approved conditions have strong scientific support for the efficacy of medical cannabis for treatment, a review of qualifying conditions in twenty states as far back as 2016 revealed that "84.6 percent had either substantial or conclusive evidence of therapeutic efficacy."[96] A more recent assessment of patients using medical cannabis found that the most prevalent conditions were pain, sleep, stress, anxiety, and depression.[97] That said, local factors instead of scientific rigor can shape decisions on which medical conditions meet the criteria for allowing cannabis use for treatment. Ohio and Pennsylvania are illustrative here. In Pennsylvania, anxiety is by far the most common qualifying condition. In 2021, 60 percent of patient certifications were for anxiety.[98] In neighboring Ohio, the state medical board has for multiple years in a row refused to add anxiety to the list of approved conditions.

Patient Regulations

Given that medical marijuana laws allow access to a federally prohibited substance, state laws also provide guidance to law enforcement. Fully comprehensive laws must provide "an affirmative defense" for patients and caregivers that excludes them from charges of drug possession. Furthermore, medical cannabis is regulated similarly to alcohol and tobacco, so its use can be prohibited in some places (e.g., near schools) or conditions (e.g., while operating heavy machinery). Protections for employment are one legal area that remains murky. Employees who use other drugs for medical needs are protected under the Americans with Disabilities Act from being denied employment or fired—with exceptions for specific jobs that might be hindered by drug use (e.g., drivers, pilots, law enforcement, etc.). Such federal protections do not exist for medical marijuana users, and state courts have ruled both for and against employees who have been terminated for the use of medical cannabis.[99]

Having considered what constitutes a fully comprehensive medical marijuana program, we now turn to describing the politics of implementation and the linkages to policy design. We use the design and implementation of medical marijuana laws in Pennsylvania, Ohio, and West Virginia to provide examples of implementation theory in action.

Medical Marijuana Policy Design in Pennsylvania, Ohio, and West Virginia

We focus this case comparison on the rules developed for regulating medical marijuana in these three states, the time it took for dispensaries to open, the number of patients registered over time, and the number of prescribing physicians. Furthermore, we discuss how Americans for Safe Access has evaluated the programs in each of these states. While these states only adopted medical marijuana in 2016 (Pennsylvania and Ohio) and 2017 (West Virginia), we now have had a few years to examine why their success at implementation has differed drastically.

Pennsylvania

It took seven years for Pennsylvania to adopt medical marijuana after the measure was introduced for the first time in 2009. The state was the twenty-fourth to adopt in April 2016. A fundamental institutional difference in Pennsylvania's adoption is that the commonwealth has no mechanism for direct initiatives or legislative referenda. Medical marijuana had to be passed through the traditional legislative process. Pennsylvania's passage was a grassroots effort led "in large part by mothers of children with hard-to-control seizures, veterans with post-traumatic stress disorder [PTSD] and patients with cancer."[100] This illustrates the changes in framing and beneficiary populations that occurred since the early adoptions in the mid- to late-1990s (discussed in more detail in chapter 1).

Republican Senator Mike Folmer proved to be pivotal in getting the bill through the Republican-controlled General Assembly. The senator had crossed state lines to obtain his own medical cannabis during a prior bout with cancer and had firsthand experience in using the product even while it was illegal in Pennsylvania.[101] The legalization effort was also boosted by support from Representative Mike Regan, a Republican and former U.S. marshal. Regan described how his father-in-law sought out marijuana on the streets to alleviate the pain from late-stage cancer treatment.[102] It still took almost a year for the House to take up the bill after it had passed in the State Senate. This delay occurred because the bill was referred to a committee that was chaired by an opponent of the legislation. After the bill was referred to a different committee it began to move again, though the House also created a task force that rewrote substantial portions of the Senate-passed bill.[103] Ultimately, both chambers passed the new version, and Democratic Governor Tom Wolf signed the bill into law on April 17, 2016.

Pennsylvania's Act 16 of 2016 initially covered sixteen medical conditions, which has increased to twenty-three conditions through Medical Marijuana Advisory Board (MMAB) action.[104] The law allowed for delivery through pills, oils, topical gels/creams/ointments, vaporization, tinctures, or liquids. The MMAB added dry leaf to this list later because it is less expensive than more concentrated oils; however, it is only legal to vaporize the dry leaf.[105] It still cannot be smoked. Both physicians and patients must register with the state to participate in the program. Grower/processor and dispensary applications also included provisions for social equity through diversity and community impact plans.[106]

Ohio

Legislators in the Ohio General Assembly reluctantly, but quickly, took up designing and adopting a medical marijuana program in 2016.[107]

Legislators rushed to adopt a program for two reasons. First, they were prompted by a ballot initiative that would have legalized medical and adult-use recreational marijuana in 2015.[108] While the initiative failed by a large margin, this was mainly because of criticism around the language in the initiative and fears that it was too ambitious to adopt both medical and adult-use recreational marijuana at the same time. Regardless, the initiative pushed marijuana onto the agenda in Ohio, and polls showed that medical marijuana was supported by 90 percent of Ohioans.[109] Second, Ohio legislators rushed to write a medical marijuana law to cut off a subsequent medical marijuana initiative effort sponsored by the Marijuana Policy Project.[110] Thus, in the spring of 2016, the Ohio legislature prioritized medical marijuana and acted.

The legislature moved in an unusually quick fashion. The House Select Committee on Medical Marijuana began its hearings on April 20. The House approved the bill by a 71–26 vote on May 10. On May 25, the State Senate approved the bill by a vote of 18 to 15.[111] Marijuana Policy Project dropped its initiative drive three days later.[112] Governor John Kasich signed the law on June 8, 2016. The governor's office announced the signing of the bill and several others without any comment.[113] They certainly did not opt for fanfare at a signing ceremony that is emblematic of a governor achieving a desired priority. While the government moved quickly to adopt a medical marijuana program, there was a sense of reluctance and skepticism from activists about whether Ohio legislators would work to faithfully execute the program.[114]

The law set a deadline of September 8, 2018, to have the program up and running. The deadline was missed by over three months, and sales began on January 16, 2019. Even so, only four of the fifty-six licensed dispensaries were ready for business on opening day, and they could only sell marijuana buds; edibles would not be available for another four months.[115] Decrying the delay, Bob Bridges, a member of Ohio's Medical Marijuana Advisory Committee, said, "Setting up a medical cannabis industry from scratch in the state of Ohio should not have been rocket science."[116]

West Virginia

West Virginia Governor Jim Justice signed the Medical Cannabis Act (SB 386) on April 19, 2017, after it was passed in the State Senate by a

28–6 vote and in the House by a 76–24 vote. The *Charleston Gazette-Mail* said the bill "might have been the legislative underdog story of the session."[117] The Senate bill was passed late in the legislative session among several other bills. In fact, before its passage, some legislators signaled that it would die in the House, where leadership had expressed opposition. However, public pressure convinced Republican Delegate Michael Folk to make a motion to bypass committee reference and take the bill straight to the House floor. It was this move, combined with constituent advocacy, that put legislators on the spot and led to its passage. As one legislator commented, "Like every other member of this body, I can't count the number of emails and phone calls I received on this subject today."[118] The legislative maneuver prevented the bill from dying in committee, but the House made changes that restricted smoking and the use of dry flower, much like in Pennsylvania's law.[119]

Governor Jim Justice signed the bill while flanked by Democratic lawmakers, including veteran State Senator Richard Ojeda, who used his own story of PTSD as well as the opioid crisis to support a medical marijuana bill. Rusty Williams was also present at the signing ceremony. A survivor of late-stage testicular cancer, Williams had shared his story about how illegally purchased marijuana helped him handle the chemotherapy. Senator Mike Woelfel noted that while the law's 2019 full activation date might be a frustration for advocates, he argued that it would allow the state to properly implement the complex program and noted that many states that moved too fast on implementation experienced major setbacks. The *Charleston Gazette-Mail* framed the law's signing by using narratives present in other recent laws: a sympathetic group of patients, an acknowledgment of the effects of current events like the opioid epidemic and the rise of PTSD among veterans, and acknowledgments about other states' experiences.[120]

The West Virginia bill restricted home grow and required purchases of pills, oils, topicals, tincture liquid, dermal patch, or non-whole plant forms for administration through a vaporizer or nebulizer. And while the law allowed applicants with sixteen conditions to apply for a card, it did not cover depression and anxiety, which are two of the most common medical reasons for cannabis use.[121] The state set an implementation date of July 1, 2019, but the program remained bogged down by delays. It was not until May of 2021 that qualifying patients could finally register for a medical cannabis patient card.[122] The delays were partly related to the law's design and partly related to politics. The law banned two of the most commonly sold products—smokable flower and edibles—scaring away many would be investors. The original bill also limited ownership to thirty dispensaries and ten growers.

There is one factor that is particularly unique to West Virginia. Mike Stuart, the Trump-appointed U.S. attorney for the Southern District of West Virginia, was an outspoken opponent of marijuana laws. It is important know that the U.S. Department of Justice appoints U.S. attorneys in each state for the purpose of enforcing federal law. Given marijuana's complicated legal status, U.S. attorneys are often placed in awkward positions. In April 2018, Stuart organized an invitation-only event portrayed as a symposium on marijuana. However, one Democratic legislator called the event a "lecture series by a handpicked list of prohibitionists who used half truths and fear tactics to further a predetermined narrative."[123] U.S. Attorney Stuart's tweets, op-eds, and legal suits had a chilling effect on those responsible for implementing the policy in the state—particularly those in the banking industry and regulators in the West Virginia Department of Health and Human Resources. West Virginia Treasurer John Perdue (D) and Attorney General Patrick Morrisey (R) went so far as to seek outside counsel with a background in medical cannabis law, criminal defense, and the Freedom of Information Act, specifically citing "potential legal issues involving the United States Attorney."[124] Cannabis attorney Sally Peebles also noted that limiting licenses and creating a merit-based application process "has placed regulators in the unfortunate position of being the primary target for litigation."[125]

Considering each of these factors, the cost of entry into the marijuana market in West Virginia was high.[126] The example of Mike Weaver is instructive. Weaver owned a poultry business and switched to growing industrial hemp.[127] As a potential grower, he had to have a minimum of $2 million in assets with $500,000 in cash. Weaver applied for a grower permit, processor permit, and two dispensary permits that each required nonrefundable application fees. He had to hire legal counsel to navigate the application process; he had to purchase growing and security equipment, hire employees, and pay for criminal background checks. In the end, he spent more than $250,000 of his retirement savings and was not awarded a license.[128] In fact, only two of the ten growing licenses were awarded to owners living in the state, even though thirteen of the forty-two applications came from within the state. Instead, most licenses were awarded to out-of-state corporations that are already invested in other states.

The West Virginia legislature passed bills in 2018 to remove licensing limitation caps. They acted in 2019 to address banking services and allowed for vertical integration.[129] Finally, in 2020, they passed SB 339, a Senate bill allowing for dried leaf or plant to be an acceptable form of medical cannabis. Meanwhile, the State Senate moved to permit edibles in April 2021, second to only dried flower in its use among medical patients.[130] The bill died in the House, however.

Evaluating Policy Design, Implementation, and Outcomes

We now transition to assessing the outcomes of these different policy designs and implementation approaches. First, however, it is important to consider the challenges in conducting such an assessment across the states. As we have discussed, federal prohibition complicates the adoption and implementation of medical marijuana and puts physicians, patients, and the industry in a legal gray area. Federal prohibition also makes data collection challenging since states do not report data about their programs in a uniform way. In this regard, Ohio's program has been the most reliable in terms of consistently reporting the program's revenue, sales, patients, and physicians monthly.

Meanwhile, Pennsylvania started releasing data about registered patients, physicians, and sales in May 2021. The Department of Health has taken a very conservative view of the confidentiality clause in Act 16:

> The department shall maintain a confidential list of patients and caregivers to whom it has issued identification cards. All information obtained by the department relating to patients, caregivers and other applicants shall be confidential and not subject to public disclosure, including disclosure under the act of February 14, 2008 (P.L.6, No.3), known as the Right-to-Know Law.[131]

While dispensary and grower and processor applications are public records under the Right-to-Know Law, the Department of Health has used the confidentiality clause to withhold even basic aggregate information about the program. By withholding data on patient counts, conditions used for patient certification, and doctor recommendations, it becomes difficult to assess the strengths and weaknesses of the program. *Spotlight PA*, a reporting outlet situated in the state capital of Harrisburg, has had some success prying information from the department through several lawsuits.[132]

In West Virginia, the first dispensaries did not open until January 2022. Thus, there is a more limited period for which data is available on the state's program. The Medical Cannabis Advisory Board holds quarterly meetings that are recorded, and some data on patient numbers, licensed physicians, and sales are provided during the presentation.

In this section, we use data roughly comparable across the states to assess implementation—but we are transparent about the limitations. Table 3.1 compares publicly available data about the implementation of medical marijuana programs in Pennsylvania, Ohio, and West Virginia. As of February 2023, Pennsylvania, with a slightly larger population than Ohio, had over double the patients per capita of Ohio and over six times the patients per capita as West Virginia. Pennsylvania also had over double the number of licensed physicians per capita compared to both Ohio and West Virginia. Interestingly, Ohio and West Virigina were nearly equal on this metric. It is difficult to compare West Virginia on sales because of the much-delayed start of the program and its smaller size. But Pennsylvania has significantly outpaced Ohio with $5 *billion* more in sales.

Table 3.1. Program Totals, as of February 2023

	Pennsylvania[a]	Ohio	West Virginia
Patients	842,021	330,280	18,660
Patients (per 1,000 population)	64.9	28.1	10.5
Licensed physicians	1,870	657	129
Licensed physicians (per 1,000 population)	0.14	0.06	0.07
Sales	$6.3 billion	$1.2 billion	$31.2 million

Sources: Medical Marijuana Advisory Board Meetings in West Virginia (2022), Pennsylvania (2022), and Ohio (2023).
[a] Pennsylvania has only reported data through November 2022.

Permitting Timing and Dispensary Openings

By June 2017, Pennsylvania regulators approved twelve companies for grower and processor permits and twenty-seven companies for dispensary permits. Keystone Canna Remedies (KCR) in Bethlehem became the first dispensary to open in January 2018, but it did not have product on its shelves until mid-February.[133] It would take another three months for the first dispensary to open in Philadelphia.[134] But even with delays, dispensaries consistently opened over time (see figure 3.2). One thing that helped dispensaries site more quickly in Pennsylvania was the lack of local control built into its law. While only a certain number of dispensaries were allowed to open in each of the six designated regions across the state, local governments were not allowed to ban medical marijuana facilities. They could use their zoning power to place additional restrictions on marijuana businesses, but they could not prohibit them outright. Pennsylvania's medical marijuana law designated growers and processors as manufacturers and dispensaries as commercial entities for the purpose of zoning.

Meanwhile, Ohio's program took nearly a year longer but started to catch up once the initial dispensaries opened. One major issue for Ohio businesses was having to deal with multiple regulatory agencies. This harkens back to the idea of fragmented organizational capacity hindering implementation. As State Senator Steve Huffman noted, "The biggest example is the Department of Pharmacy regulates dispensaries, and the Department of Commerce regulates cultivators. So if you own one of each you have to go to each one to make business decisions."[135] Local control in Ohio also added to the challenging business conditions at the start. In Marietta, citizens protested that a dispensary was too close to a high school stadium and busy intersection.[136] In Dayton, neighbors expressed concerns that dispensaries would attract crime.[137] In Marion, council members warned that extra foot traffic downtown would overwhelm the police force.[138]

On November 12, 2021, Trulieve Cannabis became the first dispensary to open in West Virginia, four years and seven months after the passage of the law, making West Virginia's law the slowest from adoption to dispensing product. The state licensed 10 growers, 10 processors, and 100 dispensaries, even though only 7,310 patients had applied at that time. More dispensaries opened shortly after Trulieve. Only 4,400 patients had registered by November 2021—not enough customers to support 100 dispensaries.[139] A year later, the number of patients tripled to 18,000, and the dispensaries also took off—increasing threefold in 2022 (figure 3.2.)

Figure 3.2 plots the dispensaries per capita over time. The top panel (figure 3.2a) shows the raw total count, and the bottom panel (figure 3.2b) shows the number of dispensaries per 100,000 residents in each state. In Ohio, the number of patients has exceeded expectations, putting a strain on access and prices. In response, the State of Ohio Board of Pharmacy approved licensing an additional 73 dispensaries, which will more than double the number of retailers and improve the geographical distribution of dispensaries.[140] While West Virginia's program looked to be faltering after a slow rollout, the industry took off in late 2022. In early 2022, few dispensaries were open, and many were concentrated near Morgantown, the state's most progressive city located a short drive from the Pennsylvania border. But dispensary openings accelerated in the summer of 2022. In fact, on a per 100,000 population basis, West Virginia now has more dispensaries per capita than either Pennsylvania or Ohio.

Contrasting Program Evaluations

Table 3.2 shows the how the three laws have been evaluated by Americans for Safe Access (ASA). The organization scores each state program "based on how well its current law and regulations accommodate patient needs, as broken down into five general categories."[141] It is worth noting that ASA is concerned with the patient experience; it is not interested in the business environment of the program. The scale is also aspirational. That is, no state earned an A after being rated on several categories. In fact, the highest score is a B–, a score given to five states. The scoring rubric developed by ASA captures policy design and implementation. In the first category, "Access to Medicine," there are policy design elements such as retail access, personal cultivation, and reciprocity (i.e., patients can obtain medical cannabis out of state); there are also ratings related to implementation. such as whether the state has enough retailers.

FROM THE STATEHOUSE TO THE DISPENSARY | 111

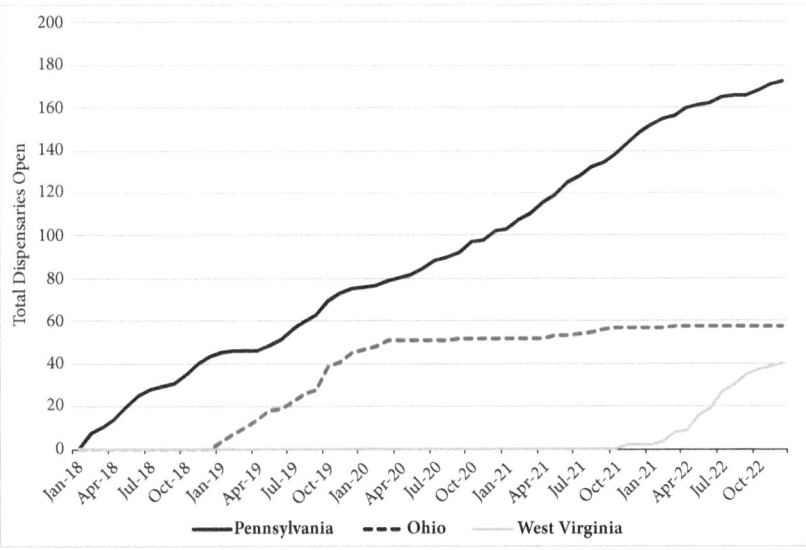

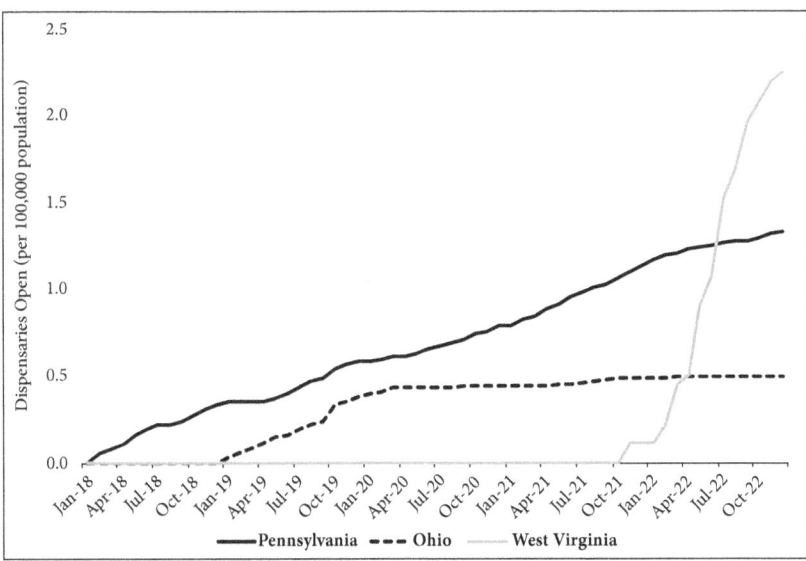

Figure 3.2a–b. Total number of dispensaries open (top) and dispensaries per 100,000 population (bottom) opened in Pennsylvania, Ohio, and West Virginia, 2018–2022. Sources: https://www.health.pa.gov/topics /Documents/Programs/Medical%20Marijuana/Medical%20Marijuana%20 Dispensaries%20in%20Pennsylvania%20with%20Product.pdf; https://www .medicalmarijuana.ohio.gov/DispensaryLocations; https://omc.wv.gov/Pages /default.aspx (under "Find a Dispensary" section). Per capita data based on population data at https://www.census.gov/data/tables/time-series/demo /popest/2020s-state-total.html.

Table 3.2. Americans for Safe Access 2022 *State of the States* Rankings

	Pennsylvania	Ohio	West Virginia
Access to Medicine	50/100	30/100	36/100
Authorizes retail access	10/10	10/10	10/10
Alternative accessibility Methods (delivery/pickup)	15/20	10/20	0/20
Personal cultivation (home grow)	0/15	0/15	0/15
Collective gardening	0/5	0/5	0/5
Sufficient number of retailers	25/30	10/30	20/30
Reciprocity	0/20	0/20	6/20
Affordability	58/100	49/100	60/100
Sales tax break for patients and caregivers	20/20	15/20	20/20
Covered by state insurance or health aid	0/20	0/20	0/20
Reasonable registration fees	18/20	14/20	20/20
Financial hardship Waivers or discounts	20/20	20/20	20/20
Donation program	0/10	0/10	0/10
Allows multiyear registrations	0/10	0/10	0/10
Program Functionality	91/100	87/100	62/100
Legal protections within a reasonable time frame	14/20	14/20	16/20
Reasonable possession limits	10/10	10/10	8/10
Reasonable purchase limits	10/10	10/10	8/10
Telemedicine for physician certification	15/15	15/15	15/15
Patient and physician representation in program decision making	20/20	20/20	0/20
Reasonable caregiver standards	4/5	5/5	5/5
Reasonable physician standards	3/5	3/5	2/5
Access to administration methods (dried flower, edibles)	10/10	10/10	3/10
Provides access to minors on school grounds	5/5	0/5	5/5
Health and Social Equity	43/100	90/100	15/100
State programs and protections	20/25	25/25	0/25
Housing protections	0/25	25/25	0/25
Access for minors	10/10	9/10	8/10
Access in underserved areas	4/10	9/10	0/10
List of qualifying conditions is exhaustive/all-inclusive	9/10	8/10	7/10
Allows patients to medicate where they choose	0/10	8/10	0/10

Table 3.2. Americans for Safe Access 2022 *State of the States* Rankings (*continued*)

	Pennsylvania	Ohio	West Virginia
Organ transplants	0/5	5/5	0/5
Ownership or employment restrictions	0/5	1/5	0/5
Consumer Protection and Product Safety	**165/200**	**151/200**	**145/200**
Grow/cultivation	36/50	35/50	33/50
Manufacturing	37/50	37/50	28/50
Dispensing	40/50	33/50	44/50
Laboratory operations	48/50	44/50	40/50
ASA grade	C+	C+	C−

Source: Americans for Safe Access, *2022 State of the States Report* (Washington, DC: ASA, 2023).

We can see how the adoption and legislative process in Pennsylvania, Ohio, and West Virginia is manifested in the ASA scorecards. Overall, Pennsylvania and Ohio's programs are both given a C+, indicating that "the state has a fair medical cannabis program that provides at least some access and protections for cannabis patients, but requires substantial improvement in one or more areas."[142] In 2021, West Virginia fell behind both states with a D grade because of "critical and substantial deficiencies in access and/or patient rights that must be addressed immediately."[143] In 2022, ASA elevated West Virginia's grade to a C− for making strides in patient registration and dispensaries. Even so, the program still scored below Ohio and Pennsylvania mainly due to a lack of patient protection in employment, housing, education, and child custody cases.

This leads us to consider the more specific ratings that exist underneath these broad categories. They include ratings related to each state's effectiveness in providing access to medicine, making the program affordable and functional, protecting health and social equity, and meeting requirements for consumer protections and product safety. With the most supportive political environment, Pennsylvania outperforms the other two states in access by providing delivery and curbside pickup and by having more retailers open that are also geographically dispersed. Pennsylvania and West Virginia are similarly affordable in terms of offering some tax breaks to marijuana businesses and having lower patient registration fees. While this measure only captures the design rather than the price of the product, from an administrative standpoint, Pennsylvania and Ohio have done more to make their programs affordable. Now that Pennsylvania and Ohio have had their dispensaries open for over three years, they have ranked high in functionality—scoring highly in every subcategory. West Virginia lags in two key areas: access to multiple administration methods and having patient and physician representation in decision making.

ASA argues that state departments of public health are the most effective in administering a medical marijuana system. They also rate whether the state has a "proven track record of patient and physician decision making in its regulatory affairs."[144] West Virginia has set up a separate Office of Medical Cannabis Advisory Board with gubernatorial appointments. While the board includes a patient advocate and physicians, several of the physicians are skeptics. Mike Pushkin, the Democratic Party chair of West Virginia and a state delegate who has been instrumental in getting West Virginia's program off the ground, argued that "Governor [Jim] Justice has weighted the program with prohibitionists."[145] This further demonstrates the power of the executive to influence policy implementation and effectiveness.

Starting in 2021, ASA created a new scoring category for health and social equity. Here, Ohio's program has surpassed the others. While Pennsylvania is the only state in our analysis that has written equity provisions into its law, it trails behind in protecting patients. Several states require drug testing to receive state assistance. Ohio and Pennsylvania have written provisions that protect the benefits of medical patients that test positive for marijuana. Similarly, patients in public housing can lose their benefits for marijuana use, but only Ohio has crafted legislation to protect patients from eviction or discrimination owing to medical cannabis use. Several hospitals have removed medical cannabis users from organ transplant lists because marijuana can increase the risk of pulmonary infections.[146] Ohio's law explicitly protects medical patients from being removed from organ donation lists based on cannabis use.

Finally, ASA rates the production of marijuana. Being patient-centered, the organization is not interested in costs or efficiency but in how many safeguards are in place to protect patients. These safeguards include employee training, facility sanitation, packaging and labeling, testing, and procedures for handling complaints, adverse events, and recalls. Overall, each of the states are similarly rated. This category is also different from the others. Whereas the other categories were about adding more protections for patients, this category is related to *restrictions* placed on producers (which in turn protect patients). But the results may signify that it is much more politically palatable to heap regulations on the industry than it is to make the program more accessible for patients.

Conclusion

Pennsylvania, Ohio, and West Virginia had different institutional environments when their laws were passed. Ohio and West Virginia had single-party government control by Republicans, and Pennsylvania had divided government with a Republican General Assembly and Democratic governor. Out of the three governors, Pennsylvania's Tom Wolf was the most supportive of legalizing medical marijuana. Ohio Republicans, including Governor John Kasich, were skeptical of medical marijuana but decided to take control of the issue in the face of a credible ballot threat from a related initiative.[147] Despite their skepticism, they worked with interest groups to create an effective bill. West Virginia Governor Jim Justice did not champion the policy but was supportive when the bill made it to his desk stating, "I'm going to sign this into law and I think all of us will feel like we're doing something good for families out there."[148] While there were questions about his commitment to the program early on, the program expanded quickly in 2022. While West Virginia lawmakers pushed it through the statehouse, they had to bypass many staunch prohibitionists in leadership. In fact, one marijuana interest group leader had stated that he would not go to West Virginia if Speaker of the House Tim Armstead is in charge.[149] The legislative maneuvering also meant that West Virginia lawmakers did not have the benefit of time or committee work to tinker with the bill. Consequently, much of the original statutory language was borrowed from Pennsylvania's law. But West Virginia lawmakers, dealing with a much smaller population, lower per capita income, and a challenging geography for transportation and access, had to rely on the rulemaking process to finally get a workable bill that included reforms to banking and business models. West Virginia is also the only state to deal with threats from a U.S. attorney, who took a decidedly different approach than other U.S. attorneys and knocked the program offtrack for two years. Even with these reforms, Delegate Mike Pushkin is not sure if the medical program will survive without West Virginia adopting an adult-use program. The majority of cannabis businesses in West Virginia are major multistate corporations that might be absorbing losses in order to be at the front of the line if an adult-use law is passed.[150] If it is not passed, however, it is not clear how long such speculators can keep losing money. Thus, the future of medical marijuana in West Virginia is decidedly mixed without further reforms.

In chapter 2, we discussed how policy adoption is a dynamic process, with conditions changing over time. The same is true with implementation. By taking a snapshot of three neighboring programs that are a few years into implementation, we can learn about the conditions that hinder or facilitate implementation. This chapter also contrasts how the federal environment has been more important for implementation than it was in adoption. This exercise surfaces several challenges in evaluating the implementation of medical marijuana, from disparities in data availability and collection to normative questions related to what makes a successful program. Nevertheless, implementation theory points out important factors to consider. A policy must be designed well, with clear and consistent goals and structure. A supportive political environment, with support from both the state legislature and the executive, is also important for providing the stability necessary to build a comprehensive medical marijuana program. Of course, resources are always needed. And not just financial resources for regulators and industry, but also political, social, and cultural resources that contribute to a supportive implementation environment and ongoing legitimacy of the policy. Informal actors like interest groups can also work to hold government accountable and promote reforms to programs when inevitable problems emerge. In fact, policy reform is but one type of feedback effect that occurs after policy adoption and implementation. We now turn to those feedback effects, completing the circle.

4

When Policy Creates Politics

States Learn as They Go

When Oklahomans voted for medical marijuana, they were sold a bill of goods. The state question was misleading, and it has tied our hands as we regulate the industry. . . . While we can't change the past, we can learn from it and improve our future. We are getting the right leaders in place and untying their hands to enforce the laws.
—Kevin Stitt, governor of Oklahoma, State of the State Address, 2022

Oklahoma's experience with medical marijuana stands out as an outlier in almost every way. In 2018, an ideologically diverse group of activists pushed for a medical marijuana initiative that was opposed by Governor Mary Fallin, the entire Oklahoma congressional delegation, and leaders in business, policing, medicine, and religion. Fallin even used her powers to push State Question 788 to a June primary ballot in hopes that would ensure a less receptive electorate. Instead, 57 percent of Oklahomans approved the measure, making Oklahoma the thirtieth state to adopt medical marijuana.[1]

With hindsight, Oklahoma officials probably wish they would have partnered with the activists rather than push them away because within months the market in "Toke-lahoma" exploded. Tom Spanier, a dispensary owner noted, "They've literally done what no other state had done: free-enterprise system, open market, wild wild west." Unlike other states, Oklahoma's policy has no set qualifying conditions for a patient card or possession or purchasing limits. The patient registration process requires a five-minute consultation. On the business side, the costs of entry are extremely low—just $2,500 for a license to grow or dispense, with no limits on licensing (so no scarcity), and local governments do not have the authority to ban marijuana businesses.[2] Within two years, nearly 10 percent of Oklahomans had acquired medical marijuana cards, the highest percentage in the country. By late 2020, more than 9,000 grow licenses had been issued—another national record. Tax revenue has been high and prices low.[3]

This laissez-faire approach to marijuana has made Oklahoma a case study for many observers. So far, there have been some major positive outcomes. When licenses are expensive or scarce, large companies have substantial advantages in the market. Many state programs get bogged down in litigation and allegations of corruption, but the low cost of entry initially kept the major multistate players out and favored Oklahoma residents. Furthermore, the low cost of entry kept prices low, allowing dispensaries to better compete with the illicit market. Consequently, illegal sales became rare. In the first year, tax revenue from the program outpaced projections.

But over time, people figured out how to game the system in Oklahoma. Some residents discovered they could make a quick buck by serving as "ghost" owners—using their residency to cover out-of-state and foreign investors. Similarly, crime syndicates have used lax rules to grow marijuana in Oklahoma and traffic it to other parts of the country. Even an early champion for legalization conceded, "The word went out on the black market that Oklahoma was a place that you could come set up shop, and they weren't going to come enforce the law, and you could do what you wanted."[4] This sentiment explains why Governor Kevin Stitt—a champion of deregulation and Fallin's successor—tried to rein in the program.

While Oklahoma represents an extraordinary policy experiment, all states monitor the implementation of their own and other states' policies so they can adjust when necessary. Furthermore, states considering adoption carefully learn from other state policies. As North Carolina's legislature considers a medical marijuana program, State Senator Bill Rabon boasted, "We have looked at other states, the good and the bad. And we have, if not perfected, we have done a better job than anyone so far."[5] Even if North Carolina's legislature really did do a better job than anyone in crafting their legislation, which has yet to be signed into law, the policy will inevitably have unexpected outcomes that must be remedied over time.

In this chapter, we consider the "final" stage of the policy process: evaluation and feedback. Final is in quotes because the process never ends. In fact, feedback theory explicitly considers how the adoption of policies creates new politics and how evaluation of policy successes and failures (i.e., policy learning) can result in additional policymaking. Round and round it goes. We begin by describing policy feedback theory, the four channels of feedback effects that occur in policymaking, and policy learning. We then consider the process of medicalization, whereby states over time have instituted a variety of mechanisms to treat marijuana more like a medicine (e.g., packaging requirements). We then consider specific problems that have emerged in the medical marijuana industry (e.g., social equity and banking) and how states have struggled to find solutions. Finally, we address two of the major feedback effects of medical marijuana legalization: first, the path that was carved for adult-use recreational programs, and second, the building pressure on the federal government to do something to address marijuana policy problems that the states cannot fix because of federal prohibition.

Policy Feedback

While there is a strong temptation to think of policies with a discrete beginning (agenda setting) and end (implementation), reality is far more complicated. In policymaking, there is rarely anything truly new under the sun. Once policies are adopted and implemented, they have many different effects on society. There are certainly the direct effects of the policy. Take medical marijuana. A state legalizes medical marijuana, and a system is established to certify patients and give them access to the product. But policies have other feedback effects, too. They reshape political debates. They change how people and groups view themselves. For example, marijuana users are no longer viewed as deviants, at least not if they are using the product through the new state system. Growers and dispensaries become small businesses that employ people, pay taxes, sponsor community events, and occupy vacant downtown buildings. Policies also shift power from some individuals and groups to others.

Debates involve new stakeholders (e.g., growers and dispensary owners) whose health or fortune is tied to any modifications in the policy. All of these considerations illustrate how policies create new politics, and they are the issues that interest scholars who focus their attention on policy feedback.[6]

There are four channels through which feedback effects occur.[7] First, policies reshape the political agenda and definitions of a policy problem. Opponents of policies often claim that adopting, X, Y, or Z policy will amount to a Pandora's box that will legitimize undesired outcomes and behaviors. Some of these claims, like the notion that same-sex marriage will somehow legitimize bestiality, are farcical. However, no policy is perfect, and opponents can inevitably point to some evidence that the downsides of a new policy are emerging just as they predicted. Success is also legitimizing, of course. We have already discussed how the expansion of medical marijuana increased the policy's legitimacy, which in turn helped it spread further. Policymakers do make decisions based on a logic of appropriateness, where they consider whether a policy is appropriate.[8] "Appropriateness" is not about the outcomes of a decision; that falls under a different logic of consequentiality (what we think of as rational decision making). Instead, a sense of appropriateness is shaped by cultural, spiritual, social, and other factors that can change. As a policy is legitimized, it becomes more appropriate and develops its own constituency. Policies also reshape our conception of what "the problem" is. In fact, policies often create new problems to solve through the effects of unintended consequences. Again, marijuana policy is instructive. Without medical marijuana policies, there is no need to be concerned about packaging that is attractive to children, product quality control, and social equity in the industry. All these problems emerged as a new industry took shape. As problems are identified, the policy process begins anew because groups jockey to get them onto decision makers' agendas.

The second channel of policy feedback effects operates by changing the influence or power of different groups. Policies can empower or disempower, and often there must be trade-offs made in who gains and loses power under new policy regimes. We commonly think of interest groups as forming to lobby for specific causes.[9] However, they will also form as a response to new policies.[10] Take the accelerated emergence of the religious right in the 1980s. Its increasing engagement in secular realms like politics and media was driven by policy choices that emphasized individual rights (e.g., abortion). Groups will also emerge, or add to their portfolio of causes, to protect new benefits conferred by policies. The American Association of Retired Persons (AARP), for example, is fiercely protective of Social Security and Medicare.[11]

The third channel of policy feedback involves changes in governance. The creation of a new policy can shape how government acts in the future through new institutional arrangements or by altering what policymakers view as the legitimate role of government in society (i.e., what is appropriate). The passage of new and especially large pieces of legislation often requires the creation of new executive entities, or reform within existing ones, for implementation. For example, the significant expansion of policies to control pollution in the United States under President Richard Nixon necessitated an administrative reorganization and the creation of the Environmental Protection Agency (EPA). Once established, the EPA has been able to continue advancing its mandate, even in the face of more hostile presidential administrations.[12] Successful agencies tend to attract more work, meaning there is positive governance feedback (e.g., more funding), whereas failure can result in negative feedback (e.g., funding cuts).

The fourth channel cuts to something fundamental in a democracy: the meaning of citizenship. Policies shape the membership, status, and identity of groups in a society.[13] Membership has many definitions and policy nuances. One place to start in defining membership is to consider the fundamental rules of who is, strictly speaking, a citizen of the polity and who is not. The United States has rules for who is a citizen and how to become one. Those rules evolved over time through both constitutional and statutory changes. The Fourteenth Amendment, passed in the aftermath of the American Civil War, guarantees birthright citizenship. Statutory immigration policy has changed dramatically over the last 150 years, often in response to feelings of an in-group threat from emergent immigrant populations.[14] Changes to the rules surrounding citizenship redefine who is a member of society and who is not. In several states, a quasi-legal gray market existed before policies were adopted that legalized marijuana. Ideally, such policies bring increased legitimacy to these stakeholders.[15]

A narrower means to consider membership is the fundamental right to vote.[16] Not all citizens are extended this right. The United States has experienced both expansion and retrenchment on who has this status. Successive expansions in enfranchisement included working-class whites, Black men, women, Native Americans, and those between eighteen and twenty years of age. However, expansions often come with de jure and de facto retrenchments, from Jim Crow laws to restrictive voting requirements. While such restrictions do not eliminate one's technical citizenship, they can substantially alter the status of groups in society.

Of course, voting rules are not the only policies that affect the status and identity of groups. For citizens to engage meaningfully in a democratic system, they need access to resources like time, education, and security.[17] But not all groups have equal access to quality education or leisure time. Policies like the War on Drugs and the growth in mass incarceration have deeply disadvantaged marginalized communities in the United States.[18] While welfare policies may not necessarily change mass opinion, their design can reinforce stereotypes that negatively affect recipients.[19] Positive feedback effects also occur, as evidenced by the research on the effects of GI Bill benefits on returning World War II veterans.[20] In each case, a policy serves to alter the status of recipients, clients, or beneficiaries in either positive or negative ways.

Finally, policies affect the identity of groups. Prominent examples include the struggle over marriage equality in the United States and the fights in states over the status of transgendered youth and adults. By banning or allowing same-sex marriage, banning sodomy, determining who can and cannot use a bathroom, and prohibiting transgender youth from participating in sports, the state is determining the bounds of acceptable behavior and identity.[21]

Medical marijuana laws have helped to bring many previous cannabis users out of the shadows. While stigma surrounding cannabis use certainly has not entirely disappeared, the expansion of medical marijuana laws has brought political legitimacy to drug liberalization and greater social legitimacy to cannabis users, especially those who use it medicinally. In fact, medical patients have been shown to specifically dissociate themselves from recreational users to avoid experiencing heightened social stigma.[22] Not to mention, awareness of the potential therapeutic effects of cannabis has increased, and medical cannabis use has consistently received more support among the public than recreational use.[23] As we discussed in chapter 1, society's view of medical cannabis users is changing. Once seen as deviants, they are now assuming more positive and influential roles in advancing policy.[24] In addition, this societal shift likely also affects how medical cannabis users perceive themselves.

Learning to Keep It Fast and Loose

Policy learning also occurs during the evaluation and feedback stage of the policy process. Not all policies are formally evaluated; however, lawmakers will draw a variety of lessons from policies implemented in their own states and by other governments. Learning occurs in a boundedly rational fashion, meaning policymakers cannot possibly consider all relevant information when updating their views on a given social problem.[25] Instead, heuristic shortcuts help them gather information quickly, even if that information is incomplete or inaccurate.[26] The primary lesson we typically think policymakers learn from evaluating policies is whether they are working. But working can mean different things to different people. It could mean effectively serving the most clients possible or maximizing tax revenue to pay for other priorities. It could also mean gaining electoral advantages in future elections.[27] Thus, policymakers will evaluate whether a policy in their state or another jurisdiction is well designed and implemented, but they will also learn lessons about post-adoption politics.[28] Such lessons can help in their own policy design or could even deter legislators from pursuing further adoption of a policy innovation.

Fear characterized some of the earliest lessons about medical cannabis policy in the states. The first era of cannabis policy adoption (1996–2000) was driven almost exclusively by ballot initiatives, with greater legislative adoptions in the second era (2000–2009).[29] Our analysis in chapter 2 showed that the initiative is still important in latter adoptions, even if it is by forcing the legislature to act. During both eras, states tended to have ambiguous laws with few details that left much discretion to patients, doctors, and implementers (e.g., California). As we discussed in chapter 3, under the administrations of Bill Clinton and, later, George W. Bush, threats to prosecute state workers and physicians recommending medical cannabis had a chilling effect on state implementation. The threat of federal legal action also discouraged states from creating comprehensive regulatory regimes for medical marijuana. It was better to keep things fast and loose rather than get too involved and attract the federal government's ire. Of course, such threats did not stop the spread of medical marijuana policy, but they did prompt states to take a hands-off approach to implementation and regulation.[30]

Medicalization and Policy Feedback Effects

We have previously discussed how federal marijuana policy enforcement shifted substantially during the Barack Obama administration. It is worth expanding on that here because this third era of medical marijuana adoption and reinvention is characterized by the states becoming bolder in regulating and medicalizing marijuana programs. Obama's Department of Justice (DOJ) issued the Odgen memo in 2009, which established a nonenforcement policy for state-legal medical marijuana.[31] The memo encouraged U.S. attorneys to not pursue medical marijuana operations that were compliant with state laws. States with medical marijuana programs were freed to engage more in regulating the nascent industry. This sparked a period of increasing medicalization, where medical marijuana rules began to resemble those in place for pharmaceuticals.[32]

The DOJ further clarified the administration's position on federal forbearance in the 2011 and 2013 Cole memos. These memorandums clarified that the feds would not pursue state-legal cannabis entities in states with *"strong and effective regulatory and enforcement systems* that will address the threat those state laws could pose to public safety, public health, and other law enforcement interests" (emphasis added).[33] The section we emphasize in italics is the key here. DOJ was saying it was not enough for states to simply legalize medical—and starting in 2012, adult-use recreational—marijuana programs. They had to provide "strong and effective regulatory and enforcement systems." This led to the states taking a far more hands-on approach in regulating medical marijuana. After leaving office, Deputy Attorney General James Cole discussed the purpose of these memos. Cole noted that U.S. attorneys had come to him for a remedy because people were "overreading" the Ogden memo. According to Cole, the Ogden memo's intent was to say that people who "really are sick, and people who give them care in that illness, are not going to be the topic of our conversations in our prosecution efforts"; furthermore, Cole's 2011 memo was an attempt to clarify that the memo "wasn't intended to say that anyone who's doing it in compliance with state law is just fine."[34]

In 2013, DOJ circled back after Colorado and Washington passed adult-use recreational marijuana programs. Cole described the DOJ's process: "What we came to was looking at these initiatives as two pieces—one was the decriminalization of marijuana in those states, and secondly, setting up a regulatory scheme, through which it can be controlled and taxed." The department decided against preempting the state laws. Cole noted:

> We also heard in our legal analysis that if you wanted to, you probably could stop the regulatory scheme because it probably could stop conduct that's illegal under federal law. And so we said, "But what's the point of that?" Because all we're going to do is cut off our nose to spite our face and help the drug cartels make lots of money.

The DOJ proceeded by spelling out some of the potential harms that can come from the marijuana industry and clarifying when U.S. attorneys should prosecute. But they also pushed the states to tighten up their regulations. According to Cole, "We were saying to the states, 'You guys have to become serious about your regulatory enforcement here.' Recognizing that it hadn't been done very well in the past, we were basically admonishing them."[35] While ensuing regulations vary considerably across the state-legal programs, states have implemented rules for product safety testing, packaging, labeling, media advertising, waste disposal, security, stock limitations, on-site consumption, caregiver and patient registration, caregiver permissions, and qualifying conditions.[36]

Feedback Channel 1: Identifying and Solving New Problems

Learning and policy feedback were evident as newly adopting states incorporated these regulations in their laws and older adopting states undertook significant updates of their laws. This can be thought of as the first channel of feedback effects: redefining the problem. Problems had emerged in regulating nascent medical marijuana programs, and states were learning how to solve them.[37] In perhaps the most visible display of policy learning, legislators from states considering medical marijuana would travel in delegations to places like Colorado to learn how to make their programs work. Site visits and so-called policy tourism are common methods of intergovernmental learning.[38] As policy learning and feedback occurred during this new era, state medical marijuana laws become more complex. We can use the provisions in those laws to illustrate how learning occurred over time.

We used a comprehensive dataset called the Prescription Drug Abuse Policy System (PDAPS) that tracks provisions in a host of state drug laws to better understand trends in state policies.[39] We begin by analyzing the number of qualifying conditions that each state law covered. Many state laws specify qualifying conditions that patients must have to access medical cannabis. These conditions can include diagnoses and symptoms like pain, glaucoma, HIV/AIDS, post-traumatic stress disorder (PTSD), among many others.[40] From 1999 to 2020, chronic pain was far and away the most common condition patients reported for accessing medical cannabis.[41] As we noted in chapter 1, one of the things that advocates did to advance medical marijuana adoptions was to expand the scope of conflict by including additional groups with conditions that were potentially treatable with medical cannabis (e.g., veterans with PTSD). In general, we see a positive trend over time in state laws, including more qualifying conditions (figure 4.1). A simple bivariate regression analysis suggests that qualifying conditions increased by 0.2 each year—or one more qualifying condition every five years. This is partly driven by new understandings of cannabis's potential to aid with certain conditions. However, it is also driven by the efforts of activists to engage with new communities that would benefit from this treatment, like veterans and mother's groups. Furthermore, some states have included broader catchall language, either deferring to a physician's judgment or including symptoms (e.g., chronic pain or nausea) that are downstream from several conditions.[42]

Next, we looked at specific provisions within each state law. The PDAPS dataset has coded over 100 unique provisions related to patients in medical marijuana laws. While it is difficult to simplify such detailed laws into a few meaningful metrics, a theme does emerge. There are

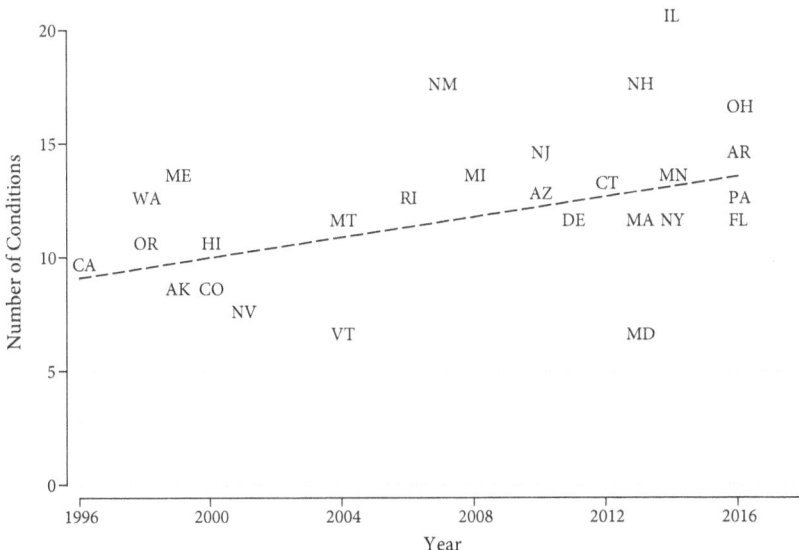

Figure 4.1. Number of qualifying conditions in medical marijuana law, 1996–2016.

parts of the laws related to patients that are expansionary, permissive, and protective of patients. They include provisions related to qualifying diseases, protections from discrimination, permission for home cultivation, and rules that provide patients with an affirmative defense for possession or cultivation under state law. Meanwhile, a second dimension emerges from the laws that contain restricting and punitive provisions. They include specific requirements for registering patients and doctors, restrictions on cannabis use in certain areas (e.g., near schools), and situations that can lead to expulsion from the medical marijuana program. We use a statistical method of exploratory factor analysis to create indices of protections and restrictions for patients so that we can observe how both changed over time (see appendix B for methodological details).

Figure 4.2 displays a distinct increase in patient protections included in medical marijuana laws over time. Figure 4.3, however, shows overall a slight decline in patient restrictions, although what it also shows is the substantial variability in late-adopter states. While the regression line fits the states well between 1998 and 2008 (save for Montana), there are two clusters of states that appear after 2008—namely, states with greater-than-average restrictions (Illinois, Delaware, New Hampshire, Arizona,

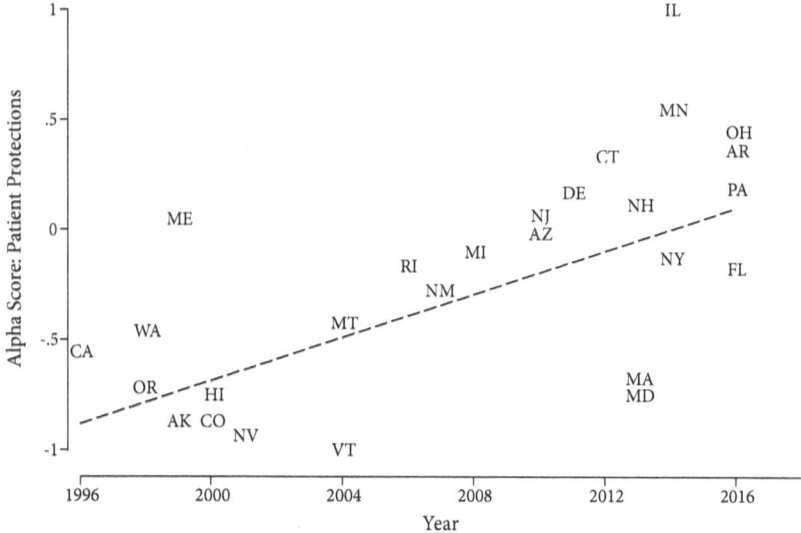

Figure 4.2. Alpha index of patient protections included in medical marijuana laws, 1996–2016.

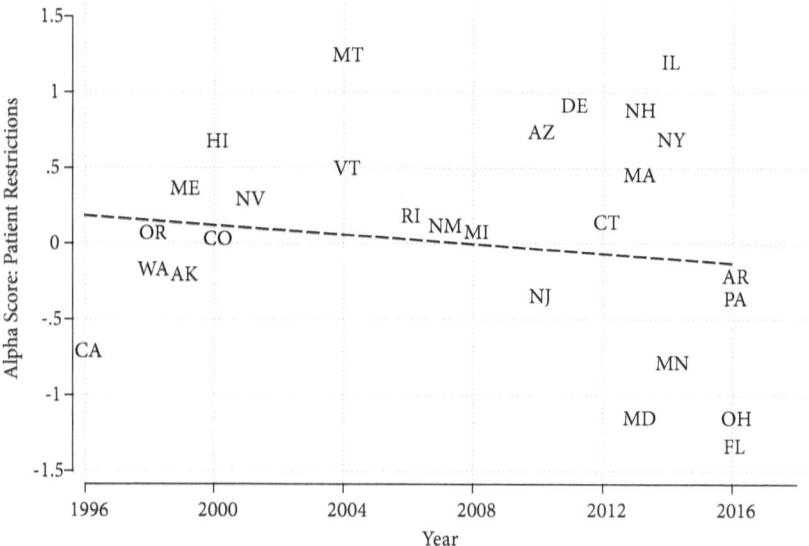

Figure 4.3. Alpha index of patient restrictions included in medical marijuana laws, 1996–2016.

New York, and Massachusetts) and those with lower-than-average restrictions (Florida, Ohio, Maryland, and Minnesota). The stark increase in patient protections illustrates the effect of medicalization on subsequent laws. Whereas early-adopter states were more apt to play it fast and loose to avoid federal intervention, late-adopter states incorporated regulations that emerged once the federal government's enforcement emphasized strong and effective regulatory and enforcement systems. The states have increasingly split, however, on whether they place restrictions on access and use of medical cannabis.

Feedback Channels 2 and 4: Power and Citizenship

As cannabis policies and the industry medicalized, the image of a marijuana user also began to change. We discussed this briefly in chapter 1, but it warrants revisiting since it is in the feedback stage where policy development reshapes future politics and group identities. State policy can have a significant effect on reshaping the political landscape, particularly when the federal government does not act.[43] Cannabis culture itself is remarkably stable, with consistent symbols, rituals, and events.[44] However, as states liberalized, that culture has become increasingly visible. The Mile High 420 Festival in Denver is a prominent example. Held every year on April 20, this large public festival is dedicated to cannabis culture in the world and includes smoking on the grounds of the state capitol building. We combined these two feedback channels because they are related: the expansion of the industry and advocacy groups (citizenship) is directly related to power.

Legalization has encouraged more cannabis content on social media.[45] Illegal sellers have used social media for promoting their business for some time, but social media influencers are increasingly promoting state-legal products.[46] Notably, while the cannabis industry and illegal sellers are predominantly men, influencers (at least on Instagram) in the United States are disproportionately women.[47] This could help to change the image of cannabis, encouraging consumption among women as "sanitized, wholesome, and healthy."[48] Beyond social media, cannabis tourism, museum displays of formerly deviant cannabis heritage, and agricultural shows help to normalize cannabis.[49] Tourism normalizes because it "facilitates the accessibility and availability, everyday prevalence, increased tolerance, and social and cultural accommodation of cannabis."[50] Including cannabis in agricultural events, like California's State Fair, helps to legitimize the industry as an agricultural enterprise.[51] California launched cannabis competitions in 2022. According to Jess Durfee, director of the state fair, "Adding cannabis cultivation alongside wine, craft beer, cheese and olive oil, was a perfect fit with the CA State Fair's history of celebrating California's rich agriculture history."[52]

Images of cannabis have also changed as more Americans have access to cannabidiol (CBD). CBD is a cannabinoid, like tetrahydrocannabinol (THC), but it is not psychoactive. Like medical marijuana more broadly, CBD has been marketed for its potential therapeutic effects, even though research support for many claims remains thin.[53] The federal government loosened restrictions on CBD in the 2018 farm bill (officially the Agriculture Improvement Act of 2018). The act established the Domestic Hemp Production Program. Hemp is a variety of *Cannabis sativa* with concentrations of delta-9-THC that are too low to have psychoactive effects.[54] The farm bill allowed for broad hemp cultivation (once restricted by the Controlled Substances Act) and the transfer and sale of hemp-derived products across state lines. The decision spurred an explosion of CBD-infused gummies, lotions, and beverages that fell into a regulatory gray area similar to supplements and cosmetics.[55] As restrictions on CBD and even medical marijuana use have eased within national and international sports regulations, athletes are touting the still-dubious recovery and performance benefits of cannabis.[56] The industry grew to nearly $6 billion by the end of 2022.[57] The debate over its regulation is ongoing, with the Food and Drug Administration seeking new regulatory authority to develop more oversight.[58] Regardless, the ubiquity of CBD products can lessen the fears or stigma of marijuana and affect the decisions states make to regulate it.

Feedback Channel 3: Governance

Another signal of cannabis's evolving political legitimacy is the frankness with which more political elites are willing to discuss their experiences with the drug. Democrat Gary Chambers smoked a large blunt in his very first television ad in the 2022 Senate primary in Louisiana.[59]

The ad's title, "37 seconds," refers to how often someone in the United States is arrested for marijuana possession. Chambers is African American, and he made the point that disproportionately, these arrests were of people who looked like him. Chambers taped that ad in New Orleans, which had decriminalized cannabis possession. That same year, Indiana State Senate candidate Tom McDermott (D) followed by smoking a cannabis joint in an ad of his own, cut for 4/20, a rallying date for advocates of legal marijuana use.[60] Such blatant use of cannabis is perhaps new among public officials, but drug confessionals are not. Elite discourse has come a long way from Bill Clinton ensuring during his 1992 presidential campaign that he "did not inhale" when he tried marijuana as a youth. By 2008, Barack Obama admitted that he did inhale and "that was the point."[61] More recently, in promoting the STATES Act, which would decriminalize and tax cannabis at the federal level, Representative Nancy Mace (R-SC) has told her personal story of using cannabis to cope with the experience of being raped in high school.[62]

Also fitting within the governance channel of feedback is the emergence of independent regulation of state-legal cannabis. Initially, states tended to vest new powers to regulate medical marijuana programs with existing agencies, like state departments of health. However, as the policy and industry matured, some states have developed entirely new agencies to regulate cannabis. California is emblematic of this evolution. Before 2021, three different regulators managed medical and recreational cannabis programs in the state: the Bureau of Cannabis Control (under the Department of Consumer Affairs), the CalCannabis Cultivation Licensing Division (under the Department of Food and Agriculture), and the Manufactured Cannabis Safety Branch (under the Department of Health). In 2021, California consolidated the three into a brand-new Department of Cannabis Control through the 2021–2022 budget. This move not only provides bureaucratic efficiencies, but it also further institutionalizes the cannabis industry in California. Figure 4.4 shows the states that either use an existing agency or department to regulate cannabis operations and those that have created independent agencies to do this work.[63] Existing agencies that are often given the authority to regulate medical or adult-use cannabis include departments of health, revenue, and licensing and state liquor control boards.

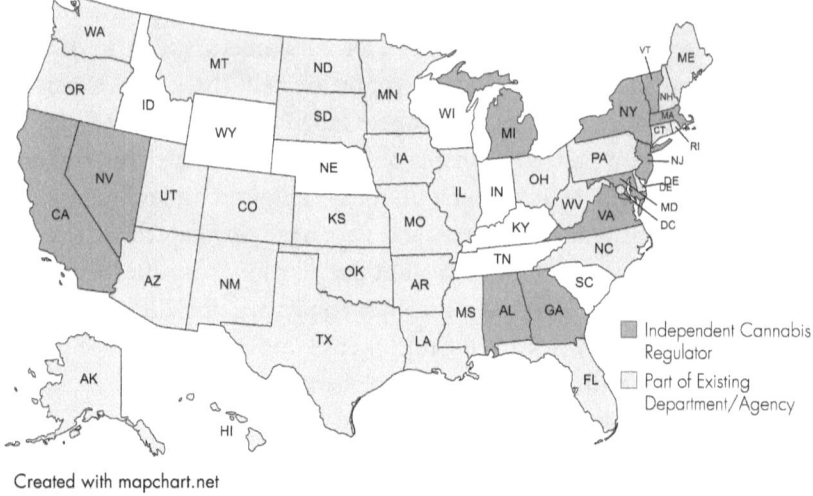

Created with mapchart.net

Figure 4.4. State cannabis regulators.

Tackling Emerging Problems in the States

Regulation and patient protection were not the only problems that emerged and created a feedback loop for further state policymaking. Notably, many problems facing the states and this new industry are only partially solvable through state action because they hinge on federal prohibition. The federal government and the states have different spheres of power. For example, the federal government regulates banks, which has made it difficult for the industry to access and store capital. States have also wrestled with the growth of "big cannabis," emergent social equity demands, and limits on research about cannabis's medical efficacy. The aim here is not to discuss every problem facing the states but to illustrate how those problems have had their own feedback effects as states learn to solve them, at least within their power to do so.

Banking

Many state programs are still operating largely on a cash basis as banks and credit card companies refuse to get involved. As of 2022, only 700 of the nearly 5,000 commercial banks reported serving the cannabis industry.[64] There has been steady growth in this number over time, however, particularly by smaller banks.⁶⁵ That said, federal rules still make life difficult for these oftentimes smaller banks. To serve cannabis businesses, banks must report "suspicious or illegal activities" to the Financial Crimes Enforcement Network (FinCEN). Since state-legal cannabis programs are illegal federally, this means reporting any banking transactions of state-legal companies. In one example of how cumbersome this can be, a small credit union in Oregon had to file 13,500 reports over two years for 500 clients.⁶⁶ Several states have carved out allowances for credit unions to take marijuana dollars. Credit unions have had a few advantages, being under fewer federal regulations as well as having a "more reasonable" regulatory body, but remain hesitant to lend to marijuana businesses for fear of the federal government seizing their assets.⁶⁷

Social Equity

In 2014, Maryland became the first state to incorporate social equity provisions into its medical marijuana law. Since the first adult-use recreational policies were passed in 2012, racial justice and social equity have become major sticking points in marijuana policy. First, racial justice has become an increasingly dominant theme in the national conversation, with attention paid to police brutality, mass incarceration, and the rise of white supremacist groups.⁶⁸ Second, leaders in the cannabis industry are disproportionately white, which is juxtaposed against the disproportionate policing of Black Americans for marijuana offenses.⁶⁹ Third, larger multistate companies are buying out local businesses, and in states with only medical marijuana, these companies are trying to establish an inside track on licensing and production if adult-use recreational marijuana is adopted.⁷⁰

Early medical marijuana laws often excluded anyone with a criminal record related to drug trafficking or possession from working in the field and from being a patient. This means that those from minority groups most deeply affected by War on Drugs policy could not benefit either financially or medically from state-legal cannabis. Minority populations have been left out of the industry, given that wealth is unevenly distributed and strongly correlated with race.⁷¹ A 2021 survey of the fourteen largest publicly traded cannabis companies in the United States and Canada found that 90 percent of executives are white (77 percent being men).[72] These results were similar to a 2017 survey conducted by Marijuana Business Daily that found 81 percent of marijuana business owners in the United States were white.[73]

As the medical and adult-use recreational markets grow, companies with long histories are better positioned to succeed. This limits opportunities for new and possibly more diverse organizations to compete. Large multistate businesses have several advantages over startups and local businesses. They have learned to navigate the regulatory process through trial and error in other states and can absorb the high costs associated with the application and licensing process. As each new state considers adopting a medical marijuana program or expanding into adult use, the old winners are positioned to maintain their dominance.

States are addressing social equity through criminal justice reforms, including by expunging records for past cannabis offenses, reinvesting tax revenue into communities most harmed by the War on Drugs, and creating a business licensing process that increases representation of people most likely to have been negatively affected by prohibition in the industry.[74] Despite such efforts, it is not clear that even these equity reforms have worked as promised.[75] In fact, there is evidence that African American men who had involvement in the criminal justice system feel even more alienated after marijuana reform.[76] As Amber Littlejohn, executive director of the Minority Cannabis Business Association, argues, "Most social equity programs have failed—even programs that were designed to yield a multitude of minority owners."[77]

In Maryland, 15 percent of applicants' scores for grower and dispensary licenses were supposed to be tied to whether the business reflected racial and gender diversity. Yet a 2020 study found that the industry lacked diversity, and the winning applicants were more likely to have ties to out-of-state marijuana companies, law enforcement, or politicians.[78] A study of Pennsylvania's program showed that diversity plan and community impact scores had no effect on the first round of dispensary licensing, despite accounting for 20 percent of the total application score.[79] But the same study also found that applicants with high diversity and community plan scores in the second round of applications were more likely to earn a dispensary license. In short, there may have been some trial and error in determining the most effective way to ensure equity in these programs. Additionally, it may have been that regulators prioritized getting the medical marijuana program up and running quickly and effectively during the first round, whereas social equity and community impact concerns were more important in the second round.[80] At the same time, even promising findings from Pennsylvania warrant caution because regulators still have issues with equity license winners selling their licenses to, or being backed by, companies that are not minority owned.[81]

Other equity approaches, like investing tax revenue in communities most harmed by the War on Drugs, have produced less data. Furthermore, these approaches are more likely to be effective in the larger and more profitable adult-use recreational marijuana markets. Even so, Amber Littlejohn argued that these programs are "shiny and pretty and everyone feels good about them, but they don't actually oftentimes kick in until the tax revenue funding comes in."[82] Shaleen Title, an attorney and thought leader on questions of restorative justice and equity, has acknowledged that no programs have immediately achieved their social equity goals as envisioned, but states are making progress. She notes that feedback is a critical component of this process: "Equity programs should contain formal mechanisms to at least annually review and adjust the programs based on participant feedback."[83]

Medical Research

In chapter 1, we discussed how federal regulations have limited medical research. In response, states started developing their own research programs. Pennsylvania created the first state-authorized medical marijuana research program when the state adopted Act 16 in 2016. All eight Pennsylvania medical schools have partnered with the state to conduct cannabis research, and the first clinical registrant who can supply cannabis to the program was approved in 2020. While the medical schools cannot administer or produce cannabis, they will use partnerships with dispensaries and patients to create a more robust understanding of medical cannabis's efficacy.[84] However, the pace of good research is slow, so it will take years to grow the body of evidence regarding cannabis's medical efficacy. In 2021, New Mexico partnered with Bright Green Corporation, a company with conditional approval from the DEA to cultivate marijuana for research purposes, to construct a $300 million facility for research.[85] And Michigan diverted $20 million of tax revenue from its adult-use program to fund a study for medical cannabis' benefits to veterans with PTSD. Positive research on the therapeutic benefits of cannabis may subsequently increase public support for at least medical cannabis policies.[86]

Banking, social equity, and efficacy research offer three examples of problems that emerged because of the adoption of medical marijuana by the states. They are certainly not the only ones, but they are illustrative of how a new policy creates new problems that then set the agenda for future policymaking. In the case of banking, the problem has not been resolved, though there is substantial pressure on both the federal government and states to reform banking regulations that penalize banks for providing financial services to marijuana businesses. In the case of social equity, the initial focus on trying to increase diversity through licensing measures was a very limited success, and the conversation about what constitutes social equity in cannabis policy has become larger and multifaceted. In short, the states are very much still feeling their way forward on it. Finally, states have also begun trying to address the limitations of efficacy research using their own state-legal medical cannabis, but research takes time, and the results of this effort will be slow. We now turn, however, to two of the most significant external feedback effects of the expansion of medical marijuana policy in the states: setting the stage for adult-use programs and building pressure for federal policy change.

Setting the Stage for Adult-Use Cannabis

A major sign of policy feedback effects has been the rapid spread of adult-use cannabis programs. The adoption of adult-use recreational programs has occurred almost entirely in states that already had comprehensive medical cannabis programs. South Dakota, through a ballot initiative, became the first state to adopt medical and adult-use programs at the same time in 2020—though, notably, South Dakota's programs were overturned by the state's Supreme Court. Aside from that instance, all the other twenty-two adult-use states had comprehensive medical programs first. The playbook for adult-use legalization is very similar to the story we have told for medical marijuana use. The ballot initiative was crucial for much of the initial adoption activity. Of the twenty-three adult-use states, fourteen adopted using either the direct initiative or legislative referral (New Jersey and Maryland).

Researchers Beau Kilmer and Robert J. MacCoun argue that medical marijuana programs eased the adoption of adult-use in five specific ways.[87] First, medical programs demonstrated the efficacy of using the direct initiative to circumvent hesitant legislatures and adopt cannabis liberalization directly. Second, there are the psychological feedback effects among the public and lawmakers that eroded the War on Drugs mentality, at least for marijuana. It is no coincidence that adult-use legalization has occurred in parallel with growing discussions of reforming the criminal justice system in the United States and reducing mass incarceration. The two are intimately connected.[88] However, public support for marijuana legalization has swung rapidly since 1996.[89] The likely reasons are both changes in the perceived risks and benefits of cannabis and wider cultural changes.[90]

Third, medical marijuana proved that many of the fears surrounding cannabis liberalization were not well founded. Research in the era of adult-use marijuana has confirmed that there have not been substantial changes in youth use, emergency room visits, or car crashes *due to legalization*.[91] Furthermore, causal evidence is still conflicting, weak, or absent for many of the potential effects of legalization.[92] Evidence suggests, however, that marijuana use has shifted among certain groups, like LGBTQ adolescents and cigarette smokers, with some negative outcomes in certain states.[93] Further, there is growing evidence of potentially positive outcomes, like increased substitution of cannabis for more addictive opioids.[94] The substitution potential became apparent at the height of the opioid epidemic, when doctors and politicians alike were searching for alternatives. It must be noted, however, that much of this evidence remains murky, and the broader societal and public health effects of cannabis legalization are yet to be fully understood.

Fourth, a "visible and active" cannabis industry has grown across the country.[95] The industry reached nearly $100 billion in direct sales and additional economic impact in 2022.[96] There were nearly half a million cannabis jobs across the United States in 2022; in fact, more is spent on cannabis in the United States than milk, orange juice, or energy drinks.[97] There are more people employed in direct and indirect

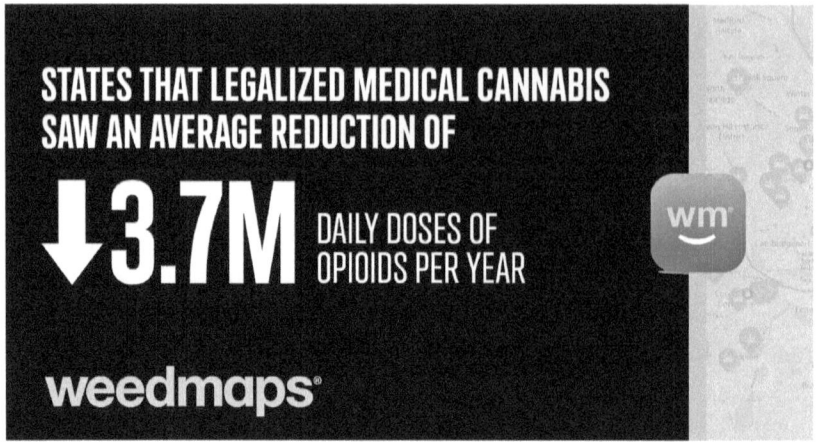

Figure 4.5. Weedmaps billboard campaign.

cannabis industry positions than there are bank tellers or hairstylists nationwide.[98] Depending on a state's advertising rules, cannabis ads can be seen frequently. Moreover, Weedmaps, a cannabis tech company, has a cross-country billboard campaign that is meant to "dispel some of the myths around cannabis and foster real dialogue about cannabis legalization" (see figure 4.5).[99] Granted, the visibility of the industry varies substantially, particularly in states that give local governments a say over whether dispensaries and growers and processors are welcome.[100]

Fifth, and finally, the expansion of medical and now adult-use marijuana programs has made apparent the federal government's willingness to allow this industry to grow and for states to make a profit. We have argued that there is a fickleness to this federal forbearance.[101] Likewise, others rightly point out that forbearance could theoretically vanish in an instant.[102] Even so, it is also difficult to conceive of the federal government putting the genie back in the bottle. Of course, legalization of adult-use recreational programs in states has had its own negative feedback effects on the older medical programs.

Patients Getting Left Behind

It is reasonable that states implementing an adult-use recreational program would look to the medical marijuana industry to learn from their experience. Those in the medical industry have already grown cannabis from seed-to-sale, produced a multitude of different products, and learned some of the best practices for quality control of the product and of caring for patients (consumers). Lawmakers naturally see that the medical industry has already laid much of the infrastructure down. However, while erecting a recreational program on top of a medical program might accelerate implementation and increase the recreational cannabis supply in the short term, patients can be left behind.

Americans for Safe Access (ASA) is an organization distinctly focused on medical marijuana. As adult-use recreational adoptions took off, ASA published the following statement:

> Issues such as access, police harassment, and the price and quality of medicine will still be relevant to the patient community despite the adoption of a policy of legalization for recreational. The federal refusal to recognize the medical efficacy of cannabis causes more harm and difficulty for patients than any failure by local or state governments to adopt policies of legalization of cannabis for recreational use. Any system of regulation should not be built on the backs of current medical cannabis laws.[103]

ASA brings up a major consideration in the future of marijuana policy and points out that recreational use "is a separate issue from safe and legal access to cannabis for therapeutic use." The consequences of a shortsighted action that combines medical and recreational programs into one are significant. Even Robert Randall, the father of the medical marijuana movement, expressed suspicion about adult-use recreational programs: "Seriously ill Americans are caught in the crossfire as drug warriors on both sides of the cultural divide try to turn the sick into cannon fodder."[104] While the legalization movement is broadly unified, Randall's warning is prescient. Even allies of drug liberalization are concerned about what will become of medical cannabis programs and patients.

When Montana voters approved an adult-use recreational marijuana program, medical dispensaries were given an eighteen-month head start over outside businesses in the recreational market. Only about 80 of Montana's 451 medical dispensaries (20 percent) opted to remain medical only. This put medical users in direct competition with adult-use consumers for product. Moreover, an adult-use recreational user is generally in the market for marijuana for pleasure, not medical necessity.

Meanwhile, medical users may not only need cannabis for relief, but they may also need very specific products. Competition on dispensary store shelves, tight supply chains, and resulting price increases can lead to disruptions for medical users. Such disruptions have a human face, like Joylynn Wright, who has used cannabis to treat pain from a spinal surgery. Wright, who is on a fixed income and commutes thirty-five minutes to purchase pre-rolled joints for $8, cannot handle a major price increase or the loss of product altogether.[105] The same issues have likewise arisen in Illinois, New Jersey, New York, and Washington as they legalized adult-use recreational marijuana.

Washington was one of the first states to adopt a medical marijuana law in 1998, and it was the first, along with Colorado, to pass an adult-use recreational law in 2012. As we previously discussed, fear of federal enforcement caused Washington State to take a hands-off approach to its medical marijuana program. Patients were allowed to grow a two-month supply of cannabis or join a collective garden with up to ten other patients.[106] Thus, the state never set up a product-testing regime and looked the other way as some of these collectives grew to service hundreds of patients. After voters approved the adult-use program in 2012, the state pushed to hold medical dispensaries to the same standards as recreational ones, including adding testing and a registration process that many patients fear could put them at greater legal risk.[107] Regulations for both programs were formally brought into alignment in 2016.[108] The medical program has not been "decimated," as opponents predicted, however conflicts remain.[109] The state has received increasing scrutiny over the availability of high-potency cannabis extracts that have been linked to psychosis and other health effects in the state.[110]

New York adopted an adult-use recreational program in 2020 but faced an institutional bottleneck in implementation that roiled patients in the medical program. The state's Office of Cannabis Management (OCM) was tasked with overseeing both medical and the new adult-use programs. Because of a delayed start in launching the adult-use market (the first legal recreational sales occurred in 2023), OCM had to put its limited resources into the new program, at the expense of medical patients.[111] Facing enrollment delays, new patients have turned to the illicit market for their cannabis. According to one patient on Reddit in 2022, "I'm approaching 45 days of attempting to register as a cannabis patient in NY state. I've tried the website, I've emailed, I've called. I even filled out a manual form given to me via email (about two weeks ago) and still am not registered. No longer getting any responses from OCM."[112] Beyond these delays, new cards did not work at dispensaries, the state's data management system was offline for weeks, companies ended their delivery programs, and 10 percent of registered patients left the system from January to June 2022.[113] Clerical errors and delays prevented patients from starting home grow for months after it was approved. Furthermore, the two-year delay in implementation led to the opening of numerous "gray market" stores.[114] These operations, especially in high-density places like New York City, cut into the financial advantages of having a state-legal license. Additionally, the cannabis sold at such facilities has been found to have high levels of *E. coli* and heavy metals, as the products are not subject to the testing requirements of the state's medical marijuana law.[115]

Other states have attempted to protect the medical industry. When Illinois passed a recreational law, it attempted to protect the medical marijuana supply. However, several dispensaries started reporting shortages a few months before the recreational market opening.[116] Some states allowed cultivators to grow more cannabis without a license prior to the launch of their new recreational programs, to prevent a crunch in supply that would negatively affect medical users.[117] Illinois did not do this. Instead, Illinois tried to rely on its existing medical program and its twenty-one existing certified cultivators to launch the adult-use recreational program. When the recreational program launched in January 2020, State Senator Heather Steans (D-Chicago), a sponsor of the legalization bill, lamented, "We do want to protect medical patients, and that certainly has been the goal, so we all share frustrations they are not having complete access to the product the way they need."[118] Six months after the launch of recreational sales, one medical marijuana patient stated, "It's been dismal for medical patients" because they "cannot consistently find the specific products that they need for their various conditions."[119] In response to these problems, the Illinois Department of Professional and Financial Regulation issued a letter to dispensaries to prioritize medical sales over recreational, however that necessarily left these decisions up to the dispensaries.[120] Illinois has six state agencies that regulate aspects of its medical and adult-use recreational cannabis programs, which has led to calls for regulatory consolidation, much like what has occurred in California and other large adult-use states.[121]

Within two months of recreational sales starting in Connecticut in January 2023, the legislature was flooded with complaints from medical marijuana patients about product scarcity. Growers were required to submit a "medical cannabis preservation" plan to ensure that medical patients will have access to products, but House Majority Leader Jason Rojas admitted that they failed to do so:

> In some ways, they didn't meet their obligation. In others, I think it's just part of the natural growing pains of standing up a new marketplace, and that's not me defending them. That's just my observation of the world. I don't know that the producers are fully built out with the additional capacity to better ensure that medical patients can continue to get their supply of medical cannabis and fulfill the (recreational) market demand as well.[122]

State leaders moved quickly to address the issue. They increased the maximum allotment for medical marijuana patients and pushed forward a bill in early 2023 that would create an "official Connecticut cannabis ombudsman" to oversee the programs and essentially act as an agent of consumer protection.[123]

States like Arizona and Michigan have also observed sharp declines in medical marijuana sales after the launch of their recreational programs. Figure 4.6 illustrates what happened in Arizona after the state implemented the recreational marijuana program adopted by voters through the ballot initiative in 2020. Adult-use recreational launched in January 2021, and very rapidly its overall sales increased. Medical sales were also increasing in the same period but quickly plateaued and then precipitously declined. The number of medical cardholders in Arizona declined from 309,479 in January 2021 to 156,647 in November 2022.[124] Granted, this likely means that many of these cardholders have switched to simply buying their product in the recreational market, but it does undercut the viability of the medical program and potential access to medical products.

Michigan likewise experienced a "collapse" of its medical program after the implementation of adult-use recreation, dropping from 284,100 patients in 2019 to 184,564 in November 2022.[125] Like Arizona, the

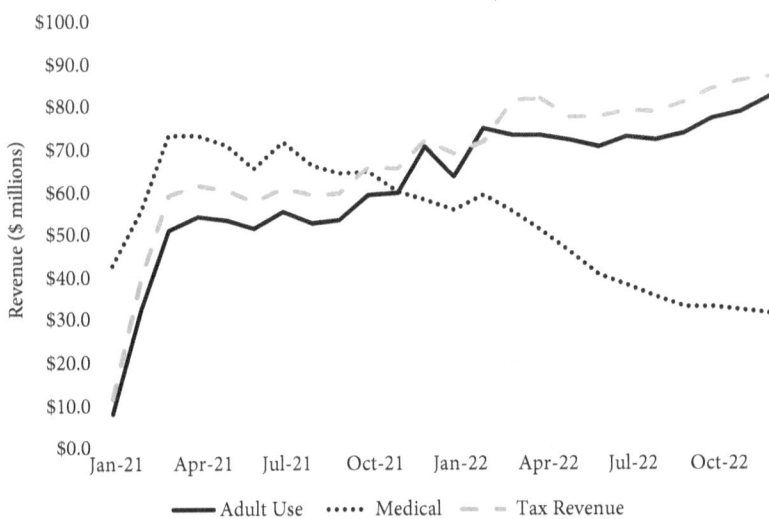

Figure 4.6. Arizona sales of recreational and medical cannabis and total excise taxes, 2021–2022. Source: Marijuana Tax Collection, Arizona Department of Revenue.

precipitous decline did not begin right away but picked up pace in 2022. More importantly for access, the number of licensed primary caregivers declined from 40,200 in 2019 to 19,916 in 2022.[126] This is the result of a dramatic decline in prices, making it less financially attractive for caregivers to grow their own cannabis plants and provide the cannabis to patients. Michigan's director of the National Organization for the Reform of Marijuana Laws (NORML), Rick Thompson, concluded that:

> You have sick children that are coming out of their pediatric stage and want to get into the adult-use market, but they may not have this medical support that they need. They may not have those specialized strains that only medical producers create that are not necessarily financially viable for a commercial cultivation operation but might be incredibly important for a particular person's significant illness. So, I see a lessening, a worsening of the compassion level in this state as the medical program goes down.[127]

The quick expansion of adult-use recreational programs can put medical growers and dispensaries in the center of the debate about a future program. On the one hand, they should be focused on serving and prioritizing their medical patients. On the other hand, they are best positioned to get an adult-use program up and running quickly. Moreover, an expanded program with new consumers can help with their margins, presumably passing down some of those savings into more affordable products. But there can also be incentives for people in the medical industry to abuse their position to maximize profits. In Arkansas, two prominent legalization activists campaigned against the state's 2022 recreational ballot initiative, which ultimately failed. The initiative, largely funded by the state's medical marijuana industry, was written in a way to allow the current medical marijuana businesses to take over adult-use with little competition from outsiders. One activist stated that "they're using money earned off the backs of patients to feed their greed."[128] States legalizing adult-use must consider how to balance getting a program off the ground quickly and effectively without leaving patients behind or creating unfair competitive advantages for the medical industry at the expense of others.

The Pressure Builds on the Federal Government

In this chapter, we have documented many (though certainly not all) of the feedback effects that the expansion of medical marijuana has had on the states, the federal government, consumers, and the industry. Each of the four channels of feedback has been, and continues to be, active in this policy. New problems emerge and set the agendas for the federal, state, and local governments. For example, cannabis policy came to the fore in an unexpected way during and after the COVID-19 pandemic. A nationwide shortage of truckers and significant and lingering disruptions to the national supply chain drew attention to the fact that many truckers were leaving their jobs out of fear of failing drug tests for marijuana. A representative of the American Trucking Association told Congress in 2023, "We're regulated by the federal government. We cannot have anyone impaired using marijuana or any other narcotic operating this equipment. So this channel conflict between the federal rules and the states allowing—this ambiguity is creating a litigious environment, and we're caught right in the middle of it."[129] Local governments are also wrestling with challenges like market failures, particularly after adult-use recreational is legalized.[130]

The expansion of medical marijuana programs to over 70 percent of Americans has also increased the power of users and slowly changed how they are depicted in popular culture. For a long time, Cheech and Chong and TV shows and movies such as *That 70s Show*, *Dazed and Confused*, and *Half Baked* dominated the portrayal of cannabis users. Today, there is a shift in the portrayal of marijuana users on television, with a more diverse representation, such as the neighbors who own a medical marijuana dispensary on *Modern Family*, and on the TV show *Bones*, a character who uses medical marijuana to ameliorate symptoms of cancer treatment. Furthermore, documentaries like *Super High Me*, CNN's *High Profits* series, and A&E's *Growing Belushi*, about actor Jim Belushi's cannabis farm, offer more serious views of the industry.[131] Something notable about Belushi's work to legitimize the industry is his argument that his brother John would not have died of an overdose had marijuana been legal. In a 2020 interview, Belushi said, "In the [1970s], if they knew what we knew today about marijuana and the healing benefits I think my brother John would still be alive."[132]

Professional athletes have also worked to destigmatize marijuana. Each of the four major sports leagues has loosened testing requirements and sanctions for athletes.[133] Former NBA player Al Harrington is one of the most outspoken voices for cannabis reform. Harrington was prescribed opioids in 2012 to manage the pain after a knee surgery. The opiates left him foggy and uncomfortable—a nurse at his clinic in Colorado suggested he try CBD to manage his pain. His recovery was revelatory, and Harrington soon formed his own cannabis company, Viola, named in honor of his grandmother who used CBD to treat her glaucoma and diabetes.[134] Harrington has also been an advocate for equity in marijuana policies and has partnered with several professional athletes on cannabis companies and products. In 2021, he announced his mission to turn 100 Black individuals into millionaires through his Viola brand incubator program.[135]

All these markers, and more, suggest a slow cultural shift that is legitimizing marijuana, at least as a medical treatment. Of course, great concern remains about the potential negative effects of positive portrayals of cannabis use, particularly on children.[136] Finally, medical marijuana, as well as the expansion of adult-use recreational marijuana, is affecting governance. Perhaps the most visible manifestation of this is the consolidation of cannabis regulatory authority in several states. However, local governments must engage with the industry on the ground, and federal agencies like the Department of Veterans Affairs are being forced to navigate the state-legal but federally illegal landscape on behalf of their clients.

5

Laboratories in Limbo

The Future of Marijuana Policy

On the brink of gaining control in Washington, Sen. Chuck Schumer said emphatically in 2020 that "I am going to do EVERYTHING I can to end the federal prohibition on marijuana" if Democrats took back the Senate. But 14 months since winning, Senate Democrats haven't even succeeded at changing the little things.
—Natalie Fertig, Reporter, *Politico*, 2022

As we close the book, the laboratories of democracy continue to address medical marijuana policy without knowing what the future holds from the federal government. Everything seemed to be in place after the 2020 election for the federal government to finally step in and provide the states with some relief and clarity. Democrats held onto their majority status in the House of Representatives and reclaimed the Senate for the first time in six years. Newly elected President Joe Biden would have two years of unified government to fulfill the Democratic Party's campaign promises. As we wrote this conclusion in March 2023, a full year after Fertig's reporting for *Politico* (quoted above), much of that commentary still rings true.[1] Two significant developments did occur in that year span, however. First, President Biden issued an executive order in October 2022 granting pardons for federal marijuana offenses and initiating a scheduling review of cannabis by the Drug Enforcement Administration and the Department of Health and Human Services.[2] Second, in December 2022, Congress passed its first-ever stand-alone marijuana law (the Medical Marijuana and Cannabidiol Research Expansion Act).[3]

But the debate about marijuana policy continues to evolve, and congressional action on various liberalization schemes appeared to stall after the president's scheduling review order. While fewer lawmakers are staunch prohibitionists, there are a wide range of opinions about what should happen next. A new conflict has emerged between those satisfied with incremental changes, as undertaken with banking reforms, and those who want ambitious reforms that would radically alter the marijuana marketplace and address the transgressions from the War on Drugs. This latest conflict typifies the history of marijuana in the United States—where the stars seem to align in times of prohibition only to fall apart when the country is on the precipice of liberalization. In this vacuum, the states march on.

We have argued that the states have been the primary engines for the expansion of cannabis policies in the United States. Furthermore, if one wants to understand marijuana policy, you should start with the states. The states have truly acted as laboratories—venues where activists test messages and institutional support, where experimental policies are formulated and adopted, where programs are implemented and evidence is collected from within the state and other states' experiences. These lessons learned affect leaders in both established programs, as they make adaptations based on their own and other states' experiments, and in yet-to-be-adopted or implemented programs, as they look for ideal models from which to craft their programs. Meanwhile, an entire ecosystem has evolved with interest groups, industry members, patients, and cannabis-centered media sharing ideas and best practices.

In this concluding chapter, we first briefly review the policy cycle and how medical marijuana policy has progressed through it. We then review the problems that have emerged due to discordant marijuana policy across the U.S. federal system. Next, we discuss possible federal action, including whether executive-driven rescheduling has lessened the pressure on Congress to find a comprehensive solution to the problem of marijuana policy. We conclude by considering the future of marijuana policy in the United States.

Medical Marijuana through the Policy Cycle

In structuring this book, we purposefully chose the policy process model—problem identification, agenda setting, policy adoption, implementation, and evaluation and feedback—as an organizing principle. It helps us boil down a very complex and chaotic process into phases that can be described. Additionally, policy process theorists tend to develop theories that are attached to specific phases.

In chapter 1, we demonstrated how medical marijuana has been framed and reframed over the years. Coverage of the policy has become more positive over time, and the faces of beneficiaries and activists have changed. But the agenda space in state legislatures is limited. As Kansas Governor Laura Kelly put it, a medical marijuana bill could pass if "everything else doesn't take up all the oxygen."[4] The Multiple Streams Framework helped make sense of how and why certain issues make it onto the government's decision-making agenda while others do not. Medical marijuana policy arrived on state agendas at least in part because of the strategic choices of key supporters and interest groups. The problem of complete marijuana prohibition was raised almost immediately after the Controlled Substances Act (CSA) was adopted in the 1970s, but the issues with medicinal use of marijuana grew over the ensuing decades. As the policy spread and received greater legitimacy, media narratives shifted to involve groups viewed positively by society. Among these positively socially constructed groups were those with significant political power in more conservative states: veterans and moms. Over time, marijuana policy began to break away from a purely moral framing, and groups like the Marijuana Policy Project mobilized to provide ready-made policy solutions to legislators and activists advancing medical marijuana policy through the legislature or the ballot initiative.

In chapter 2, we focused further on how the institutional mechanism of the popular initiative helped drive the adoption of medical marijuana in the states. Getting around reluctant legislatures helped advocates defiantly advance this policy innovation. However, as the policy spread and gained more acceptance, we argue that each subsequent adoption was less and less defiant. State-legal marijuana was emerging as the dominate policy regime in the United States, even in the face of continued federal prohibition. Another important conclusion from chapter 2, particularly for scholars of policy diffusion, is that as the observed window of diffusion expands, our conclusions about the determinants of adoption can change substantially. This finding is in line with work on how determinants of adoption change across the diffusion life course, but it raises important questions about when a diffusion analysis of a single innovation should be done.[5]

In chapter 3, we noted that the policymaking process does not stop when a policy is adopted. It must be effectively implemented. Implementation theory helps us think about the different resources and supports necessary for effective implementation, as well as how policy design choices affect implementation. Using the cases of Ohio, Pennsylvania, and West Virginia, states that adopted medical marijuana policies within a year of each other, we demonstrated how differences in political, social, and financial supports led to starkly different implementation experiences. We also demonstrated how the changing landscape of federal forbearance on prohibition enforcement affected the choices the states made in both policy design and implementation. In fact, the Barack Obama administration's specific forbearance for well-regulated programs helped to medicalize and legitimize a policy that remains contrary to federal law.

Finally, in chapter 4 we discussed how policies have a variety of feedback effects. While states medicalized in response to the Obama administration's guidance on forbearance, they also revised their programs in light of emerging problems like banking, safety, labeling, and social inequity in ownership and profits. Policies inevitably create new problems that can find their way back on the government's decision agenda. Additionally, state governments have invested in their own significant governance infrastructure for regulating medical marijuana programs. Two major feedback effects of the spread of medical marijuana policies have been the initiation, and more rapid expansion, of adult-use recreational programs and the growing pressure on the federal government to *do something* about the many problems created by state-legal and federally illegal marijuana. Before considering what federal action may look like, we first want to touch on how the policy cycle is repeating for adult-use recreational marijuana. The issues that we have discussed for medical use do have application for this innovation.

Wash, Rinse, Repeat?

The same policy process model offers a vantage into the dynamics of spreading adult-use recreational programs. Advocates for these programs face similar challenges when it comes to stigma and public safety and health concerns. Successful medical marijuana policies have aided in dispelling some of the worst fears about legal marijuana and have legitimized the actors that implement these programs. Similarly, policymakers and advocates must deal with the problems that federal prohibition creates. At the same time, there are distinct differences. While medical marijuana programs have diffuse goals related to sustaining businesses and expanding access, their primary goal is to provide medicine needed by patients. With adult-use recreational programs, the goals are access and profit. There is no underlying moral dimension to providing marijuana beyond cutting off an illicit market. The clearer goal of profit, juxtaposed with the social, financial, and personal costs of the War on Drugs in communities of color, has made social equity concerns far more central to state efforts to legalize adult-use recreational.

The adoption of adult-use recreational marijuana policies has outpaced the adoption of medical marijuana policies. Figure 5.1 provides a snapshot of the first ten years of adoptions by comparing the diffusion of medical marijuana laws after the initial adoption by California in 1996 to the spread of adult-use recreational laws after the initial adoptions by Colorado and Washington in 2012. The policies spread at a similar

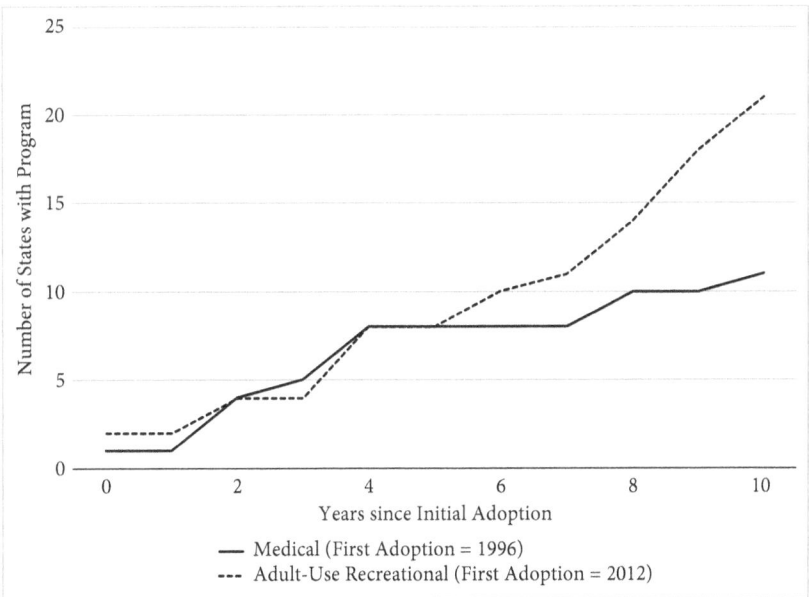

Figure 5.1. Cumulative adoption of medical marijuana laws and adult-use recreational laws in first ten years.

rate in the first five years before adult-use recreational policies eclipsed medical adoptions in the latter five years. Myriad factors explain the quicker expansion of adult-use recreational policies, but a principal factor is the existence of medical marijuana policies that paved the way.[6] While medical marijuana has diffused at a more typical pace for policy innovations, recreational is enjoying a much more rapid increase.[7] It is notable that when a policy innovation is compatible with existing policies, governments are more likely to take up that innovation, and more quickly, than if there is no compatible policy.[8]

The expansion of adult-use recreational programs has followed a similar arc, with early-adopter states being driven by the initiative. The first eight policies were adopted by initiative, and state legislatures are increasingly taking up the issue. At the implementation stage, states have relied on lessons from the implementation of medical marijuana, although the larger scale of the programs has come with complications. The feedback stage has some similarities to medical marijuana in terms of evaluating how the program works from the supply chain to the testing of products. But the major difference has been the scrutiny of the industry and how that has called for reforms related to equity and restorative justice. Early-adopter states have had to develop ways to address this issue while pushing forward with their program, while equity has set the terms of the debate in late-adopter states.

Is a Green Rush Inevitable?

As of this writing, thirty-eight states have legalized the medical use of cannabis, and twenty-three states have legalized adult-use recreational cannabis. It seems inevitable that the dam will ultimately break at the federal level. Kevin Sabet, the president and CEO of Smart Approaches to Marijuana (SAM)—a group in opposition to the legalization movement—stated:

> Inevitability is the number-one talking point of the legalization movement.... That's a really powerful talking point for them, because if people think something is inevitable, even if they're against it, they're likely to surrender it because it's not worth their time to deal with it or fight. But I think what goes up must also come down. I think these things come in

cycles. In the 1970s, we had the exact same thing happen with support for legalization. Maybe not as much as we have now, but we did see a dramatic change from the 1950s to the 1970s—in the same way you've seen a change from the 1990s to the 2010s. And that reversed for all sorts of reasons after the 1970s. It might reverse this time, but it might not.[9]

Given public opinion on medical cannabis and the size of the market, it can be difficult to imagine a federal rollback.[10]

However, there are many failed projections, especially when it comes to some liberal hegemonic future in the United States. Emily Dufton's book is aptly titled *The Rise and Fall and Rise of Marijuana in America*. She sketches out the immediate backlash against marijuana prohibition under the CSA and the opening of marijuana policies in the mid-1970s, when the government nearly went in a scientifically informed direction. However, the sudden backlash resulting from the parents movement merging with the culture war politics of Ronald Reagan, brought on the "Just Say No" era. Not only Reagan, but George H. W. Bush, Bill Clinton, and George W. Bush ramped up the global and domestic War on Drugs—a war that has cost the United States over $1 trillion.[11] Amid this doubling down, however, medical necessity and sympathetic and relatable advocates led to a quarter of a century rise in cannabis liberalization. But could there be another fall?

In the early 2010s, it was common to read about a new liberal order.[12] The United States was becoming more diverse and tolerant. Barack Obama was elected president twice, and the commentary largely focused on a Republican Party that was out of step with demographic and cultural trends.[13] The LGBTQ+ rights movement saw major victories in the Supreme Court with the *United States v. Windsor* (2013) and *Obergefell v. Hodges* (2015) decisions. Yet, contrary to most predictions, the GOP has become more conservative and leaned into the culture wars *with* electoral success. These electoral victories helped conservatives flip the ideological direction of the Supreme Court, that has since struck down the constitutional right to abortion and sided with social conservatives on several high-profile decisions related to guns and religious liberty. Such developments would have been unthinkable to most observers just ten years ago. Could a Republican administration or conservative court drop the hammer on marijuana?

We certainly find that scenario unlikely, especially considering the substantial infrastructure that has been built around these programs in the states. However, organizations like SAM continue to mobilize against marijuana liberalization. Alex Berenson's popular book *Tell Your Children: The Truth about Marijuana, Mental Illness, and Violence* was published in 2019 and repeated many of the claims that the antimarijuana propogandist movie *Reefer Madness* made in 1936. Moreover, Laura Ingraham, an influential host on Fox News, dedicated a number of segments in 2022 to connecting marijuana to psychosis and violence. Just a week after a school shooting in Uvalde, Texas, Ingraham argued that the perpetrator's cannabis use was being covered up as part of a "pro-marijuana" conspiracy.[14] Additionally, both Ingraham and Tucker Carlson (before he left Fox) picked up on a narrative of marijuana and psychosis in suggesting that a 2022 mass shooting in Chicago during July 4 celebrations might have been brought on by the shooter's marijuana use. Carlson stated, "They are high on government-endorsed weed, 'smoke some more, it's good for you.' They're numbed by the endless psychotropic drugs that are handed out at every school in the country by crackpots posing as counselors."[15] Such hyperbole might sound unserious, but Ingraham and Carlson have high viewership and are representative of the broader conservative media ecosystem. It is possible that a major focusing event linked to marijuana, or even a collection of smaller events that are hyped by conservative media, could chill or even reverse the slow shift of conservative support toward legalized marijuana. And given that medical and adult-use recreational programs are often lumped together, a sweeping condemnation of marijuana more broadly could lead to rollbacks or, at minimum, a stalling of these policies.

Even though some of the criticisms are exaggerated, states have run into very significant and legitimate issues, especially when expanding from medical into adult-use recreational marijuana. California adopted adult-use recreational marijuana in 2016. The new program did little to control the size of farms, and prices plummeted to the point that only the largest farms could remain sustainable. Six years after legalization, 60 percent of the farms in Humboldt County, once the epicenter of cannabis farming, had shut down.[16] Moreover, an illicit market that was nearly quashed during the quasi-legal gray market has returned. This gray market encompasses violent cartels but also businesses in the legal market that make illicit sales on the side to prop up their business.[17] Similarly, Oregon has had to crack down on illegal growers who have been accused of violating environmental regulations, mistreating migrant workers, and serving as fronts for international crime syndicates.[18] Washington State saw armed robbery attempts more than double in 2022, with more than 100 robberies and the first fatality of a dispensary worker.[19]

Additionally, the view of medical marijuana as a "gateway policy" for adult-use recreational is not determinative. In 2022, adult-use recreational marijuana policies were approved in Maryland and Missouri but voted down in Arkansas, North Dakota, and South Dakota. In a special election in 2023, Oklahoma voters overwhelmingly rejected adult-use recreational marijuana, with 61 percent of voters against the measure.[20] Despite the "yes" campaign spending $4.9 million compared to a mere $219,000 against, the measure failed to get majority support in each of Oklahoma's seventy-seven counties. As we noted in chapter 4, Oklahoma had become the "wild west" of medical marijuana, with a loosely regulated system that exploded since it was adopted in 2018. Pat McFerron, campaign manager of the anti-legalization effort, tied the failure of the adult-use recreational vote to this already wide-open medical marijuana program: "The medical program we received from voters is not what they voted for to begin with. . . . So in the voter's mind, there should be a difference between medical and recreational. So, I think this is a repudiation of how far the quote unquote, medical system we have in place has gone."[21] The narrative that the recreational vote is a repudiation of the medical program has helped the governor and legislature, both Republican, to argue for the need to crack down on the medical side.[22] These examples bring into question the *inevitability* of adult-use recreational programs in the states.

Finally, we must return to where cannabis scheduling started: America's participation in the 1961 Single Convention on Narcotic Drugs. In issuing its 2022 annual report, the International Narcotics Control Board (INCB) called out countries and the states that have legalized marijuana access for nonmedical (i.e., recreational) use as being in contravention to the treaty.[23] The INCB does not push back against medical use, and it has recommended decriminalization and depenalization instead of legalization for reducing drug-related offenses; nonetheless, its report is a reminder that countries like the United States are still technically beholden to treaties that view cannabis as highly addictive with little to no medicinal value. As countries like Canada and Uruguay have legalized, and others like Germany and the United States are actively considering legalization, new treaties are likely necessary to prevent erosion of the basis of global efforts to fight dangerous and illicit drugs. Just as cannabis scheduling has become increasingly untenable in the United States, marijuana liberalization, at least in Western developed countries, undermines scheduling internationally.

Federal Remedies to the Green Rush

The federal government largely continues a piecemeal approach of fickle forbearance in enforcing prohibition, even as pressure builds with each state adoption. However, as we noted earlier in this chapter, there were two significant departures in 2022: Biden's rescheduling and expungement executive order for marijuana-related offenses and Congress's standalone marijuana research law. While the rescheduling review might result in significant changes in the future, as of our writing, it seems to have reduced the pressure on Congress to enact major reforms in marijuana policy. While proponents of marijuana banking legislation are still advocating for those fixes, efforts to address the larger federal-state policy morass appear to be on hold. This behavior aligns with what we have observed happening at the state level in terms of policy innovation. In considering how local governments shape state-level policy adoption, Charles Shipan and Craig Volden proposed two different effects that result when pressure bubbles up from below.[24] Either a snowball effect can occur, where the state responds positively by taking up an innovation that is spreading among local governments (e.g., smoking bans), or a pressure valve effect occurs, where local adoption reduces the state's incentive to act. In the first case, the likelihood of state policy innovation increases and in the second, it decreases.

Pressure is building for federal action, but will it result in a snowball effect? While state adoption of medical and recreational marijuana programs has exerted pressure on the federal government to act, it is actually the related issues that have arisen (e.g., banking, bankruptcy laws, tax breaks) that are driving demand for action. In many respects, the adoption of medical and adult-use cannabis programs at the state level has also taken some pressure off the federal government. There are myriad problems and inefficiencies in the current state-to-state approach coupled, as it is, with federal prohibition. Yet medical marijuana patients and recreational marijuana users are getting their products in states where there has been enough support to pass either program. Furthermore, both types of programs continue to expand. Now, the executive branch has also relieved pressure on Congress by unilaterally initiating a scheduling review. This brings us back to the question of whether federal action is truly inevitable. The easing of political pressure certainly slows down any sense of inevitability. Additionally, unilateral rescheduling could scramble the deck of ideas that are feasible for federal marijuana policy reform through Congress. Considering this, we will review the major pieces of legislation proposed in Congress that could alter the landscape for medical marijuana.

Rescheduling

The most likely short-term scenario may involve the U.S. Department of Health and Human Services (DHHS), the Drug Enforcement Administration (DEA), and the Food and Drug Administration (FDA) rescheduling cannabis in response to Biden's executive order. Currently, cannabis (marijuana) is listed as a Schedule I drug with heroin, LSD, ecstasy, methaqualone, and peyote. Rescheduling cannabis to Schedule II would still define it as having "a high potential for abuse, with use potentially leading to severe psychological or physical dependence," but would remove it from being classified as having "no currently accepted medical use." It would also move cannabis into a category with several opiates, cocaine, methadone, Adderall, and Ritalin.[25]

Rescheduling would relinquish some of the bureaucratic barriers related to medical research and would be the lightest touch from the federal government. It would not create an FDA-approved pharmaceutical, nor would it remove the industry from the legal gray market. Rescheduling cannabis to Schedule II would also not eliminate Section 280E of the U.S. tax code, which states that no deductions or credits are allowed for tax purposes for businesses engaged in the trafficking of controlled substances, specifically Schedule I and II of the CSA. State-legal businesses would only be able to take advantage of typical business tax breaks if cannabis were moved to Schedule III (where DHHS ultimately recommended it to be placed)—the category with codeine, ketamine, anabolic steroids, and testosterone.[26] But the effects on medical research could be a game changer in terms of how proponents and opponents understand medical cannabis.

Rescheduling can happen in two ways. Congress can reschedule cannabis by passing legislation that amends the Controlled Substances Act. In fact, a bill to amend the CSA and reschedule cannabis was first introduced in 1981, but Congress has not earnestly considered amending the CSA. The second route would occur through the executive branch. The secretary of DHHS or an outside interested party can file a petition to the attorney general to reschedule. Then DHHS would be tasked with conducting an assessment through the FDA and return a recommendation to the attorney general. The attorney general, through the DEA, conducts a separate investigation on whether the drug should be rescheduled or removed entirely from drug scheduling. If there is sufficient evidence that a change is warranted, the attorney general can initiate the change through rulemaking consistent with the Administrative Procedures Act. Finally, the rule would go to the White House, which assesses the rule change through the Office of Management and Budget's Office of Information and Regulatory Affairs. Then the attorney general's office will determine whether cannabis should or should not be controlled. If the finding is that cannabis should still be controlled, the attorney general would determine the appropriate schedule.[27]

Rescheduling could produce some unintended consequences, which may explain why the status quo on marijuana policy has held even though access continues to expand through the states. Currently, states have worked around the FDA by having doctors "recommend" rather than "prescribe" marijuana. Rescheduling could put the state programs under FDA regulations (Schedules II through V), which are more stringent than the current testing regimens.

Descheduling

Many reformers have pushed for descheduling marijuana, which would remove marijuana from its classification as a controlled substance. The Controlled Substances Act established five classifications—or schedules—for various substances. Only Schedule I drugs are deemed to have no accepted medical use. Schedule II through V drugs are classified to have medical use but vary from "high potential of abuse" (Schedule II) to "low potential of abuse" (Schedule V). Further, the potential of "psychological or physical dependence" ranges from "severe" (Schedule II) to "limited" (Schedule V). Any drug on Schedule II through V is available legally through a doctor's prescription and can be fulfilled by a licensed pharmacy.[28]

If marijuana were descheduled, it could be regulated like alcohol and tobacco. In such a regulatory environment, the federal government can establish rules and regulations ranging from setting excise tax rates to limiting certain products or capping potencies. Meanwhile, states and localities would retain authority to regulate marijuana production and sales. In the case of alcohol, there is wide variation across the states in terms of where, when, and how a person can consume alcohol. Such a move could retain the federal nature of marijuana policy in the states. The Congressional Cannabis Caucus, a bipartisan coalition of twenty-nine members of Congress, has endorsed descheduling.[29]

But some fear that descheduling would still require significant federal intervention to prevent "unlimited commercialization and a corporate free-for-all."[30] Furthermore, descheduling could roll back the progress made in establishing markets and advancing equity and social justice. In fact, large tobacco and alcohol companies have started to invest in marijuana companies and lobby the federal government for a role in the regulation of marijuana. Shaleen Title of the Parabola Center for Law and Policy writes about how "Big Marijuana" could undo years of deliberate and careful progress made by activists within the states:

> Over past decades, beginning with a small group of AIDS activists and their loved ones fighting for their right to medicine, the marijuana law reform movement has fought for credibility and won new laws in state after state, with these big industries either opposing us or nowhere to be found. Now with much of the work done and most of the country in support of legalization, those corporations are suddenly elbowing their way in to design a market structure in their favor. They didn't create this young industry, and we don't need to let them take over and ruin it like many of them ruined their own industries.[31]

Marijuana Opportunity Reinvestment and Expungement (MORE) Act

The MORE Act was first passed by the Democrat-controlled U.S. House of Representatives in December 2020, but it has yet to see legislative action in the Senate. In April 2022, the House passed the bill again with the support of only three Republicans. The MORE Act goes a step further than rescheduling and would remove marijuana from the list of scheduled substances in the CSA. The act would decriminalize marijuana at the federal level and retroactively expunge federal cannabis arrests, charges, and convictions.

The measure would also address social equity in several ways. It would impose a 5 percent tax on retail sales that would go into an opportunity trust fund. It would create the Office of Cannabis Justice to oversee social equity provision in the law.[32] It will allow the Small Business Administration to make loans and other services available for cannabis businesses. And it would direct several agencies to study the impact of legalization, including the Department of Education, Government Accountability Office, National Highway Traffic Safety Administration, and the Occupational Safety and Health Administration.[33]

The MORE Act has been viewed as too bold by most Republican legislators. Key Republican allies on marijuana reform, like Representative Nancy Mace (R-SC), believe questions of equity should be left to the states to resolve.[34] Representative David Joyce (R-OH), the Republican cochair of the Congressional Cannabis Caucus, explained why he would not support the MORE Act:

> Since the House last voted on the MORE Act, a number of more targeted, bipartisan cannabis reform proposals have been introduced. By forsaking these bills for an all-or-nothing approach, congressional leadership is perpetuating federal cannabis prohibition and allowing the unsustainable patchwork of federal and state cannabis laws to fester.[35]

The reaction to the MORE Act in Congress embodies the partisan fault lines in the marijuana debate. The debate is not just over fundamental beliefs about whether marijuana can be used as an effective and legitimate medicine. It is instead wrapped up in broader themes ranging from the wisdom of recreational use to racial justice.

Other Proposals

There are numerous other proposals that address federal marijuana prohibition in some way. While different in their core details, the bills also differ in their political centers of gravity. For example, the Strengthening the Tenth Amendment through Entrusting States (STATES) Act was introduced in 2018 by Senators Cory Gardner (R-CO) and Elizabeth Warren (D-MA) and Representatives Earl Blumenauer (D-OR) and David Joyce (D-OH). The act would have amended the CSA to protect individuals and companies participating in state-legal cannabis programs from federal prosecution, essentially leaving cannabis up to the states. It also contained banking requirements that eventually became the Secure and Fair Enforcement (SAFE) Banking Act. This was an early approach, however, as it did not contain the more comprehensive reforms in more recent proposals addressing issues like social equity. That said, it received bipartisan co-sponsorship in both chambers of Congress and support from a dozen governors.

Representative Nancy Mace's States Reform Act was a game changer in some respects. Introduced in 2021, the act would decriminalize cannabis federally by removing it from the CSA. Adult-use cannabis would be regulated like alcohol, and medical cannabis would be regulated by the FDA. It also includes veteran protections for federal hiring and Veterans Administration benefits. It is not these details, however, that represent sweeping change; rather, it is Mace's championing the bill. Mace is a Republican from South Carolina, a state that has not yet itself legalized either medical or adult-use marijuana. This puts her in a strong position to perhaps bring enough Republicans on board to advance such a major reform, which is similar to what was observed in Pennsylvania, when a key Republican champion jumped on board with medical legalization.

Narrower Reforms

There are also numerous narrower reforms circulating. Since 2013, some version of the SAFE Banking Act has been passed five times by the House of Representatives. It was most recently passed as a stand-alone bill in 2022 with all 215 Democrats and 101 Republicans voting in favor. The House then attached the SAFE Banking Act to the 2022 National

Defense Authorization Act, but it was removed in the Senate. The SAFE Banking Act has the most bipartisan support of any federal legislation dealing with marijuana policy. The bill would free up banks to work with "legitimate cannabis-related businesses" without fear of federal encroachment.[36] This law would allow banks and ancillary services to deal with cannabis businesses. It would allow patients to use credit cards and free the industry from dealing with large amounts of cash that create additional security concerns. The bill would also allow for easier tracking and monitoring by law enforcement, national security organizations, and state tax authorities.

The SAFE Banking Act appears to have bipartisan support and provides a simple and immediate solution to one of the most pressing issues facing the industry. So, why has it stalled in the Senate? The answer lies with Senators Charles Schumer and Mitch McConnell. For Senate Majority Leader Schumer (D-NY), allowing the SAFE Banking Act to pass without restorative justice measures put in place is viewed as a half measure. His position is supported by one of the most influential cannabis supporters, Senator Cory Booker (D-NJ), who fears that allowing the SAFE Banking Act through will alleviate pressure to take broader action that Booker, Schumer, and others view as nonnegotiable (i.e., a pressure valve effect). Meanwhile, Senate Minority Leader McConnell (R-KY) did not put any of the nine Republican cosponsors on the conference committee in 2021. This was a clear signal of his unwillingness to get the legislation passed. Despite this, pressure continues to mount on Democratic and Republican leadership to pass the SAFE Banking Act. The number 3 Senate Democrat, Patty Murray (D-WA), has championed the policy, and several state attorneys general of both parties have implored Congress to act.[37]

As noted above, Congress passed the first stand-alone cannabis bill in its history in 2022: the Medical Marijuana and Cannabidiol Research Expansion Act. The intent of this narrow piece of cannabis legislation is to ease the restrictions on medical research. The act requires the federal government to ensure an adequate and timely supply of research-grade cannabis for scientists doing medical research. Universities and other research institutions will be able to obtain a license to "grow, manufacture, distribute, dispense and possess [cannabis] for research purposes."[38] Currently, researchers must obtain their supply from a single national source, the National Institute on Drug Abuse's Drug Supply

Program at the University of Mississippi. After much delay, the DEA followed through on a 2016 promise to expand its sources of cannabis for medical research.[39] The 2022 act may render such efforts moot if institutions chose to grow their own cannabis. Beyond supply, the act also encouraged the FDA to pursue cannabis-derived medicines and for DHHS to study the potential health effects of cannabidiol (CBD). Finally, the act allows physicians to discuss the known harms and benefits of marijuana. Importantly, the act does not allow researchers to obtain cannabis from state-legal programs, which is the approach that state-based research programs like that in Pennsylvania have taken (see chapter 4).

Beyond banking and research, several bills proposed in Congress focus specifically on veterans: the Medicinal Cannabis Research Act, the Veterans Equal Access Act, the Veterans Medical Marijuana Safe Harbor Act, and the Fully Informed Veteran Act. These bills would allow the Veterans Administration to conduct research using medical cannabis and protect veterans from being sanctioned for using state-legal cannabis.[40] The Preparing Regulators Effectively for a Post-Prohibition Adult-Use Regulated Environment (PREPARE) Act would establish a commission under the U.S. attorney general (Department of Justice) to develop federal regulations for cannabis. Our aim here is not to account for every piece of possible legislation but to illustrate that while there is clearly pressure on the federal government to do something, it is not yet clear which of the somethings are feasible politically and practically.

Be Careful What You Wish For

The marijuana industry in the United States is unique because in many respects, it must be contained within a state's borders. This does not discount the fact that large cross-state cannabis companies have emerged, but even neighboring states with similar programs cannot combine production or businesses. The seed-to-sale model means that once a medical marijuana policy is passed, marijuana is grown in a statewide system that monitors the product from cultivation to the end sale.

The in-state requirement would become irrelevant if marijuana were legalized by the federal government. Would that lead to mass consolidations of production? On the positive side, the changes could produce a more efficient system that would lower prices and improve access across the country. Moreover, the change could lead to production in natural climates instead of in energy-inefficient greenhouses, where 80 percent of cannabis is currently grown.[41] But there are several negative repercussions, too. A federal change in marijuana policy could leave small businesses behind. The cannabis industry has already been characterized by major buyouts and mergers. A federally regulated industry could quickly crash several states' markets, especially on the cultivation and production side. Just as Walmart wiped out local retailers and Amazon shuttered independent bookstores, state cannabis producers could sign their own death warrant by supporting a change in federal law. Scholars at the RAND Corporation have long argued that federal legalization and commercialization could backfire. Beau Kilmer wrote:

> If the really big companies are allowed to enter the market (think alcohol and tobacco companies, big food producers, Amazon, national supermarket chains), they will be able to produce [and] sell at a mass scale that will drive down prices even more.... We've estimated that you could produce all of the cannabis consumed in the US on a few dozen–industrial sized farms—that's it.[42]

Large cannabis companies will likely have significant political leverage with states, creating the conditions for a race to the bottom where states compete with other states to offer the most generous subsidies to the industry.

Thus, state leaders and some stakeholders in the industry might prefer incremental measures from the federal government rather than a major departure from the status quo. Moreover, state legislatures may be prone to pass protectionist policies in the wake of federal liberalization. Heather Steppe, president of the Kansas Cannabis Chamber of Commerce, argued that Kansas needed to ensure it passed a program "that is able to support small businesses and family farmers out in western Kansas just as much as ... [the] industrial and large operations in our Wichita and Kansas City areas."[43]

The Future of Cannabis Policy in the States

On the day after Donald Trump's surprising election to president in 2016, Jann Wenner of *Rolling Stone* sat down with President Obama to discuss his legacy and the policies left unfinished. Wenner did not mince words. "You can now buy marijuana legally on the entire West Coast. So why are we still waging the War on Drugs? It is a colossal failure. Why are we still dancing around the subject and making marijuana equivalent to a Schedule I drug?" Obama responded:

> Look, I've been very clear about my belief that we should try to discourage substance abuse. And I am not somebody who believes that legalization is a panacea. But I do believe that treating this as a public-health issue, the same way we do with cigarettes or alcohol, is the much smarter way to deal with it. Typically how these classifications are changed are not done by presidential edict but are done either legislatively or through the DEA. As you might imagine, the DEA, whose job it is historically to enforce drug laws, is not always going to be on the cutting edge about these issues.

Wenner pressed. "What about you? Are you gonna get on the cutting edge?" President Obama expounded.

> Look, I am now very much in lame-duck status. I will have the opportunity as a private citizen to describe where I think we need to go. But in light of these referenda passing, including in California, I've already said . . . that it is untenable over the long term for the Justice Department or the DEA to be enforcing a patchwork of laws, where something that's legal in one state could get you a 20-year prison sentence in another. So this is a debate that is now ripe, much in the same way that we ended up making progress on same-sex marriage. There's something to this whole states being laboratories of democracy and an evolutionary approach. You now have about a fifth of the country where this is legal.[44]

Obama's response, and his record in the White House, left many hopeful marijuana advocates disappointed.[45]

Wenner continued to press. "You got up there and said legalize same-sex marriage, and you pushed it right over the edge." Obama cut him off and pushed back, noting that he first changed laws around hospital visitations for same-sex partners, got buy-in from the Joint Chiefs of Staff before repealing "don't ask, don't tell," and filed a brief in opposition to California's marriage ban.

It has been eight years since that interview, and the federal government continues to "dance around the subject." While President Obama conceded that the status quo is untenable, the federal government's approach to marijuana has been slow and cautious. Meanwhile, state lawmakers continue to lead by partnering with interest groups and other parties to develop workable systems providing significant medical relief to over five million people.[46] Until the federal government steps up and changes the status quo, the states—advocates, patients, and policy entrepreneurs—will continue to erode the prohibitionist foundation of the War on Drugs. Regardless of what the federal government does, the story of cannabis liberalization belongs to the states.

ACKNOWLEDGMENTS

In May 2015, we sat down for a cup of coffee at the HUB-Robeson Center at Penn State and were looking ahead. At the end of the summer, Dan was heading to Stockton University in Galloway, New Jersey, and Lee was on his way to Wright State University in Dayton, Ohio. Lee set up this meeting to discuss the article that he was writing on the adoption of medical marijuana laws. It had promise—but he needed Dan's expertise on policy diffusion to refine it. At that point, neither of us had given much thought to marijuana policy, but it made for a good case study in state policy adoption. As we chatted, we uncovered more and more interesting aspects of marijuana policy and discovered questions that we wanted to answer. It took two years for us to slog through the writing and publication process for that first article in *Policy Studies Journal*. But it left us captivated by the intricacies of medical marijuana policies that were both practically and theoretically interesting. That meeting and our partnership since has culminated in this book. We are indebted to the scholars and, maybe even more so, journalists who continue to uncover new wrinkles in these policies and give us more to think about as we try to understand such a dynamic policy and what it means for state politics, policy theory, and federalism.

It has been nearly a decade since we started asking those initial questions, and we have made it to this point thanks to the contributions of many. We start by thanking our joint community from Penn State University. We are grateful for the guidance and support that we received, during our time as graduate students, from Dave Lowery, Eric Plutzer, Michael Berkman, Marie Hojnacki, Michael Nelson, Suzanna Linn, and others. They truly taught us how to be professionals and gave us the time and resources to become independent scholars. Their kindness and generosity helped launch us into rewarding careers. Not only have we remained in touch with many of these mentors, but we remain close to several friends from our time in graduate school and still benefit from their points of view and advice. We are grateful for Christopher Ojeda, Eleanor Schiff, Amanda Parks, Kevin Reuning, Anne Whitesell, Mike Kenwick, and Molly Ariotti for being consistent and steadfast friends and colleagues, always willing to read a draft or provide advice as we navigate academia. We are also indebted to Chris Devine, who provided invaluable advice about the book writing and proposal process.

We must also thank Sonia Tsuruoka and the team at New York University Press for supporting us through this endeavor. We are honored to publish our first book with a press that publishes excellent and timely work. Sonia's feedback and advice during revisions has improved this book markedly. And we thank Karen Brogno for careful and thoughtful copyediting. We would also like to thank the Drug and Policy Enforcement Center at the Ohio State Moritz College of Law for providing grant support that allowed us to hire some exceptional undergraduate students at Wright State. We particularly thank Erin Fisher for research assistance that was critical in providing the data for our chapter 1.

Dan would personally like to thank his colleagues at Penn State Harrisburg—particularly, Marvin Overby, director of the School of Public Affairs, for his mentorship and Eric Best for his friendship. Dan and Eric spent many an afternoon together complaining about work, sharing their challenges and joys at home, and encouraging each other. Dan's students encountered marijuana policy as a recurring example in his classes and generously shared their perspectives on the topic, for which he is thankful. He must also extend gratitude to his family: to his wife, Rebecca, for her endless support throughout these busy and stressful early career years and to Peter, Noah, and Anna for helping him understand how much more there is to life than writing books.

Lee would like to recognize his colleagues at Wright State University in the School of Social Sciences and International Studies. He has had two excellent chairs, December Green and Laura Luehrmann, who encouraged him and fought for him at every major milestone in his career. Furthermore, Lee is thankful for Mandy Shannon, associate university librarian, who helped to track down so many critical resources and databases for his research. Lee is grateful to have been granted a sabbatical by the university to finish this book, and for colleagues who have been collegial from day one. Finally, Lee wishes to acknowledge his students, who have tolerated his marijuana policy tangents in class and remained his audience in mind when writing this book. For their support and patience throughout this process, Lee would especially like to thank his wife, Jillian, and sons Henry and Paul. Much of this book was written in the home office. Despite the occasional distraction, it brought him delight to be able to experience his son Henry in action—singing, playing make-believe, or planning to sneak up on him. Henry's joy and curiosity are contagious and certainly Paul's will be, too, in due time. Lee is also grateful for his parents, Alfred and Susan Hannah, whose unconditional love and support have brought him to this point.

APPENDIX A

Full Models

The original analysis we conducted included state medical marijuana law adoptions from 1996 to 2014.[1] In January 2023, we updated our dataset through the end of 2022 to capture the substantial number of additional adoptions that have occurred since. By December 2022, thirty-seven states had passed medical marijuana laws (MMLs), either by voter initiative or statute. Figure 2.4 showed the states that were included in the original sample of twenty-three adopting states and the new sample of thirty-seven adopting states.

We also simplified the set of independent variables included in the analysis. This was done for two reasons. First, we removed many of the internal factors that theory pointed to as potentially relevant but were not statistically significant in the original analysis (e.g., glaucoma rates). Second, several independent variables have not been updated since 2014, most notably the number of federal seizures of marijuana per year. Table A.1 presents the variables included in our updated analysis, their sources, and their mean and standard deviation (SD). We used event history analysis (EHA) to examine the relationship between the internal and external predictors of adoption included in table A.1.

Full Results

Table A.2 provides results from two logistic EHA models predicting MML adoption. The first presents the results from our original sample and the second the results from the new sample. The results are presented as odds ratios with their 95 percent confidence intervals.

Table A.1. Variable Descriptions, Summary Statistics, and Sources

Variable	Description	Mean	Standard Deviation
Initiative availability[a]	Dummy = 1 if the direct initiative is available in the state.	0.36	0.48
State citizen liberalism[b]	Ideology score for state government and citizens based on Berry et al. (1998) revised 1960–2013 citizen ideology series.	46.62	14.46
Evangelical rate[c]	Rates of adherents in evangelical churches per 1,000 population.	178.22	118.16
Proportion of neighbors with MMLs[a]	Proportion of geographic neighbors with MMLs at start of year.	0.14	0.23
Relative ideology[a,b]	Distance between a state's ideology (Berry et al. 1998) and the average ideology of previously adopting states, as calculated by Cruz-Aceves and Mallinson (2019).	13.35	10.38
Time from first adoption[a]	Number of years since first law passed in 1996.	10.56	7.18
Bush administration[a]	Dummy = 1 if year = 2001:2008	0.35	0.48
Obama administration[a]	Dummy = 1 if year = 2009:2016	0.28	0.45
Trump administration[a]	Dummy = 1 if year = 2017:2020	0.08	0.27
Biden administration[a]	Dummy = 1 if year = 2021:2022	0.03	0.17

[a] Constructed by authors.
[b] Constructed by authors based on data from Richard C. Fording, "State Ideology Data," June 19, 2018, https://rcfording.wordpress.com/state-ideology-data/. See also William D. Berry et al., "Measuring Citizen and Government Ideology in the American States, 1960–93," *American Journal of Political Science* 42, no. 1 (1998). For relative ideology, see also Victor D. Cruz-Aceves and Daniel J. Mallinson, "Clarifying the Measurement of Relative Ideology in Policy Diffusion Research," *State and Local Government Review* 51, no. 3 (2019), https://journals.sagepub.com.
[c] Constructed by authors based on data from the Association of Religion Data Archives.

Table A.2. Results of Logistic Regression Model Predicting Medical Marijuana Policy Adoption in the U.S. States, 1996–2022

	1996–2018	1996–2022
Federal Signals		
Bush administration	0.021* [0.001, 0.408]	0.001* [0.000, 0.009]
Obama administration	0.008 [0.000, 1.211]	0.023* [0.003, 0.184]
Trump administration		0.004 [0.000, 0.258]
Biden administration		0.001* [0.000, 0.082]
Ecological Capacity		
Initiative availability	3.029* [1.084, 8.464]	3.157* [1.478, 6.743]
Citizen liberalism	1.097* [1.031, 1.167]	1.061* [1.027, 1.097]
Evangelical rate	0.989 [0.974, 1.003]	0.997 [0.992, 1.003]
Diffusion		
Proportion of state neighbors with MML	1.176 [0.070, 1.973]	2.874 [0.472, 17.507]
Relative ideology of states adopting MML	0.881* [0.799, 0.965]	0.972 [0.933, 1.012]
Time after first adoption	1.662* [1.160, 2.382]	1.430* [1.163, 1.758]
Constant	1.78 (4.93)	−7.316 (1.314)*
N	768	924
Log likelihood	−74.48	−125.84
Wald c^2	33.3*	34.1*

Note: Robust standard errors reported in parentheses; 95 percent confidence intervals reported in brackets.
* Indicates statistical significance at $p < 0.10$ (two-tailed); ** $p < 0.05$.

APPENDIX B

Additional Information

We used data from the Prescription Drug Abuse Policy System (pdaps.org) on medical marijuana laws created by Sarah Klieger and colleagues for the analysis in chapter 4.[1] Two legal researchers coded each state's medical marijuana law *as it existed* on February 1, 2017, and created three empirical datasets. The datasets include information on twenty-eight medical marijuana laws that were currently in force in the states in 2017. The three datasets focus on state laws governing marijuana patients, product safety, and dispensaries.

The legal researchers identified over 110 unique provisions related to patients in medical marijuana laws and used binary variables to indicate whether each state law contained such a provision. These provisions fit into broader categories. For example, the team coded twenty-four specific diagnoses that qualify for medical marijuana use. These range from diagnoses that appear in most laws, like AIDS and cancer (both appear in 93 percent of laws), to diagnoses that are less common, such as muscular dystrophy (appears in 11 percent of laws). Meanwhile, many states include grounds for revoking access to medical marijuana. For example, there are five unique provisions that dictate when patients can have their access revoked for violations, including forging a physician's diagnosis (35 percent) and using a fraudulent ID (43 percent). Considering all three categories, the measures provide a thorough depiction of the state laws, at least in 2017.

We use a standardized measure of provisions in each category (x_i—*mean/standard deviation*). Since some categories have more provisions than others, this method ensures that laws that score high are broad in their scope and not just detailed in one category that happens to have several provisions. As previously mentioned, the most thorough law on qualifying diagnoses contains twenty of twenty-four possible provisions.

Table B.1. Patient Protection Dimension of Medical Marijuana Laws

Category	Provision(s)	Item-Rest Correlation
Patient diagnoses	Indicates whether specific diagnoses qualify patient for MM: cancer, AIDS, glaucoma, MS, epilepsy, etc.	0.52
Shield laws	MM patient is protected from discrimination in employment, parental rights, property rights, educational rights	0.46
Home cultivation	MM patient is allowed to grow their own supply of marijuana	0.38
Affirmative defense	Possession by MM patient is an affirmative defense	0.33
	Scale reliability (α)	0.61
	N	28

Table B.2. Patient Restriction Dimension of Medical Marijuana Laws

Category	Provision(s)	Item-Rest Correlation
Requirements to qualify	State residency, minimum duration of disease/symptoms, documentation of ineffectiveness of standard treatment or medication, etc.	0.45
Requirements to register	Criminal background check, fee to apply, proof of physician, etc.	0.50
Requirements to renew	Physical exam to renew, new prescription, etc.	0.51
Use restrictions	Prohibits use near schools, in correctional facilities, public places, public transit, etc.	0.45
Procedure for revoking card	For-profit sale of marijuana, physician voiding prescription, fraudulent card, etc.	0.49
	Scale reliability (α)	0.72
	N	28

Meanwhile, the most thorough law that protects patients from discrimination contains four of four possible provisions. Tables B.1 and B.2 display the specific provisions in each law as well as diagnostics of the scale. The item-rest correlations indicate how well each item correlates with a scale computed of the other items. The correlations suggest that the items contribute to the scale. The Cronbach's alpha coefficients indicate the scale reliability of the two dimensions and are sufficiently high.[2]

NOTES

INTRODUCTION

1 The terms "cannabis" and "marijuana" are often used interchangeably, though experts now tend to prefer "cannabis" because of the racist and stigmatizing use of the term "marijuana" in the past. We will use cannabis when referring to the plant itself and marijuana when talking about policy and politics.
2 "Drug Czar under Fire over Pot 'Propaganda,'" *Wired*, updated January 6, 1997, www.wired.com.
3 Carey Goldberg, "Medical Marijuana Use Winning Backing," *New York Times*, October 30, 1996, A, www.nytimes.com.
4 Adam Nagourney, "Attacking Drugs, Dole Takes on Entertainment Industry," *New York Times*, September 19, 1996, B, www.nytimes.com.
5 "Medical Marijuana in California: A History," *Los Angeles Times*, March 6, 2009, www.latimes.com.
6 "Where President Donald Trump Stands on Marijuana," *Marijuana Moment*, September 29, 2020, www.marijuanamoment.net.
7 Jacob Felson, Amy Adamczyk, and Christopher Thomas, "How and Why Have Attitudes about Cannabis Legalization Changed So Much?" *Social Science Research* 78 (2019), www.sciencedirect.com; Daniel G. Orenstein and Stanton A. Glantz, "The Grassroots of Grass: Cannabis Legalization Ballot Initiative Campaign Contributions and Outcomes, 2004–2016," *Journal of Health Politics, Policy and Law* 45, no. 1 (2020), https://read.dukeupress.edu/; Ashley C. Bradford and David W. Bradford, "Factors Driving the Diffusion of Medical Marijuana Legalisation in the United States," *Drugs: Education, Prevention and Policy* 24, no. 1 (2017), www.tandfonline.com; Gook Jin Kim, "Examining the Predictors of Medical Marijuana Legalization in the United States Using an Empirically Based Taxonomy Approach," *Policy Studies* 43, no. 2 (2022), www.tandfonline.com; Joanne Spetz, Susan A. Chapman, Timothy Bates, Matthew Jura, and Laura A. Schmidt, "Social and Political Factors Associated with State-Level Legalization of Cannabis in the United States," *Contemporary Drug Problems* 46, no. 2 (2019), https://journals.sagepub.com.
8 Clayton Mosher and Scott Akins, *In the Weeds: Demonization, Legalization, and the Evolution of U.S. Marijuana Policy* (Philadelphia: Temple University Press, 2019); Nikolay Anguelov, *From Criminalizing to Decriminalizing Marijuana: The Politics of Social Control* (Lanham, MD: Lexington Books, 2018); John Hudak,

Marijuana: A Short History (Washington, DC: Brookings Institution Press, 2016); Peter Hecht, *Weed Land* (Berkeley: University of California Press, 2014); Martin A. Lee, *Smoke Signals* (New York: Scribner, 2012).

9 Louis Brandeis, New State Ice Co. v. Liebmann, argument for appellant, October term, 1931, 285 U.S. 262, dissenting opinion, https://tile.loc.gov/storage-services/service/ll/usrep/usrep285/usrep285262/usrep285262.pdf.

10 A. Lee Hannah and Daniel J. Mallinson, "Defiant Innovation: The Adoption of Medical Marijuana Laws in the American States," *Policy Studies Journal* 46, no. 2 (2018), https://onlinelibrary.wiley.com.

11 Erin Ryan, *Federalism and the Tug of War Within* (New York: Oxford University Press, 2011).

12 Steven R. Weisman, "Reagan Signs Law Linking Federal Aid to Drinking Age," *New York Times*, July 18, 1984.

13 Mosher and Akins, *In the Weeds: Demonization, Legalization, and the Evolution of U.S. Marijuana Policy*.

14 J. Russell Reynolds, "On the Therapeutical Uses and Toxic Effects of Cannabis Indica," *The Lancet* 135, no. 3473 (1890), www.sciencedirect.com/science/article/pii/S014067360218723X.

15 David T. Courtwright, "A Century of American Narcotic Policy," in *Treating Drug Problems*, ed. D. R. Gerstein and H. J. Harwood (Washington, DC: National Academies Press, 1992), 1–62.

16 Michelle Newhart and William Dolphin, *The Medicalization of Marijuana: Legitimacy, Stigma, and the Patient Experience* (New York: Routledge, 2019).

17 Courtwright, "A Century of American Narcotic Policy."

18 Lee, *Smoke Signals*.

19 Anguelov, *From Criminalizing to Decriminalizing Marijuana: The Politics of Social Control*; Hudak, *Marijuana: A Short History*.

20 Anguelov, *From Criminalizing to Decriminalizing Marijuana: The Politics of Social Control*.

21 Mosher and Akins, *In the Weeds: Demonization, Legalization, and the Evolution of U.S. Marijuana Policy*, 30.

22 Sandra Bass, "Policing Space, Policing Race: Social Control Imperatives and Police Discretionary Decisions," *Social Justice* 28, no. 1 (83) (2001), www.jstor.org.

23 Newhart and Dolphin, *The Medicalization of Marijuana: Legitimacy, Stigma, and the Patient Experience*.

24 Lee, *Smoke Signals*, 52.

25 Activist organizations like the National Organization for the Reform of Marijuana Laws (NORML) and Marijuana Policy Project (MPP) and many other supporters of marijuana reform continue to use the term *marijuana*, even though it is rooted in this dark history.

26 Mosher and Akins, *In the Weeds: Demonization, Legalization, and the Evolution of U.S. Marijuana Policy*, 40.

27 Mosher and Akins, *In the Weeds: Demonization, Legalization, and the Evolution of U.S. Marijuana Policy*, 32.
28 Louis Gasnier, dir., *Reefer Madness* (Motion Pictures Ventures, 1936), enhanced video posted April 10, 2015, Inter-Pathé, YouTube, 1:08:18, https://youtu.be/zhQlcMHhF3w.
29 Bass, "Policing Space, Policing Race: Social Control Imperatives and Police Discretionary Decisions."
30 Michael L. Rosino and Matthew W. Hughey, "The War on Drugs, Racial Meanings, and Structural Racism: A Holistic and Reproductive Approach," *American Journal of Economics and Sociology* 77, no. 3–4 (2018), https://onlinelibrary.wiley.com.
31 Dave Bewley-Taylor, Tom Blickman, and Martin Jelsma, *The Rise and Decline of Cannabis Prohibition* (Amsterdam: Transnational Institute, 2014), 17–18, www.tni.org/files/download/rise_and_decline_web.pdf.
32 Bewley-Taylor, Blickman, and Jelsma, *The Rise and Decline of Cannabis Prohibition*.
33 Richard J. Bonnie and Charles H. Whitebread II, *The Marihuana Conviction: A History of Marihuana Prohibition in the United States* (Charlottesville: University Press of Virginia, 1974), 51.
34 Bonnie and Whitebread, *The Marihuana Conviction: A History of Marihuana Prohibition in the United States*, 51.
35 Mosher and Akins, *In the Weeds: Demonization, Legalization, and the Evolution of U.S. Marijuana Policy*, 41.
36 W. H. Lawrence, "President Launches Drive on Narcotics; President Opens War on Drugs; Names 5 in Cabinet to New Panel," *New York Times*, November 28, 1954, www.nytimes.com.
37 David Bewley-Taylor and Martin Jelsma, "Regime Change: Re-visiting the 1961 Single Convention on Narcotic Drugs," *International Journal of Drug Policy* 23, no. 1 (2012): 76, www.sciencedirect.com.
38 Bewley-Taylor and Jelsma, "Regime Change: Re-visiting the 1961 Single Convention on Narcotic Drugs," 77.
39 Controlled Substance Schedules, Diversion Control Division, Drug Enforcement Administration, U.S, Department of Justice, August 2023, https://www.deadiversion.usdoj.gov/schedules. Emphasis added.
40 Michael Decourcy Hinds, "States Seek Tougher Drug Forfeit Laws," *New York Times*, July 16, 1990, www.nytimes.com.
41 Charles O. Jones, *An Introduction to the Study of Public Policy* (Belmont, CA: Wadsworth, 1970); Harold Lasswell, *A Pre-View of the Policy Sciences* (New York: American Elsevier, 1971).
42 See, for example, Thomas A. Birkland, *An Introduction to the Policy Process: Theories, Concepts, and Models of Public Policy Making*, 5th ed. (New York: Routledge, 2020).

43 Kevin B. Smith and Christopher W. Larimer, *The Public Policy Theory Primer* (New York: Westview Press, 2017).
44 Michael Howlett, M. Ramesh, and Anthony Perl, *Studying Public Policy* (New York: Oxford University Press, 2009).
45 Bryan D. Jones and Frank R. Baumgartner, *The Politics of Attention: How Government Prioritizes Problems* (Chicago: University of Chicago Press, 2005).
46 Howlett, Ramesh, and Perl, *Studying Public Policy*.
47 See Nicole Herweg, Nikolaos Zahariadis, and Reimut Zohlnhöfer, "The Multiple Streams Framework: Foundations, Refinements, and Empirical Applications," in *Theories of the Policy Process*, ed. Christopher M. Weible and Paul A. Sabatier (New York: Westview Press, 2018), 17–54; Frank Baumgartner, Bryan D. Jones, and Peter B. Mortensen, "Punctuated Equilibrium Theory: Explaining Stability and Change in Public Policymaking," in *Theories of the Policy Process*, ed. Christopher M. Weible and Paul A. Sabatier (New York: Westview Press, 2018), 55–102.
48 Frances Stokes Berry and William D. Berry, "Innovation and Diffusion Models in Policy Research," in *Theories of the Policy Process*, ed. Christopher M. Weible and Paul A. Sabatier (New York: Westview Press, 2018), 253–300.
49 Anne Schneider and Helen Ingram, "Social Construction of Target Populations: Implications for Politics and Policy," *American Political Science Review* 87, no. 2 (1993); Anne L. Schneider, Helen Ingram, and Peter deLeon, "Democratic Policy Design: Social Construction of Target Populations," in *Theories of the Policy Process*, ed. Christopher M. Weible and Paul A. Sabatier (New York: Westview Press, 2014), 105–150; Anne L. Schneider and Helen M. Ingram, "Social Constructions, Anticipatory Feedback Strategies, and Deceptive Public Policy," *Policy Studies Journal* 47, no. 2 (2019), https://onlinelibrary.wiley.com/; Rebecca J. Kreitzer and Candis Watts Smith, "Reproducible and Replicable: An Empirical Assessment of the Social Construction of Politically Relevant Target Groups," *PS: Political Science & Politics* 51, no. 4 (2018), www.cambridge.org/core/; Rebecca J. Kreitzer, Elizabeth A. Maltby, and Candis Watts Smith, "Fifty Shades of Deservingness: An Analysis of State-Level Variation and Effect of Social Constructions on Policy Outcomes," *Journal of Public Policy* 42, no. 3 (2022), www.cambridge.org/core/; Elizabeth Maltby and Rebecca J. Kreitzer, "How Racialized Policy Contact Shapes the Social Constructions of Policy Targets," *Policy Studies Journal* 51, no. 1 (2023), https://onlinelibrary.wiley.com.
50 Joe Soss, Richard C. Fording, and Sanford F. Schram, *Disciplining the Poor: Neoliberal Paternalism and the Persistent Power of Race* (Chicago: University of Chicago Press, 2011); Sanford F. Schram, Joe Brian Soss, and Richard Carl Fording, eds., *Race and the Politics of Welfare Reform* (Ann Arbor: University of Michigan Press, 2003).
51 Deborah Stone, *Policy Paradox*, 3rd ed. (New York: W. W. Norton, 2012).
52 Malcolm L. Goggin, Ann O'M Bowman, James P. Lester, and Laurence J. O'Toole, Jr., *Implementation Theory and Practice: Toward a Third Generation* (New York: Harper Collins, 1990).

53 Suzanne Mettler and Mallory SoRelle, "Policy Feedback Theory," in *Theories of the Policy Process*, ed. Christopher M. Weible and Paul A. Sabatier (New York: Westview Press, 2018), 103–134.
54 Edella Schlager and Michael Cox, "The IAD Framework and the SES Framework: An Introduction an Assessment of the Ostrom Workshop Frameworks," in *Theories of the Policy Process*, ed. Christopher M. Weible and Paul Sabatier (New York: Westview Press, 2018), 215–252.
55 Hank Jenkins-Smith and Paul Sabatier, "The Study of the Policy Process," in *Policy Change and Learning: An Advocacy Coalition Approach*, ed. Paul Sabatier and Hank Jenkins-Smith (Boulder, CO: Westview Press, 1993), 1–9; Hank C. Jenkins-Smith, Daniel Nohrstedt, Christopher M. Weible, and Karin Ingold, "The Advocacy Coalition Framework: An Overview of the Research Program," in *Theories of the Policy Process*, ed. Christopher M. Weible and Paul A. Sabatier (New York: Westview Press, 2018), 135–172; Paul Sabatier and Hank C. Jenkins-Smith, eds., *Policy Change and Learning: An Advocacy Coalition Approach* (Boulder, CO: Westview Press, 1993).
56 Rainer Eising, Daniel Rasch, and Patrycja Rozbicka, "Institutions, Policies, and Arguments: Context and Strategy in EU Policy Framing," *Journal of European Public Policy* 22, no. 4 (2015), www.tandfonline.com.
57 Frank Baumgartner, Suzanna De Boef, and Amber Boydstun, *The Decline of the Death Penalty and the Discovery of Innocence* (New York: Cambridge University Press, 2008).
58 Hannah and Mallinson, "Defiant Innovation: The Adoption of Medical Marijuana Laws in the American States."
59 Lawrence J. Grossback, Sean Nicholson-Crotty, and David A. M. Peterson, "Ideology and Learning in Policy Diffusion," *American Politics Research* 32, no. 5 (2004); Victor D. Cruz-Aceves and Daniel J. Mallinson, "Clarifying the Measurement of Relative Ideology in Policy Diffusion Research," *State and Local Government Review* 51, no. 3 (2019), https://journals.sagepub.com; Daniel J. Mallinson, "Who Are Your Neighbors? The Role of Ideology and Decline of Geographic Proximity in the Diffusion of Policy Innovations," *Policy Studies Journal* 49, no. 1 (2021).
60 Daniel J. Mallinson and A. Lee Hannah, "Policy and Political Learning: The Development of Medical Marijuana Policies in the States," *Publius: The Journal of Federalism* 50, no. 3 (2020).
61 James M. Cole, "Guidance Regarding the Ogden Memo in Jurisdictions Seeking to Authorize Marijuana for Medical Use," Office of the Deputy Attorney General, memorandum, Washington, DC, 2011; James M. Cole, "Guidance Regarding Marijuana Enforcement," memorandum, Washington, DC, 2013; David W. Ogden, "Investigations and Prosecutions in States Authorizing the Medical Use of Marijuana," Office of the Deputy Attorney General, memorandum, Washington, DC, 2009.
62 Mettler and SoRelle, "Policy Feedback Theory."

63 Jonathan H. Adler, ed., *Marijuana Federalism: Uncle Sam and Mary Jane* (Washington, DC: Brookings Institution Press, 2020); Daniel J. Mallinson, A. Lee Hannah, and Gideon Cunningham, "The Consequences of Fickle Federal Policy: Administrative Hurdles for State Cannabis Policies," *State and Local Government Review* 52, no. 4 (2020), https://journals.sagepub.com; Daniel J. Mallinson and A. Lee Hannah, "Introduction to the Special Issue on Cannabis Policy in the United States: Challenges and Opportunities for Public Administration and Policy," *Public Administration Quarterly* 47, no. 3 (2023), https://doi.org/10.37808/paq.47.3.1.

CHAPTER 1. SELLING POT

Epigraph: Emily Dufton, *Grass Roots: The Rise and Fall and Rise of Marijuana in America* (New York: Basic Books, 2017), 208.

1 Kathleen Ferraiolo, "State Policy Innovation and the Federalism Implications of Direct Democracy," *Publius: The Journal of Federalism* 38, no. 3 (2008), http://publius.oxfordjournals.org.
2 Nikolay Anguelov, *From Criminalizing to Decriminalizing Marijuana: The Politics of Social Control* (Lanham, MD: Lexington Books, 2018).
3 Quoted in Joshua Clark Davis, "The Business of Getting High: Head Shops, Countercultural Capitalism, and the Marijuana Legalization Movement," *The Sixties* 8, no. 1 (2015): 31, www.tandfonline.com.
4 Sean J. Belouin and Jack E. Henningfield, "Psychedelics: Where We Are Now, Why We Got Here, What We Must Do," *Neuropharmacology* 142 (2018), www.sciencedirect.com.
5 Emily Dufton, *Grass Roots: The Rise and Fall and Rise of Marijuana in America* (New York: Basic Books, 2017), 36.
6 Clayton Mosher and Scott Akins, *In the Weeds: Demonization, Legalization, and the Evolution of U.S. Marijuana Policy* (Philadelphia: Temple University Press, 2019).
7 Martin A. Lee, *Smoke Signals* (New York: Scribner, 2012), 121.
8 Mosher and Akins, *In the Weeds: Demonization, Legalization, and the Evolution of U.S. Marijuana Policy*.
9 National Commission on Marihuana and Drug Abuse, *A Signal of Misunderstanding: First Report of the National Commission on Marihuana and Drug Abuse* (Washington, DC: Government Printing Office, 1972), 140.
10 National Commission on Marihuana and Drug Abuse, *A Signal of Misunderstanding*, 167.
11 National Commission on Marihuana and Drug Abuse, *A Signal of Misunderstanding*, 176.
12 Fred P. Graham, "National Commission to Propose Legal Private Use of Marijuana," *New York Times*, February 13, 1972, www.nytimes.com.
13 Roger A. Roffman, "Marijuana and Its Control in the Late 1970s," *Contemporary Drug Problems* 6, no. 4 (1977).
14 Dufton, *Grass Roots: The Rise and Fall and Rise of Marijuana in America*.

15 Associated Press, "Carter Asks Congress to Decriminalize Marijuana Possession," *New York Times*, March 14, 1977, www.nytimes.com.
16 Robert Reinhold, "Smoking of Marijuana Wins Wider Acceptance," *New York Times*, May 23, 1977, www.nytimes.com.
17 Dufton, *Grass Roots: The Rise and Fall and Rise of Marijuana in America*.
18 Dufton, *Grass Roots*.
19 Dufton, *Grass Roots*.
20 Dufton, *Grass Roots*.
21 John W. Kingdon, *Agendas, Alternatives and Public Policies*, 2nd ed. (New York: Longman, 2011); Nicole Herweg, Nikolaos Zahariadis, and Reimut Zohlnhöfer, "The Multiple Streams Framework: Foundations, Refinements, and Empirical Applications," in *Theories of the Policy Process*, ed. Christopher M. Weible and Paul A. Sabatier (New York: Westview Press, 2018), 17–54.
22 Thomas A. Birkland, *An Introduction to the Policy Process: Theories, Concepts, and Models of Public Policy Making*, 5th ed. (New York: Routledge, 2020).
23 Frank R. Baumgartner and Bryan D. Jones, *Agendas and Instability in American Politics*, 2nd ed. (Chicago: University of Chicago Press, 2009); Bryan D. Jones and Frank R. Baumgartner, *The Politics of Attention: How Government Prioritizes Problems* (Chicago: University of Chicago Press, 2005).
24 Jones and Baumgartner, *The Politics of Attention: How Government Prioritizes Problems*.
25 Kingdon, *Agendas, Alternatives and Public Policies*, 127.
26 Herweg, Zahariadis, and Zohlnhöfer, "The Multiple Streams Framework: Foundations, Refinements, and Empirical Applications."
27 Kingdon, *Agendas, Alternatives and Public Policies*, 179.
28 Graeme Zielinski, "Activist Robert C. Randall Dies," *Washington Post*, June 8, 2001, www.washingtonpost.com.
29 Zielinski, "Activist Robert C. Randall Dies."
30 Dufton, *Grass Roots: The Rise and Fall and Rise of Marijuana in America*, 217.
31 Michael Pollan, "Living with Medical Marijuana," *New York Times*, July 20, 1997, www.nytimes.com.
32 Anne Schneider and Helen Ingram, "Social Construction of Target Populations: Implications for Politics and Policy," *American Political Science Review* 87, no. 2 (1993).
33 Daniel Forbes, "Fighting 'Cheech & Chong' Medicine," Salon, July 27, 2000, www.salon.com.
34 Ohio Senate, Third Consideration Hearing for H.B. 523, 131st General Assembly 2nd sess., May 24, 2016.
35 William Cummings, "Nebraska Gov. Ricketts Warns: 'If You Legalize Marijuana, You're Going to Kill Your Kids,'" *USA Today*, March 12, 2021, www.usatoday.com.
36 Lee O. Sanderlin, "Gov. Tate Reeves Signs Mississippi Medical Marijuana Bill into Law," *Clarion Ledger*, February 2, 2022, www.clarionledger.com.
37 John Zaller, *The Nature and Origins of Mass Opinion* (Cambridge: Cambridge University Press, 1992).

38 Casey T. Harris and Jeff Gruenewald, "News Media Trends in the Framing of Immigration and Crime, 1990–2013," *Social Problems* 67, no. 3 (2019), https://academic.oup.com/socpro.
39 Anguelov, *From Criminalizing to Decriminalizing Marijuana: The Politics of Social Control*.
40 Robert A. Mikos and Cindy D. Kam, "Has the 'M' Word Been Framed? Marijuana, Cannabis, and Public Opinion," *PLOS ONE* 14, no. 10 (2019), https://journals.plos.org/plosone.
41 Mikos and Kam, "Has the 'M' Word Been Framed?"
42 Harvey Molotch and Marilyn Lester, "Accidental News: The Great Oil Spill as Local Occurrence and National Event," *American Journal of Sociology* 81, no. 2 (1975): 236, www.journals.uchicago.edu.
43 Baumgartner and Jones, *Agendas and Instability in American Politics*, 25–26.
44 The specific search syntax used was as follows. Search terms: headline(cannabis OR marijuana w/5 medic*) and publication(abc news/cbs news/nbc news); Search type: Terms and Connectors.
45 "Nation's Drug Czar Says Marijuana Will Stay on the Government's List of Illegal Drugs," *NBC News at Sunrise*, aired March 18, 1999.
46 "Hawaii Becomes the Latest State to Approve Use of Marijuana for Medical Purposes," *CBS Morning News*, aired April 27, 2000.
47 Robert M. Entman, "Framing: Toward Clarification of a Fractured Paradigm," *Journal of Communication* 43, no. 4 (1993), https://onlinelibrary.wiley.com.
48 Hwalbin Kim and Sei-Hill Kim, "Framing Marijuana: How U.S. Newspapers Frame Marijuana Legalization Stories (1995–2014)," *Preventative Medicine Reports* 11 (2018).
49 Kim and Kim, "Framing Marijuana: How U.S. Newspapers Frame Marijuana Legalization Stories (1995–2014)."
50 Guy J. Golan, "Editorials, Op-ed Columns Frame Medical Marijuana Debate," *Newspaper Research Journal* 31, no. 3 (2010), https://journals.sagepub.com.
51 William L. Benoit, Kevin A. Stein, and Glenn J. Hansen, "New York Times Coverage of Presidential Campaigns," *Journalism & Mass Communication Quarterly* 82, no. 2 (2005), https://journals.sagepub.com.
52 We follow the process originally published in A. Lee Hannah, "The Politics of Passing and Implementing Medical Marijuana in Ohio," *Ohio Journal of Economics and Politics* 24, no. 1 (2018), https://papers.ssrn.com.
53 Schneider and Ingram, "Social Construction of Target Populations: Implications for Politics and Policy."
54 Patrick Corrigan, "How Stigma Interferes with Mental Health Care," *American Psychologist* 59, no. 7 (October 2004).
55 Janet S. St. Lawrence, Brenda A. Husfeldt, Jeffrey A. Kelly, Harold V. Hood, and Steve Smith Jr., "The Stigma of AIDS," *Journal of Homosexuality* 19, no. 3 (1990), www.tandfonline.com.
56 Bernice A. Pescosolido, John Monahan, Bruce G. Link, Ann Stueve, and Saeko Kikuzawa, "The Public's View of the Competence, Dangerousness, and Need for

Legal Coercion of Persons with Mental Health Problems," *American Journal of Public Health* 89, no. 9 (1999), https://ajph.aphapublications.org.

57 Daniel J. Mallinson and Francisco Puello, "Veterans and Medical Cannabis: A Perfect Federalism Storm," *Public Administration Quarterly* 47, no. 3 (2023), 347–373, https://doi.org/10.37808/paq.47.3.6.

58 Ariana Eunjung Cha, "'Mommy Lobby' Emerges as a Powerful Advocate for Medical Marijuana for Children," *Washington Post*, March 2, 2014, www.washingtonpost.com.

59 Aneri Pattani, "Veterans Push for Medical Marijuana in Conservative South," *USA Today*, August 10, 2021, www.usatoday.com; Patrik Jonsson, "As War Vets Enter the Fray, Stigma Lessens around Cannabis," *Christian Science Monitor*, July 5, 2018, www.csmonitor.com.

60 See Marcus A. Bachhuber, Brendan Saloner, Chinazo O. Cunningham, and Colleen L. Barry, "Medical Cannabis Laws and Opioid Analgesic Overdose Mortality in the United States, 1999–2010," *JAMA Internal Medicine* 174, no. 10 (2014), https://jamanetwork.com/; Ashley C. Bradford and W. David Bradford, "Medical Marijuana Laws Reduce Prescription Medication Use in Medicare Part D," *Health Affairs* 35, no. 7 (2016), www.healthaffairs.org; Yuyan Shi, "Medical Marijuana Policies and Hospitalizations Related to Marijuana and Opioid Pain Reliever," *Drug and Alcohol Dependence* 173 (2017), www.sciencedirect.com/science.

61 Beth Wiese and Adrianne R. Wilson-Poe, "Emerging Evidence for Cannabis' Role in Opioid Use Disorder," *Cannabis and Cannabinoid Research* 3, no. 1 (2018), www.liebertpub.com; Theodore L. Caputi and Kevin A. Sabet, "Population-Level Analyses Cannot Tell Us Anything about Individual-Level Marijuana-Opioid Substitution," *American Journal of Public Health* 108, no. 3 (2018), https://ajph.aphapublications.org; Alex H. S. Harris, Keith Humphreys, and John W. Finney, "State-Level Relationships Cannot Tell Us Anything about Individuals," *American Journal of Public Health* 105, no. 4 (2015), https://ajph.aphapublications.org; Caroline A. MacCallum, Lauren de Freitas, Lauren Eadie, and Samer N. Narouze, "Cannabinoids as a Substitute for Opioids: Basic Science and Clinical Evidence," in *Cannabinoids and Pain*, ed. Samer N. Narouze (Cham: Springer International Publishing, 2021).

62 Daniel J. Mallinson and A. Lee Hannah, "Policy and Political Learning: The Development of Medical Marijuana Policies in the States," *Publius: The Journal of Federalism* 50, no. 3 (2020).

63 Ted Van Green, "Americans Overwhelmingly Say Marijuana Should Be Legal for Recreational or Medical Use," Pew Research Center, November 22, 2022, www.pewresearch.org.

64 Kevin B. Smith and Christopher W. Larimer, *The Public Policy Theory Primer* (Boulder, CO: Westview Press, 2017); Kevin B. Smith, "Typologies, Taxonomies, and the Benefits of Policy Classification," *Policy Studies Journal* 30, no. 3 (2002), https://onlinelibrary.wiley.com.

65 Theodore J. Lowi, "American Business, Public Policy, Case-Studies, and Political Theory," review of *American Business and Public Policy: The Politics of Foreign*

Trade, by Raymond A. Bauer, Ithiel de Sola Pool, and Lewis A. Dexter, *World Politics* 16, no. 4 (1964), www.jstor.org; Theodore J. Lowi, "Four Systems of Policy, Politics, and Choice," *Public Administration Review* 32, no. 4 (1972), www.jstor.org.

66 Smith, "Typologies, Taxonomies, and the Benefits of Policy Classification"; Christopher Z. Mooney and Richard G. Schuldt, "Does Morality Policy Exist? Testing a Basic Assumption," *Policy Studies Journal* 36, no. 2 (2008).

67 Kathleen Ferraiolo, "From Killer Weed to Popular Medicine: The Evolution of American Drug Control Policy, 1937–2000," *Journal of Policy History* 19, no. 2 (2007): 350, www.cambridge.org/core.

68 "U.S. Cannabis Economic Impact," *MJBizDaily*, April 2023, https://mjbizdaily.com/us-cannabis-sales-estimates.

69 A. Lee Hannah and Daniel J. Mallinson, "Defiant Innovation: The Adoption of Medical Marijuana Laws in the American States," *Policy Studies Journal* 46, no. 2 (2018), https://onlinelibrary.wiley.com.

70 Grant W. Neeley and Lilliard E. Richardson Jr., "Marijuana Policy Bundles in the American States Over Time and Their Impact on the Use of Marijuana and Other Drugs," *Evaluation Research* 46, no. 2 (2022), https://journals.sagepub.com; Grant W. Neeley and Lilliard E. Richardson Jr., "Cannabis Policy Adaptation: Exploring Frameworks of State Policy Characteristics," *Public Administration Quarterly* 47, no. 3 (2023), https://paq.spaef.org.

71 Mallinson and Hannah, "Policy and Political Learning: The Development of Medical Marijuana Policies in the States."

72 Pollan, "Living with Medical Marijuana."

73 Kyle Jaeger, "Marijuana Use Is More Moral than Porn, Gay Relations and Wearing Animal Fur, Americans Say," *Marijuana Moment*, June 23, 2020, www.marijuanamoment.net.

74 Mark Regnerus, David Gordon, and Joseph Price, "Documenting Pornography Use in America: A Comparative Analysis of Methodological Approaches," *Journal of Sex Research* 53, no. 7 (2016), www.tandfonline.com.

75 Matt Reid, "A Qualitative Review of Cannabis Stigmas at the Twilight of Prohibition," *Journal of Cannabis Research* 2, no. 1 (2020), https://jcannabisresearch.biomedcentral.com.

76 Nicole Herweg, "Clarifying the Concept of Policy-Communities in the Multiple-Streams Framework," in *Decision-Making under Ambiguity and Time Constraints: Assessing the Multiple Streams Framework*, ed. Reimut Zohlnhöfer and Friedbert W. Rub (Colchester: ECPR Press, 2016), 125–145.

77 Livia Johannesson and Martin Qvist, "Navigating the Policy Stream: Contested Solutions and Organizational Strategies of Policy Entrepreneurship," *International Review of Public Policy* 2, no. 1 (2020), https://doi.org/10.4000/irpp.740.

78 Peter Bachrach and Morton S. Baratz, "Two Faces of Power," *The American Political Science Review* 56, no. 4 (1962), www.jstor.org.

79 This assumption is a point of active debate among MSF scholars. See Gary Mucciaroni, "The Garbage Can Model and the Study of Policy Making: A Critique,"

Polity 24, no. 3 (1992), www.journals.uchicago.edu/; Scott E. Robinson and Warren S. Eller, "Participation in Policy Streams: Testing the Separation of Problems and Solutions in Subnational Policy Systems," *Policy Studies Journal* 38, no. 2 (2010), https://onlinelibrary.wiley.com.

80   Rosalie Liccardo Pacula, Priscillia Hunt, and Anne Boustead, "Words Can Be Deceiving: A Review of Variation among Legally Effective Medical Marijuana Laws in the United States," *Journal of Drug Policy Analysis* 7, no. 1 (2014), www.ncbi.nlm.nih.gov/pubmed.

81   Cha, "'Mommy Lobby' Emerges as a Powerful Advocate for Medical Marijuana for Children."

82   Jesse Elliott, Deirdre DeJean, Tammy Clifford, Doug Coyle, Beth K. Potter, Becky Skidmore, Christine Alexander, et al., "Cannabis-Based Products for Pediatric Epilepsy: An Updated Systematic Review," *Seizure* 75 (2020), www.sciencedirect.com.

83   Cha, "'Mommy Lobby' Emerges as a Powerful Advocate for Medical Marijuana for Children."

84   Jan Hefler, "Taking Steps to Get Their Sick Children Usable Pot," *Philadelphia Inquirer*, December 22, 2014, www.inquirer.com.

85   Dufton, *Grass Roots: The Rise and Fall and Rise of Marijuana in America*, 150.

86   Patrik Jonsson, "As War Vets Enter the Fray, Stigma Lessens around Cannabis," *Christian Science Monitor*, July 5, 2018, www.csmonitor.com.

87   Mallinson and Puello, "Veterans and Medical Cannabis: A Perfect Federalism Storm."

88   Tony Newman, "Governor Andrew Cuomo Signs Bill on Veterans Day to Allow Patients with Post-Traumatic Stress Disorder Access to Medical Marijuana in New York," Drug Policy Alliance, news release, November 14, 2017.

89   Rachael Herndon Dunn, "VFW of Missouri Endorses Amendment 2," *Missouri Times*, October 25, 2018, https://themissouritimes.com.

90   Pattani, "Veterans Push for Medical Marijuana in Conservative South."

91   Kyle Jaeger, "Congressional Analysis Finds Veterans Marijuana Research Bill Would Come at Little Cost," *Marijuana Moment*, December 22, 2021, www.marijuanamoment.net.

92   Dufton, *Grass Roots: The Rise and Fall and Rise of Marijuana in America*; Emily Dufton, "Why the 1970s Effort to Decriminalize Marijuana Failed," *Smithsonian Magazine*, April 25, 2019, www.smithsonianmag.com.

93   A. Lee Hannah, Daniel J. Mallinson, and Lauren Azevedo, "Maximizing Social Equity as a Pillar of Public Administration: An Examination of Cannabis Dispensary Licensing in Pennsylvania," *Public Administration Review* 83, no. 1 (2023), https://onlinelibrary.wiley.com.

94   Shaleen Title, "Fair and Square: How to Effectively Incorporate Social Equity into Cannabis Laws and Regulations," Drug Enforcement and Policy Center, December 6, 2021, https://papers.ssrn.com; Katherine Hendy, Amanda I. Mauri, and Melissa Creary, "Bounded Equity: The Limits of Economic Models of Social

Justice in Cannabis Legislation," *Contemporary Drug Problems* 50, no. 1 (2023), https://journals.sagepub.com.

95 Hannah, Mallinson, and Azevedo, "Maximizing Social Equity as a Pillar of Public Administration: An Examination of Cannabis Dispensary Licensing in Pennsylvania."

96 Kingdon, *Agendas, Alternatives and Public Policies*.

97 Daniel J. Mallinson, A. Lee Hannah, and Gideon Cunningham, "The Consequences of Fickle Federal Policy: Administrative Hurdles for State Cannabis Policies," *State and Local Government Review* 52, no. 4 (2020), https://journals.sagepub.com; Mallinson and Hannah, "Policy and Political Learning: The Development of Medical Marijuana Policies in the States."

98 Robert S. Erikson, Michael B. Mackuen, and James A. Stimson, *The Macro Policy* (Cambridge: Cambridge University Press, 2002).

99 Julianna Pacheco, "The Thermostatic Model of Responsiveness in the American States," *State Politics & Policy Quarterly* 13, no. 3 (2013), http://journals.sagepub.com; Christopher Wlezien, "The Public as Thermostat: Dynamics of Preferences for Spending," *American Journal of Political Science* 39, no. 4 (1995), www.jstor.org.

100 Baumgartner and Jones, *Agendas and Instability in American Politics*.

101 Thomas T. Holyoke, Heath Brown, and Jeffrey R. Henig, "Shopping in the Political Arena: Strategic State and Local Venue Selection by Advocates," *State and Local Government Review* 44, no. 1 (2012), https://journals.sagepub.com.

102 Nicole Herweg, Christian Huß, and Reimut Zohlnhöfer, "Straightening the three Streams: Theorising Extensions of the Multiple Streams Framework," *European Journal of Political Research* 54, no. 3 (2015), https://ejpr.onlinelibrary.wiley.com.

103 Ed Mahon, "Pa. Senator Says He Used Medical Marijuana despite Ban," *York Daily Record*, December 14, 2016, www.ydr.com.

104 Interview with Fred Sembach, former chief of staff for Senator Mike Folmer.

105 "Meet the Blunt-Smoking Louisiana Senate Candidate Determined to Take Down the Republican 'Foghorn Leghorn,'" *Rolling Stone*, January 20, 2022, www.rollingstone.com.

106 Reid, "A Qualitative Review of Cannabis Stigmas at the Twilight of Prohibition."

107 Herweg, Huß, and Zohlnhöfer, "Straightening the Three Streams: Theorising Extensions of the Multiple Streams Framework."

108 Baumgartner and Jones, *Agendas and Instability in American Politics*.

109 Daniel J. Mallinson, "Policy Innovation Adoption across the Diffusion Life Course," *Policy Studies Journal* 49, no. 2 (2021), https://onlinelibrary.wiley.com.

CHAPTER 2. DEFIANT INNOVATION

Epigraph: Quoted in Suntrop, Jack, "Marijuana Backes Preparing for Victory After Decades of Disappointment in Missouri," *St. Louis Post-Dispatch*, October 31, 2018.

1 Andy Marso, "Missouri Voters Approve Medical Marijuana with a Constitutional Amendment," *The Kansas City (MO) Star*, November 6, 2018.

2   Rachael Herndon Dunn, "VFW of Missouri Endorses Amendment 2," *Missouri Times*, updated October 25, 2018, https://themissouritimes.com.
3   Christopher Z. Mooney, *The Study of U.S. State Policy Diffusion: What Hath Walker Wrought?* (Cambridge: Cambridge University Press, 2021), www.cambridge.org/core.
4   Everett M. Rogers, *Diffusion of Innovations*, 5th ed. (New York: Free Press, 2003).
5   Frances Stokes Berry and William D. Berry, "Innovation and Diffusion Models in Policy Research," in *Theories of the Policy Process*, ed. Christopher M. Weible and Paul A. Sabatier (New York: Westview Press, 2018), 253–297.
6   Daniel J. Mallinson, "Growth and Gaps: A Meta-Review of Policy Diffusion Studies in the American States," *Policy & Politics* 49, no. 3 (2021), https://bristoluniversitypressdigital.com.
7   Mallinson, "Growth and Gaps: A Meta-Review of Policy Diffusion Studies in the American States."
8   Daniel J. Mallinson, "Who Are Your Neighbors? The Role of Ideology and Decline of Geographic Proximity in the Diffusion of Policy Innovations," *Policy Studies Journal* 49, no. 1 (2021); Daniel J. Mallinson, "Policy Innovation Adoption across the Diffusion Life Course," *Policy Studies Journal* 49, no. 2 (2021), https://onlinelibrary.wiley.com; Daniel J. Mallinson, "Building a Better Speed Trap: Measuring Policy Adoption Speed in the American States," *State Politics & Policy Quarterly* 16, no. 1 (March 2016), https://journals.sagepub.com/; Sean Nicholson-Crotty, "The Politics of Diffusion: Public Policy in the American States," *Journal of Politics* 71, no. 1 (2009); Todd Makse and Craig Volden, "The Role of Policy Attributes in the Diffusion of Innovations," *Journal of Politics* 73, no. 1 (2011); Aravind Menon and Daniel J. Mallinson, "Policy Diffusion Speed: A Replication Study Using the State Policy Innovation and Diffusion Database," *Political Studies Review* 20, no. 4 (2022), https://journals.sagepub.com.
9   Mallinson, "Growth and Gaps: A Meta-Review of Policy Diffusion Studies in the American States."
10 Daniel J. Mallinson, "Identifying and Explaining Instability in the General Model of Policy Innovation Diffusion" (diss., The Pennsylvania State University, 2015); Erin R. Graham, Charles R. Shipan, and Craig Volden, "The Diffusion of Policy Diffusion Research in Political Science," *British Journal of Political Science* 43, no. 3 (2013); Martino Maggetti and Fabrizio Gilardi, "Problems (and Solutions) in the Measurement of Policy Diffusion Mechanisms," *Journal of Public Policy* 36, no. 1 (2016).
11 William D. Berry and Brady Baybeck, "Using Geographic Information Systems to Study Interstate Competition," *American Political Science Review* 99, no. 4 (2005); Julianna Pacheco, "The Social Contagion Model: Exploring the Role of Public Opinion on the Diffusion of Antismoking Legislation across the American States," *Journal of Politics* 74, no. 1 (2012).
12 Lawrence J. Grossback, Sean Nicholson-Crotty, and David A. M. Peterson, "Ideology and Learning in Policy Diffusion," *American Politics Research* 32, no. 5 (2004);

Victor D. Cruz-Aceves and Daniel J. Mallinson, "Clarifying the Measurement of Relative Ideology in Policy Diffusion Research," *State and Local Government Review* 51, no. 3 (2019), https://journals.sagepub.com.

13 Susan Welch and Kay Thompson, "The Impact of Federal Incentives on State Policy Innovation," *American Journal of Political Science* 24, no. 4 (1980); Frank R. Baumgartner, Virginia Gray, and David Lowery, "Federal Policy Activity and the Mobilization of State Lobbying Organizations," *Political Research Quarterly* 62, no. 3 (2009).

14 Andrew Bell and Daniel J. Mallinson, "Constraints on Policy Learning: Designing the Regional Greenhouse Gas Initiative in Pennsylvania," *Policy Design and Practice* (2021), www.tandfonline.com/; Peter J. May, "Policy Learning and Failure," *Journal of Public Policy* 12, no. 4 (1992), www.jstor.org; Grossback, Nicholson-Crotty, and Peterson, "Ideology and Learning in Policy Diffusion."

15 Sean Nicholson-Crotty and Sanya Carley, "Effectiveness, Implementation, and Policy Diffusion: Or 'Can We Make That Work for Us?'" *State Politics & Policy Quarterly* 16, no. 1 (2016), https://journals.sagepub.com.

16 Daniel M. Butler, Craig Volden, Adam M. Dynes, and Boris Shor, "Ideology, Learning, and Policy Diffusion: Experimental Evidence," *American Journal of Political Science* 61, no. 1 (2017), https://onlinelibrary.wiley.com.

17 Berry and Baybeck, "Using Geographic Information Systems to Study Interstate Competition."

18 Frances Stokes Berry and William D. Berry, "State Lottery Adoptions as Policy Innovations: An Event History Analysis," *American Political Science Review* 82, no. 4 (1990); Frederick J. Boehmke and Richard Witmer, "Disentangling Diffusion: The Effects of Social Learning and Economic Competition on State Policy Innovation and Expansion," *Political Research Quarterly* 57, no. 1 (March 2004), https://journals.sagepub.com.

19 Berry and Baybeck, "Using Geographic Information Systems to Study Interstate Competition."

20 Craig Volden, "The Politics of Competitive Federalism: A Race to the Bottom in Welfare Benefits?," *American Journal of Political Science* 46, no. 2 (2002), www.jstor.org; Eri Saikawa, "Policy Diffusion of Emission Standards: Is There a Race to the Top?" *World Politics* 65, no. 1 (2013), https://muse.jhu.edu; Daniel J. Mallinson and Darrell Lovell, "Race to the Top and the Diffusion of State Education Intervention Policy in the American States," *Politics & Policy* 50, no. 6 (2022), https://onlinelibrary.wiley.com.

21 Pacheco, "The Social Contagion Model: Exploring the Role of Public Opinion on the Diffusion of Antismoking Legislation across the American States."

22 Pacheco, "The Social Contagion Model: Exploring the Role of Public Opinion on the Diffusion of Antismoking Legislation across the American States."

23 Mallinson, "Identifying and Explaining Instability in the General Model of Policy Innovation Diffusion."

24 Joshua M. Jansa, Eric R. Hansen, and Virginia H. Gray, "Copy and Paste Lawmaking: Legislative Professionalism and Policy Reinvention in the States," *American Politics Research* 47, no. 4 (2019), https://journals.sagepub.com.
25 Eric R. Hansen and Joshua M. Jansa, "Complexity, Resources and Text Borrowing in State Legislatures," *Journal of Public Policy* 41, no. 4 (2021), www.cambridge.org/core.
26 Robert M. Dorrell and Joshua M. Jansa, "Copy, Paste, Legislate, Succeed? The Effect of Policy Plagiarism on Policy Success," *Policy & Politics* 50, no. 4 (March 2022), https://bristoluniversitypressdigital.com.
27 Kristin N. Garrett and Joshua M. Jansa, "Interest Group Influence in Policy Diffusion Networks," *State Politics & Policy Quarterly* 15, no. 3 (September 1, 2015), https://journals.sagepub.com.
28 Welch and Thompson, "The Impact of Federal Incentives on State Policy Innovation"; Neal D. Woods and Ann O'M. Bowman, "Blurring Borders: The Effect of Federal Activism on Interstate Cooperation," *American Politics Research* 39, no. 5 (2011), https://journals.sagepub.com/; Pamela J. Clouser McCann, Charles R. Shipan, and Craig Volden, "Top-Down Federalism: State Policy Responses to National Government Discussions," *Publius: The Journal of Federalism* 45, no. 4 (Fall 2015), https://academic.oup.com/publius; Andrew Karch, "National Intervention and the Diffusion of Policy Innovations," *American Politics Research* 34, no. 4 (2006).
29 A. Lee Hannah and Daniel J. Mallinson, "Defiant Innovation: The Adoption of Medical Marijuana Laws in the American States," *Policy Studies Journal* 46, no. 2 (2018), https://onlinelibrary.wiley.com.
30 Daniel J. Mallinson, A. Lee Hannah, and Gideon Cunningham, "The Consequences of Fickle Federal Policy: Administrative Hurdles for State Cannabis Policies," *State and Local Government Review* 52, no. 4 (2020), https://journals.sagepub.com.
31 Malcolm L. Goggin, Ann O'M. Bowman, James P. Lester, and Laurence J. O'Toole Jr., *Implementation Theory and Practice: Toward a Third Generation* (New York: Harper Collins, 1990).
32 Goggin et al., *Implementation Theory and Practice: Toward a Third Generation*; Mahalley D. Allen, Carrie Pettus, and Donald P. Haider-Markel, "Making the National Local: Specifying the Conditions for National Government Influence on State Policymaking," *State Politics & Policy Quarterly* 4, no. 3 (2004).
33 Goggin et al., *Implementation Theory and Practice: Toward a Third Generation*.
34 National Commission on Terrorist Attacks upon the United States, *The 9/11 Commission Report* (New York: W. W. Norton, 2004).
35 Jason Litalien, "Why Some States Won't Comply with REAL ID Requirements," *iapp*, January 30, 2017, https://iapp.org/news.
36 Priscilla M. Regan and Christopher J. Deering, "State Opposition to REAL ID," *Publius: The Journal of Federalism* 39, no. 3 (Summer 2009), https://academic.oup.com/publius.

37. Department of Homeland Security, "DHS Announces Extension of REAL ID Full Enforcement Deadline," news release, December 5, 2022, https://www.dhs.gov/news.
38. John Dinan, "The Institutionalization of State Resistance to Federal Directives in the 21st Century," *The Forum* 18, no. 1 (2020), www.degruyter.com.
39. David M Konisky and Paul Nolette, "The State of American Federalism, 2020–2021: Deepening Partisanship amid Tumultuous Times," *Publius: The Journal of Federalism* 51, no. 3 (Summer 2021), https://academic.oup.com/publius; Jessica Bulman-Pozen and Heather K. Gerken, "Uncooperative Federalism," *Yale Law Journal* 118, no. 7 (2009); Timothy J. Conlan and Paul L. Posner, "American Federalism in an Era of Partisan Polarization: The Intergovernmental Paradox of Obama's 'New Nationalism,'" *Publius: The Journal of Federalism* 46, no. 3 (Summer 2016), https://academic.oup.com/publius.
40. Paul Nolette, *Federalism on Trial* (Lawrence: University of Kansas Press, 2015); Shanna Rose and Greg Goelzhauser, "The State of American Federalism 2017–2018: Unilateral Executive Action, Regulatory Rollback, and State Resistance," *Publius: The Journal of Federalism* 48, no. 3 (Summer 2018), https://academic.oup.com/publius; "How State AGs Became a Check on the President," *Governing*, updated September 30, 2021, 2021, accessed July 8, 2022, www.governing.com.
41. Shanna Rose, "Opting In, Opting Out: The Politics of State Medicaid Expansion," *The Forum* 13, no. 1 (2015), www.degruyter.com; Elizabeth Rigby, "State Resistance to 'ObamaCare,'" *The Forum* 10, no. 2 (2012), www.degruyter.com; Alexander Hertel-Fernandez, Theda Skocpol, and Daniel Lynch, "Business Associations, Conservative Networks, and the Ongoing Republican War over Medicaid Expansion," *Journal of Health Politics, Policy and Law* 41, no. 2 (April 2016), https://read.dukeupress.edu.
42. Lawrence R. Jacobs and Timothy Callaghan, "Why States Expand Medicaid: Party, Resources, and History," *Journal of Health Politics, Policy and Law* 38, no. 5 (October 2013), https://read.dukeupress.edu.
43. Hannah and Mallinson, "Defiant Innovation: The Adoption of Medical Marijuana Laws in the American States."
44. John Brehm and Schott Gates, *Working, Shirking, and Sabotage: Bureaucratic Response to a Democratic Public* (Ann Arbor: University of Michigan Press, 1997).
45. Greg Lucas, "Bills on Pot, Needles Die in Flurry of Vetoes—Wilson Acts at Last Minute on Controversial Measures," *San Francisco Chronicle*, October 1, 1994.
46. Arika Herron, "Gov. Eric Holcomb Admits He's Smoked Marijuana, Still Doesn't Support Legalization," *Indianapolis Star*, February 27, 2019, www.indystar.com.
47. Sam Kamin, "The Battle of the Bulge: The Surprising Last Stand against State Marijuana Legalization," *Publius: The Journal of Federalism* 45, no. 3 (Summer 2015), http://publius.oxfordjournals.org.
48. Mallinson, "Policy Innovation Adoption across the Diffusion Life Course."
49. "Drug Czar Warns Doctors That U.S. Would Prosecute," *Los Angeles Times*, October 30, 1996, www.latimes.com.

50 Michael Pollan, "Living with Medical Marijuana," *New York Times*, July 20, 1997, www.nytimes.com.
51 Richard Lacayo, "Marijuana: Where There's Smoke, There's Fire," *CNN*, October 28, 1996, www.cnn.com.
52 "San Francisco Pot Raid Raises Politicians' Ire," *Las Vegas Sun*, August 7, 1996, https://lasvegassun.com; National Drug Strategy Network, "State Agents Raid Cannabis Buyers' Club in San Francisco," *News Briefs*, September 1996, https://www.ndsn.org/SEPT96/CBC.html.
53 "The San Francisco Cannabis Buyers' Club Raid," *MarijuanaLibrary.org*, archived e-mails, August 4, 1996, http://www.marijuanalibrary.org/080496_SF_CBC_raid.html.
54 Tim Golden, "Medical Use of Marijuana to Stay Illegal in Arizona," *New York Times*, April 17, 1997.
55 Lewis A. Grossman, "Life, Liberty, [and the Pursuit of Happiness] Medical Marijuana Regulation in Historical Context," *Food and Drug Law Journal* 74, no. 2 (2019): 306, www.jstor.org.
56 Expressing the Sense of Congress That Marijuana Is a Dangerous and Addictive Drug and Should Not Be Legalized for Medicinal Use., 1998 H.J. Res. 117, 105th Cong. (1998).
57 Mark Eddy, *Medical Marijuana: Review and Analysis of Federal and State Policies* (Washington, DC: Congressional Research Service, 2010).
58 Eddy, *Medical Marijuana: Review and Analysis of Federal and State Policies*.
59 Golden, "Medical Use of Marijuana to Stay Illegal in Arizona"; Grossman, "Life, Liberty, [and the Pursuit of Happiness] Medical Marijuana Regulation in Historical Context."
60 Norman Runnion, "Runnion's View on Montpelier," *The Herald*, May 27, 2004, www.ourherald.com.
61 Runnion, "Runnion's View on Montpelier."
62 Runnion, "Runnion's View on Montpelier."
63 Kyle Kondik, *The Bellwether: Why Ohio Picks the President* (Athens: Ohio University Press, 2016).
64 Jackie Borchardt, "Issue 3 Backers Spent $21.5 Million on Failed Ohio Marijuana Legalization Amendment," *Cleveland Plain Dealer*, December 11, 2015, www.cleveland.com.
65 David A. Graham, "Why Did Ohio's Marijuana-Legalization Push Fail?" *The Atlantic*, November 3, 2015, www.theatlantic.com.
66 Jackie Borchardt, "4 Reasons Why Ohio Issue 3 Failed," *Cleveland.com*, November 5, 2015, www.cleveland.com.
67 Robert Higgs, "Ohio Voters Favor Legalizing Marijuana, Huge Majority Supports Medical Use, Poll Finds," *Cleveland Plain Dealer*, April 6, 2015, www.cleveland.com.
68 Jackie Borchardt, "5 Ways New Medical Marijuana Initiative Changes the Game in Ohio: Analysis," *Cleveland Plain Dealer*, January 22, 2016, www.cleveland.com.

69 Edward L. Lascher Jr., Michael G. Hagen, and Steven A. Rochlin, "Gun behind the Door? Ballot Initiatives, State Policies, and Public Opinion," *Journal of Politics* 58, no. 3 (1996).
70 .
71 A. Lee Hannah, "The Politics of Passing and Implementing Medical Marijuana in Ohio," *Ohio Journal of Economics and Politics* 24, no. 1 (2018), https://papers.ssrn.com.
72 Lyle Denniston, "Two States Sue to Block Colorado Marijuana Markets," *SCOTUSblog*, September 30, 2014, /www.scotusblog.com.
73 Paul Monies, "How Recreational Is Oklahoma's Medical Marijuana Market?" *Oklahoma Watch*, January 19, 2020, 2020, https://oklahomawatch.org.
74 Paul Monies, "How Recreational Is Oklahoma's Medical Marijuana Market?"
75 Paul Demko, "How One of the Reddest States Became the Nation's Hottest Weed Market," *Politico*, November 27, 2020, www.politico.com.
76 Bill Shapard, "Poll: Oklahomans Views of Marijuana Are Changing," *SoonerPoll.com*, September 23, 2013.
77 Demko, "How One of the Reddest States Became the Nation's Hottest Weed Market."
78 Demko, "How One of the Reddest States Became the Nation's Hottest Weed Market."
79 Demko, "How One of the Reddest States Became the Nation's Hottest Weed Market."
80 Marijuana Policy Project, "Model State Medical Cannabis Bill," n.d., accessed March 20, 2023, www.mpp.org. [*Insert State Name*] added by authors.
81 New Jersey Legislature, *New Jersey Compassionate Use Medical Marijuana Act*, January 18, 2010, https://pub.njleg.gov/bills/2008/PL09/307_.HTM.
82 Marijuana Policy Project, "Model State Medical Cannabis Bill."
83 Standing Akimbo, LLC, et al. v. United States, 594 U.S. (2021) (Thomas, C. dissenting), 1.
84 Ibid., 4–5.
85 David B. Magleby, "Taking the Initiative: Direct Legislation and Direct Democracy in the 1980s," *PS: Political Science & Politics* 21, no. 3 (1988).
86 Eric D. Lawrence, Todd Donovan, and Shaun Bowler, "Adopting Direct Democracy: Tests of Competing Explanations of Institutional Change," *American Politics Research* 37, no. 6 (2009), https://journals.sagepub.com; Gabor Simonovits, Andrew M. Guess, and Jonathan Nagler, "Responsiveness without Representation: Evidence from Minimum Wage Laws in U.S. States," *American Journal of Political Science* 63, no. 2 (2019), https://onlinelibrary.wiley.com.
87 Daniel A. Smith and Dustin Fridkin, "Delegating Direct Democracy: Interparty Legislative Competition and the Adoption of the Initiative in the American States," *American Political Science Review* 102, no. 3 (2008), www.jstor.org; Shaun Bowler and Todd Donovan, "Measuring the Effect of Direct Democracy on State

Policy: Not All Initiatives Are Created Equal," *State Politics & Policy Quarterly* 4, no. 3 (2004), www.jstor.org.

88 Note that the map in figure 2.2 does not include states (e.g., Pennsylvania, New Jersey) whose legislatures place constitutional amendments on the ballot. This is relevant for New Jersey, which legalized adult-use recreational marijuana through a constitutional amendment that required a supportive public vote. See National Conference of State Legislatures, "Initiative and Referendum Processes," January 2022, www.ncsl.org.

89 Joshua J. Dyck and Edward L. Lascher Jr., *Initiatives without Engagement: A Realistic Appraisal of Direct Democracy's Secondary Effects* (Ann Arbor: University of Michigan Press, 2019).

90 Bowler and Donovan, "Measuring the Effect of Direct Democracy on State Policy: Not All Initiatives Are Created Equal."

91 "Ballot Measures Cost per Required Signatures Analysis," *Ballotpedia*, accessed March 20, 2023, https://ballotpedia.org.

92 Geoff Pender and Bobby Harrison, "Mississippi Supreme Court Overturns Medical Marijuana Initiative 65," *Mississippi Today*, May 14, 2021, https://mississippitoday.org.

93 Todd Donovan, Caroline J. Tolbert, and Daniel A. Smith, "Priming Presidential Votes by Direct Democracy," *Journal of Politics* 70, no. 4 (2008), www.journals.uchicago.edu; Shaun Bowler, Reagan Dobbs, and Stephen Nicholson, "Direct Democracy and Political Decision Making," *Oxford Research Encyclopedia of Politics*, September 28, 2020, https://oxfordre.com; Arthur Lupia and John G. Matsusaka, "Direct Democracy: New Approaches to Old Questions," *Annual Review of Political Science* 7, no. 1 (2004), www.annualreviews.org; Daniel R. Biggers, *Morality at the Ballot: Direct Democracy and Engagement in the United States* (New York: Cambridge University Press, 2014); Dyck and Lascher, *Initiatives without Engagement: A Realistic Appraisal of Direct Democracy's Secondary Effects*.

94 Lucas Leemann and Fabio Wasserfallen, "The Democratic Effect of Direct Democracy," *American Political Science Review* 110, no. 4 (2016): 750, www.cambridge.org/core.

95 Devin Caughey and Christopher Warshaw, "Policy Preferences and Policy Change: Dynamic Responsiveness in the American States, 1936–2014," *American Political Science Review* 112, no. 2 (2018), www.cambridge.org/core.

96 Simonovits, Guess, and Nagler, "Responsiveness without Representation: Evidence from Minimum Wage Laws in U.S. States"; John G. Matsusaka, "Popular Control of Public Policy: A Quantitative Approach," *Quarterly Journal of Political Science* 5, no. 2 (2010), https://ideas.repec.org; Kevin Arceneaux, "Direct Democracy and the Link between Public Opinion and State Abortion Policy," *State Politics & Policy Quarterly* 2, no. 4 (2002); Elisabeth R. Gerber, "Legislative Response to the Threat of Popular Initiatives," *American Journal of Political Science* 40, no. 1 (1996); Christian Caron, "Public Opinion and Death Penalty Policy under Direct

Democracy Institutions: A Longitudinal Analysis of the American States," *American Politics Research* 49, no. 1 (2021), https://journals.sagepub.com.
97 Jeffrey Lax and Justin Phillips, "Gay Rights in the States: Public Opinion and Policy Responsiveness," *American Political Science Review* 103, no. 3 (2009); Daniel C. Lewis, "Direct Democracy and Minority Rights: Same-Sex Marriage Bans in the U.S. States," *Social Science Quarterly* 92, no. 2 (2011), https://onlinelibrary.wiley.com; Daniel C. Lewis and Matthew L. Jacobsmeier, "Evaluating Policy Representation with Dynamic MRP Estimates: Direct Democracy and Same-Sex Relationship Policies in the United States," *State Politics & Policy Quarterly* 17, no. 4 (2017), https://www.cambridge.org/.
98 John Hudak and Christine Stenglein, "Public Opinion and America's Experimentation with Cannabis Reform," in *Marijuana Federalism: Uncle Sam and Mary Jane*, ed. Jonathan H. Adler (Washington, DC: Brookings Institution Press, 2020), 15–34.
99 Ted Van Green, "Americans Overwhelmingly Say Marijuana Should Be Legal for Recreational or Medical Use," Pew Research Center, November 22, 2022, www.pewresearch.org.
100 Kyle Jaeger, "Majority of Republicans Support Variety of Marijuana Reforms, New Poll Finds as GOP Congressman Talks Bipartisan Next Steps," *Marijuana Moment*, September 15, 2022, www.marijuanamoment.net.
101 Bethany Rodgers, "Utah Has a New Medical Marijuana Law—but Not the One Approved by Voters in the Recent Election," *The Salt Lake Tribune*, December 4, 2018, www.sltrib.com; Kyle Jaeger, "Mississippi Supreme Court Overturns Medical Marijuana Legalization Ballot That Voters Approved," *Marijuana Moment*, May 14, 2021, www.marijuanamoment.net.
102 Bowler and Donovan, "Measuring the Effect of Direct Democracy on State Policy: Not All Initiatives Are Created Equal."
103 Kathleen Ferraiolo, "State Policy Innovation and the Federalism Implications of Direct Democracy," *Publius: The Journal of Federalism* 38, no. 3 (2008), http://publius.oxfordjournals.org.
104 Frederick J. Boehmke, "Approaches to Modeling the Adoption and Diffusion of Policies with Multiple Components," *State Politics & Policy Quarterly* 9, no. 2 (2009); Berry and Berry, "State Lottery Adoptions as Policy Innovations: An Event History Analysis"; Mallinson, "Growth and Gaps: A Meta-Review of Policy Diffusion Studies in the American States."
105 Berry and Berry, "State Lottery Adoptions as Policy Innovations: An Event History Analysis"; Janet M. Box-Steffensmeier and Brandford S. Jones, *Event History Modeling: A Guide for Social Scientists* (New York: Cambridge University Press, 2004).
106 Virginia Gray, "Innovation in the States: A Diffusion Study," *American Political Science Review* 67, no. 4 (1973).
107 Mallinson, "Policy Innovation Adoption across the Diffusion Life Course"; Mallinson, "Who Are Your Neighbors? The Role of Ideology and Decline of Geographic Proximity in the Diffusion of Policy Innovations."

108 Hannah and Mallinson, "Defiant Innovation: The Adoption of Medical Marijuana Laws in the American States."
109 Mallinson, "Policy Innovation Adoption across the Diffusion Life Course."
110 Hannah and Mallinson, "Defiant Innovation: The Adoption of Medical Marijuana Laws in the American States."
111 William D. Berry, Evan J. Ringquist, Richard C. Fording, and Russell L. Hanson, "Measuring Citizen and Government Ideology in the American States, 1960–93," *American Journal of Political Science* 42, no. 1 (1998).
112 Mallinson, "Policy Innovation Adoption across the Diffusion Life Course."
113 Daniel J. Mallison and Lee Hannah, "Marijuana Is on the Ballot in Four States, but Legalization May Soon Stall, Researchers Say," *The Conversation*, updated November 6, 2018, 2018, https://theconversation.com; Mallinson, Hannah, and Cunningham, "The Consequences of Fickle Federal Policy: Administrative Hurdles for State Cannabis Policies."
114 Regan and Deering, "State Opposition to REAL ID"; Daniel Palazzolo, Vincent G. Moscardelli, Meredith Patrick, and Doug Rubin, "Election Reform after HAVA: Voter Verification in Congress and the States," *Publius: The Journal of Federalism* 38, no. 3 (Summer 2008), https://academic.oup.com/publius; Steven J. Balla and Christopher J. Deering, "Salience, Complexity and State Resistance to Federal Mandates," *Journal of Public Policy* 35, no. 3 (2015), www.cambridge.org/core.
115 Magleby, "Taking the Initiative: Direct Legislation and Direct Democracy in the 1980s."
116 For how and why policies do not fully diffuse, see Andrew Karch, "Examining Episodes of Limited Diffusion: The Politics of Embryonic Stem Cell Research" (Annual Meeting of the American Political Science Association, Washington, DC, 2010). For motivation changes, see Rogers, *Diffusion of Innovations*; Mallinson, "Policy Innovation Adoption across the Diffusion Life Course."
117 See, for example, H.R. 83, the Mobilizing against Sanctuary Cities Act, 115th Congress (2017–2018); Ruari Arrieta-Kenna, "Sanctuary Cities Stand Firm against Trump," *Politico*, December 12, 2016, www.politico.com.
118 Kamin, "The Battle of the Bulge: The Surprising Last Stand against State Marijuana Legalization."
119 Donald F. Kettl, *The Divided States of America: Why Federalism Doesn't Work* (Princeton, NJ: Princeton University Press, 2020); Donald F. Kettl, "States Divided: The Implications of American Federalism for COVID-19," *Public Administration Review* 80, no. 4 (2020), https://onlinelibrary.wiley.com.

CHAPTER 3. FROM THE STATEHOUSE TO THE DISPENSARY
Epigraph: Darryl Isherwood, "State Making Progress on Medical Marijuana, Governor Says." *Observer*, April 17, 2012, https://observer.com/2012/04/state-making-progress-on-medical-marijuana-governor-says/.
1 Claire Heininger, "N.J. Medical Marijuana Law Is Signed by Gov. Corzine," *NJ.com*, January 19, 2010 .

2   Olivia Nuzzi and Abby Haglage, "Chris Christie to the Drug War: I Wish I Knew How to Quit You," *The Daily Beast*, June 18, 2014, www.thedailybeast.com.
3   Susan K. Livio, "NJ Medical Marijuana Program Struggling, with Worries Growing over Few Doctors, Patients Enrolled," *NJ.com*, June 15, 2014; Amanda Hoover and Payton Guion, "N.J. Medical Marijuana Program Expansion Approved for Its 50K Patients," *NJ.com*, June 20, 2019.
4   Hoover and Guion, "N.J. Medical Marijuana Program Expansion Approved for Its 50K Patients."
5   Tom Angell, "New Jersey Governor Orders Medical Marijuana Expansion," *Marijuana Moment*, January 23, 2018, www.marijuanamoment.net.
6   Marcela Ospina Maziarz, "NJ's Medicinal Marijuana Program Triples Patient Count since Start of Murphy Administration," news release, July 24, 2019, www.nj.gov/health/news.
7   Dustin Racioppi, "NJ Medical Marijuana Program to Expand, Says Murphy, as Legal Weed Push Continues," *NorthJersey.com*, March 27, 2018.
8   Joe Evans, "This NJ Dispensary Is Booming Thanks to Pennsylvania's Bad Weed Laws," *Leafly*, May 13, 2022, www.leafly.com.
9   Amanda Eustice, "Pennsylvanians Flock to New Jersey for Legal Weed," *WNEP*, April 21, 2022, www.wnep.com; Susan Shapiro, "Customers Line Up in New Jersey to Purchase Legal Marijuana," *WGAL*, May 11, 2022, www.wgal.com.
10 Malcolm L. Goggin, Ann Bowman, James Lester, and Lawrence O'Toole, *Implementation Theory and Practice: Toward a Third Generation*, (New York: Harper Collins, 1990), 13.
11 Jon Pierre and B. Guy Peters, *The SAGE Handbook of Public Administration* (London: Sage, 2012), http://digital.casalini.it/4913727.
12 Matthew Williams, *How Language Works in Politics: The Impact of Vague Legislation on Policy* (Bristol, UK: Bristol University Press, 2018).
13 Harald Saetren, "Facts and Myths about Research on Public Policy Implementation: Out-of-Fashion, Allegedly Dead, but Still Very Much Alive and Relevant," *Policy Studies Journal* 33, no. 4 (2005), https://onlinelibrary.wiley.com; Harald Saetren, "Implementing the Third Generation Research Paradigm in Policy Implementation Research: An Empirical Assessment," *Public Policy and Administration* 29, no. 2 (2014), https://journals.sagepub.com.
14 Frank J. Thompson, "The Rise of Executive Federalism: Implications for the Picket Fence and IGM," *American Review of Public Administration* 43, no. 1 (2013), https://journals.sagepub.com.
15 It is notable that there are three generations of implementation research and that we are drawing from the third generation. The first generation was characterized as atheoretical and largely focused on case studies. The second generation developed theoretical frameworks, but the testing of hypotheses derived from these frameworks was limited. Finally, the third generation, prompted by Malcolm Goggin and colleagues in 1990, sought to integrate the empirical and theoretical work in a way that would allow for better theory development and testing. (See

Goggin et al., *Implementation Theory and Practice: Toward a Third Generation*.) Contrary to popular opinion, implementation research has not died and remains vibrant in policy studies. See Saetren, "Facts and Myths about Research on Public Policy Implementation: Out-of-Fashion, Allegedly Dead, but Still Very Much Alive and Relevant."
16 Goggin et al., *Implementation Theory and Practice: Toward a Third Generation*.
17 Giliberto Capano and Michael Howlett, "The Knowns and Unknowns of Policy Instrument Analysis: Policy Tools and the Current Research Agenda on Policy Mixes," *SAGE Open* 10, no. 1 (2020): 1, https://journals.sagepub.com.
18 Grant W. Neeley and Lilliard E. Richardson Jr., "Marijuana Policy Bundles in the American States over Time and Their Impact on the Use of Marijuana and Other Drugs," *Evaluation Review* 46, no. 2 (2022), https://journals.sagepub.com; Sarah B. Klieger, Abraham Gutman, Leslie Allen, Rosalie Liccardo Pacula, Jennifer K. Ibrahim, and Scott Burris, "Mapping Medical Marijuana: State Laws Regulating Patients, Product Safety, Supply Chains and Dispensaries, 2017," *Addiction* 112, no. 12 (2017), https://onlinelibrary.wiley.com; Rosalie Liccardo Pacula, David Powell, Paul Heaton, and Eric L. Sevigny, "Assessing the Effects of Medical Marijuana Laws on Marijuana Use: The Devil Is in the Details," *Journal of Policy Analysis and Management* 34, no. 1 (Winter 2015), www.ncbi.nlm.nih.gov.
19 Grant W. Neeley and Lilliard E. Richardson Jr., "Cannabis Policy Adaptation: Exploring Frameworks of State Policy Characteristics," *Public Administration Quarterly* 47, no. 3 (2023), https://doi.org/10.37808/paq.47.3.2.
20 Neeley and Richardson, "Cannabis Policy Adaptation: Exploring Frameworks of State Policy Characteristics"; Klieger et al., "Mapping Medical Marijuana: State Laws Regulating Patients, Product Safety, Supply Chains and Dispensaries, 2017"; Pacula et al., "Assessing the Effects of Medical Marijuana Laws on Marijuana Use: The Devil Is in the Details."
21 Jacob S. Hacker, "Privatizing Risk without Privatizing the Welfare State: The Hidden Politics of Social Policy Retrenchment in the United States," *American Political Science Review* 98, no. 2 (2004), www.jstor.org.
22 John Brehm and Schott Gates, *Working, Shirking, and Sabotage: Bureaucratic Response to a Democratic Public* (Ann Arbor: University of Michigan Press, 1997).
23 Elisabeth R. Gerber, Arthur Lupia, and Mathew D. McCubbins, "When Does Government Limit the Impact of Voter Initiatives? The Politics of Implementation and Enforcement," *Journal of Politics* 66, no. 1 (2004), www.journals.uchicago.edu.
24 Douglas B. Marlowe, Amiram Elwork, David S. Festinger, and A. Thomas McLellan, "Drug Policy by Popular Referendum: This, Too, Shall Pass," *Journal of Substance Abuse Treatment* 25, no. 3 (2003): 213, www.sciencedirect.com.
25 Curtis J. VanderWaal, Jamie F. Chriqui, Rachel M. Bishop, Duane C. McBride, and Douglas Y. Longshore, "State Drug Policy Reform Movement: The Use of Ballot Initiatives and Legislation to Promote Diversion to Drug Treatment," *Journal of Drug Issues* 36, no. 3 (2006), https://journals.sagepub.com.
26 Goggin et al., *Implementation Theory and Practice: Toward a Third Generation*.

27 Peter Bachrach and Morton S. Baratz, "Two Faces of Power," *The American Political Science Review* 56, no. 4 (1962), www.jstor.org.
28 Carolyn Bourdeaux, "Do Legislatures Matter in Budgetary Reform?" *Public Budgeting & Finance* 26, no. 1 (2006), https://onlinelibrary.wiley.com.
29 Cody A. Drolc and Lael R. Keiser, "The Importance of Oversight and Agency Capacity in Enhancing Performance in Public Service Delivery," *Journal of Public Administration Research and Theory* 31, no. 4 (2020), https://academic.oup.com.
30 Donald M. Linhorst, "The Legislative Structuring of Insanity Acquittee Policies," *Journal of Mental Health Administration* 24, no. 2 (1997), https://link.springer.com.
31 Michael Barber, Alexander Bolton, and Sharece Thrower, "Legislative Constraints on Executive Unilateralism in Separation of Powers Systems," *Legislative Studies Quarterly* 44, no. 3 (2019), https://onlinelibrary.wiley.com.
32 Paul A. Sabatier, "An Advocacy Coalition Framework of Policy Change and the Role of Policy-Oriented Learning Therein," *Policy Sciences* 21, no. 2/3 (1988), www.jstor.org/stable.
33 Goggin et al., *Implementation Theory and Practice: Toward a Third Generation*.
34 Andreas Dur and Dirk De Bievre, "The Question of Interest Group Influence," *Journal of Public Policy* 27, no. 1 (2007), www.cambridge.org/core.
35 Emily Dufton, *Grass Roots: The Rise and Fall and Rise of Marijuana in America* (New York: Basic Books, 2017), 36.
36 Benjamin L. Crosby, "Policy Implementation: The Organizational Challenge," *World Development* 24, no. 9 (1996), www.sciencedirect.com.
37 X. Wu, M. Ramesh, and M. Howlett, "Policy Capacity: A Conceptual Framework for Understanding Policy Competences and Capabilities," *Policy and Society* 34, no. 3–4 (2015), https://academic.oup.com/policyandsociety; Charles Barrilleaux, Richard Feiock, and Robert E. Crew, "Measuring and Comparing American States' Administrative Characteristics," *State & Local Government Review* 24, no. 1 (1992), www.jstor.org.
38 Michael M. Ting, "Organizational Capacity," *Journal of Law, Economics, and Organization* 27, no. 2 (2009): 246, https://academic.oup.com/jleo.
39 "Florida Governor Wants Ban on Smokable Medical Pot Ended," *Yahoo*, January 18, 2019, 2019, https://www.yahoo.com/entertainment/florida-governor-wants-ban-smokable-104739088.html.
40 Goggin et al., *Implementation Theory and Practice: Toward a Third Generation*.
41 National Commission on Terrorist Attacks upon the United States, *The 9/11 Commission Report* (New York: W. W. Norton, 2004).
42 Eric M. Patashnik and R. Kent Weaver, "Policy Analysis and Political Sustainability," *Policy Studies Journal* 49, no. 4 (2021), https://onlinelibrary.wiley.com.
43 William D. Berry, Evan J. Ringquist, Richard C. Fording, and Russell L. Hanson, "Measuring Citizen and Government Ideology in the American States, 1960–93," *American Journal of Political Science* 42, no. 1 (1998); Jack L. Walker, "The Diffusion of Innovations among the American States," *American Political Science Review* 63, no. 3 (1969); Frederick J. Boehmke and Paul Skinner, "State Policy

Innovativeness Revisited," *State Politics & Policy Quarterly* 12, no. 3 (2012); Daniel J. Elazar, *American Federalism: A View from the States* (New York: Thomas Y. Crowell, 1966).

44 Eric B. Herzik, "The Legal-Formal Structuring of State Politics: a Cultural Explanation," *Western Political Quarterly* 38, no. 3 (1985), https://journals.sagepub.com.

45 Walker, "The Diffusion of Innovations among the American States"; Boehmke and Skinner, "State Policy Innovativeness Revisited."

46 Daniel J. Mallinson, "Agenda Instability in Pennsylvania Politics: Lessons for Future Replication," *Research & Politics* 3, no. 1 (2016), https://journals.sagepub.com; Bryan D. Jones and Frank R. Baumgartner, "Representation and Agenda Setting," *Policy Studies Journal* 32, no. 1 (2004), https://onlinelibrary.wiley.com.

47 William T. Gormley, "Regulatory Issue Networks in a Federal System," *Polity* 18, no. 4 (1986); Matthew Eshbaugh-Soha, "The Conditioning Effects of Policy Salience and Complexity on American Political Institutions," *Policy Studies Journal* 34, no. 2 (2006).

48 Rebecca Bromley-Trujillo and Andrew Karch, "Salience, Scientific Uncertainty, and the Agenda-Setting Power of Science," *Policy Studies Journal* 49, no. 4 (2021), https://onlinelibrary.wiley.com; Rebecca Bromley-Trujillo and John Poe, "The Importance of Salience: Public Opinion and State Policy Action on Climate Change," *Journal of Public Policy* 40, no. 2 (2020), www.cambridge.org/core; James H. Kuklinski and Donald J. McCrone, "Policy Salience and the Causal Structure of Representation," *American Politics Quarterly* 8, no. 2 (1980), https://journals.sagepub.com.

49 Sean Nicholson-Crotty, "The Politics of Diffusion: Public Policy in the American States," *Journal of Politics* 71, no. 1 (2009); Daniel J. Mallinson, "Building a Better Speed Trap: Measuring Policy Adoption Speed in the American States," *State Politics & Policy Quarterly* 16, no. 1 (March 2016), https://journals.sagepub.com; Aravind Menon and Daniel J. Mallinson, "Policy Diffusion Speed: A Replication Study Using the State Policy Innovation and Diffusion Database," *Political Studies Review* 20, no. 4 (2022); Graeme Boushey, *Policy Diffusion Dynamics in America* (New York: Cambridge University Press, 2010).

50 Aneta Spendzharova and Esther Versluis, "Issue Salience in the European Policy Process: What Impact on Transposition?" *Journal of European Public Policy* 20, no. 10 (2013), www.tandfonline.com.

51 Woodrow Wilson, "The Study of Administration," *Political Science Quarterly* 2, no. 2 (1887).

52 Granted, states have been increasing prescription controls as a means of combating successive waves of the opioids abuse epidemic in the United States.

53 Saahir Shafi and Daniel J. Mallinson, "A Decade in Drug Policy and Research: Evaluating Trends from 2010 to 2020 and Presenting Major Policy Developments," *Policy Studies Yearbook* 12, no. 1 (2022).

54 Conant v. Walters, 309 F.3d 629 (9th Cir. 2002), cert. denied Oct. 14, 2003. See also Conant v. McCaffrey, 172 F.R.D. 681 (N.D. Cal. 1997), and Conant v. McCaffrey, 2000 WL 1281174 (N.D. Cal. Sept. 7, 2000).

55 Marijuana Policy Project, "'Prescribing' versus 'Recommending' Medical Cannabis," 2016, accessed March 22, 2023, www.mpp.org.
56 Paul. T. Kocis and Kent. E. Vrana, "Delta-9-Tetrahydrocannabinol and Cannabidiol Drug-Drug Interactions," *Medical Cannabis and Cannabinoids* 3, no. 1 (2020), www.karger.com.
57 Sara Rosenbaum, "Law and the Public's Health," *Public Health Reports* 120, no. 6 (2005), https://journals.sagepub.com.
58 Jacob Sullum, "Commercial Potential," *Reason*, October 8, 2004, https://reason.com; Sara Rosenbaum, "Gonzales v. Raich: Implications for Public Health Policy," *Public Health Reports* 120, no. 6 (November–December 2005).
59 Bob Dreyfuss, "Bush's War on Pot," *Rolling Stone*, August 11, 2005, www.rollingstone.com.
60 Dreyfuss, "Bush's War on Pot."
61 Christopher Cambron, Katarina Guttmannova, and Charles B. Fleming, "State and National Contexts in Evaluating Cannabis Laws: A Case Study of Washington State," *Journal of Drug Issues* 47, no. 1 (2017), https://journals.sagepub.com.
62 Committee on the Judiciary, United States Senate, *Conflicts between State and Federal Marijuana Laws*, (Washington, DC: U.S. Government Publishing Office, 2013).
63 Committee on the Judiciary, United States Senate, *Conflicts between State and Federal Marijuana Laws*.
64 Caroline Cournoyer, "Medical Marijuana: Do States Know How to Regulate It?" *Governing*, July 25, 2012, www.governing.com.
65 Scott Imler, "A Success, Yes, but There Are Many Unintended Consequences," *Los Angeles Times*, March 6, 2009, www.latimes.com.
66 Jessica Bulman-Pozen and Gillian E. Metzger, "The President and the States: Patterns of Contestation and Collaboration under Obama," *Publius: The Journal of Federalism* 46, no. 3 (Summer 2016), http://publius.oxfordjournals.org.
67 David W. Ogden, "Investigations and Prosecutions in States Authorizing the Medical Use of Marijuana," Office of the Deputy Attorney General, memorandum, Washington, DC, 2009; James M. Cole, "Guidance Regarding the Ogden Memo in Jurisdictions Seeking to Authorize Marijuana for Medical Use," Office of the Deputy Attorney General, memorandum, Washington, DC, 2011; James M. Cole, "Guidance Regarding Marijuana Enforcement," memorandum, Washington, DC, 2013. See also Sam Kamin, "The Battle of the Bulge: The Surprising Last Stand against State Marijuana Legalization," *Publius: The Journal of Federalism* 45, no. 3 (Summer 2015), http://publius.oxfordjournals.org.
68 Daniel J. Mallinson and A. Lee Hannah, "Policy and Political Learning: The Development of Medical Marijuana Policies in the States," *Publius: The Journal of Federalism* 50, no. 3 (2020); Daniel J. Mallinson, A. Lee Hannah, and Gideon Cunningham, "The Consequences of Fickle Federal Policy: Administrative Hurdles for State Cannabis Policies," *State and Local Government Review* 52, no. 4 (2020), https://journals.sagepub.com; Klieger et al., "Mapping Medical Marijuana: State Laws Regulating Patients, Product Safety, Supply Chains and Dispensaries, 2017";

Rosalie Liccardo Pacula, Priscillia Hunt, and Anne Boustead, "Words Can Be Deceiving: A Review of Variation among Legally Effective Medical Marijuana Laws in the United States," *Journal of Drug Policy Analysis* 7, no. 1 (2014), www.ncbi.nlm.nih.gov/pubmed.

69 Zachary S. Price, "Federal Enforcement: A Dubious Precedent," in *Marijuana Federalism: Uncle Sam and Mary Jane*, ed. Jonathan H. Adler (Washington, DC: Brookings Institution Press, 2020), 123–138.

70 Christopher Ingraham, "Trump's Pick for Attorney General: 'Good People Don't Smoke Marijuana,'" *Washington Post*, November 18, 2016, www.washingtonpost.com.

71 House Amendment 748, 113th Cong. (2013–2014), https://www.congress.gov/amendment/113th-congress/house-amendment/748.

72 Christopher Ingraham, "Jeff Sessions Asked Congress to Let Him Prosecute Medical Marijuana Providers," *Philadelphia Inquirer*, updated June 13, 2017, www.inquirer.com.

73 Camila Domonoske, "Colorado Sen. Cory Gardner Continues His Standoff with Jeff Sessions over Marijuana," *NPR*, January 10, 2018, www.npr.org.

74 Susan Davis, "On 4/20, Chuck Schumer to Introduce Bill to Decriminalize Marijuana," *NPR*, April 20, 2018, www.npr.org.

75 Christopher Ingraham, "It Took Jeff Sessions Just One Month to Turn Obama Era Drug Policy on Its Head," *Washington Post*, June 2, 2017, www.washingtonpost.com.

76 Eric Sandy, "Differing Views: U.S. Attorneys Address Cole Memo Repeal," *Cannabis Business Times*, January 12, 2018, www.cannabisbusinesstimes.com.

77 Kyle Jaeger, "GOP Senator Reveals What Trump Said about Jeff Sessions's Anti-Marijuana Moves," *Marijuana Moment*, February 23, 2019, www.marijuanamoment.net.

78 Kyle Jaeger, "One Year after Jeff Sessions Rescinded a Federal Marijuana Memo, the Sky Hasn't Fallen," *Marijuana Moment*, January 4, 2019, www.marijuanamoment.net.

79 Greg Walters, "Trump's Department of Justice Is Harassing Legal Weed Companies Because Bill Barr Hates Pot," *Vice*, June 24, 2020, www.vice.com.

80 Kyle Jaeger, "U.S. Attorney General Reiterates That Marijuana Enforcement Wastes Department Resources, but Declines to Comment on Formal Guidance," *Marijuana Moment*, April 26, 2022, www.marijuanamoment.net.

81 Aysha Bagchi, "Medical Marijuana Business Deduction Ban Upheld by Tax Court," *Bloomberg Tax*, October 23, 2019, https://news.bloombergtax.com.

82 Paul Posner, "The Politics of Coercive Federalism in the Bush Era," *Publius: The Journal of Federalism* 37, no. 3 (Summer 2007), http://publius.oxfordjournals.org; John Kincaid, "From Cooperative to Coercive Federalism," *The ANNALS of the American Academy of Political and Social Science* 509, no. 1 (1990), https://journals.sagepub.com; John Kincaid, "Why Coercion and Cooperation Coexist in American Federalism," in *Intergovernmental Relations in Transition*, ed. Carl W. Stenberg and David K. Hamilton (New York: Routledge, 2018), 35–57.

83 Greg Goelzhauser and David M. Konisky, "The State of American Federalism 2019–2020: Polarized and Punitive Intergovernmental Relations," *Publius: The Journal of Federalism* 50, no. 3 (2020): 311, https://academic.oup.com/publius.
84 Dale Krane, "The Middle Tier in American Federalism: State Government Policy Activism during the Bush Presidency," *Publius: The Journal of Federalism* 37, no. 3 (Summer 2007), 469, www.jstor.org.
85 "Cannabis Testing Requirements: A State-by-State Guide," *Leafly*, February 24, 2020, www.leafly.com.
86 Schuyler A. Pruyn, Qiang Wang, Charles G. Wu, and Cassandra L. Taylor, "Quality Standards in State Programs Permitting Cannabis for Medical Uses," *Cannabis and Cannabinoid Research* 7, no. 6 (2022), www.liebertpub.com.
87 Omar Sacirbey, "Vertical Integration Props Up Businesses when Orders Slow Down," *MJBizDaily*, December 17, 2021, https://mjbizdaily.com.
88 Klieger et al., "Mapping Medical Marijuana: State Laws Regulating Patients, Product Safety, Supply Chains and Dispensaries, 2017."
89 A. Lee Hannah, Daniel J. Mallinson, and Lauren Azevedo, "Maximizing Social Equity as a Pillar of Public Administration: An Examination of Cannabis Dispensary Licensing in Pennsylvania," *Public Administration Review* 83, no. 1 (2023), https://onlinelibrary.wiley.com.
90 Jackie Borchardt, "Ohio Medical Marijuana: Minority Quota for Dispensary Licenses Struck Down," *Cincinnati Enquirer*, November 8, 2019, www.cincinnati.com.
91 Jackie Borchardt, "Ohio Medical Marijuana: 'Racial Quota' for Grow Licenses Ruled Unconstitutional," *Cincinnati Enquirer*, November 16, 2018, www.cincinnati.com.
92 Jackie Borchardt, "Medical Marijuana: Ohio Moves Forward with Dispensary License Applications as Black Lawmakers and Business Owners Push for More Diversity," *Cincinnati Enquirer*, September 14, 2021, www.cincinnati.com.
93 Deborah Stone, *Policy Paradox*, 3rd ed. (New York: W. W. Norton, 2012).
94 "MCBA National Cannabis Equity Map," Minority Cannabis Business Association, n.d., accessed March 23, 2023, https://minoritycannabis.org/equitymap.
95 Since the advent of medical cannabis programs in 1996, doctors have been specifically allowed to recommend but not prescribe cannabis. This is because "prescribe" has a particular application to federally approved prescription drugs. Since cannabis is illegal federally, doctors would be in legal jeopardy for writing a "prescription" for cannabis use. Thus, states have gotten around this by allowing physicians to "recommend" cannabis. See Marijuana Policy Project, "'Prescribing' versus 'Recommending' Medical Cannabis."
96 Kevin F. Boehnke, Saurav Gangopadhyay, Daniel J. Clauw, and Rebecca L. Haffajee, "Qualifying Conditions of Medical Cannabis License Holders In the United States," *Health Affairs* 38, no. 2 (2019): 295, www.healthaffairs.org.
97 Gwen T. Lapham, Theresa E. Matson, David S. Carrell, Jennifer F. Bobb, Casey Luce, Malia M. Oliver, Udi E. Ghitza, et al., "Comparison of Medical Cannabis Use Reported on a Confidential Survey vs. Documented in the Electronic Health

Record among Primary Care Patients," *JAMA Network Open* 5, no. 5 (2022), https://jamanetwork.com.
98 Ed Mahon, "A Behind-the-Scenes Look at Spotlight PA's Analysis of 1 Million Medical Marijuana Certifications," *Spotlight PA*, January 31, 2023, www.spotlightpa.org.
99 Marijuana Policy Project, "Medical Marijuana Law and Anti-Discrimination Provisions," February 7, 2022, www.mpp.org.
100 David Wenner, "One Year after Pa.'s Historic Medical Marijuana Passage: Where We Are, How We Got Here," *Pennlive*, updated May 22, 2019, www.pennlive.com.
101 Ed Mahon, "Pa. Senator Says He Used Medical Marijuana despite Ban," *York Daily Record*, December 14, 2016, www.ydr.com.
102 Wenner, "One Year after Pa.'s Historic Medical Marijuana Passage: Where We Are, How We Got Here."
103 Kurt Bresswein, "Pennsylvania Medical Marijuana Hopes Are in Hands of Bipartisan Panel," *Lehigh Valley Live*, July 8, 2015, www.lehighvalleylive.com; Chris Goldstein, "Pennsylvania House Passes Medical Marijuana Bill," *Freedom Leaf*, March 16, 2016, www.freedomleaf.com.
104 Associated Press, "Pa. Adds Anxiety to Qualifying Conditions for Medical Pot," *Pennlive*, July 11, 2019, www.pennlive.com.
105 David Wenner, "Pa. Begins Dry Leaf Medical Marijuana Sales, Reminds Users Not to Smoke It," *Pennlive*, August 1, 2018, www.pennlive.com.
106 Hannah, Mallinson, and Azevedo, "Maximizing Social Equity as a Pillar of Public Administration: An Examination of Cannabis Dispensary Licensing in Pennsylvania."
107 A. Lee Hannah, "The Politics of Passing and Implementing Medical Marijuana in Ohio," *Ohio Journal of Economics and Politics* 24, no. 1 (2018), https://papers.ssrn.com.
108 Jackie Borchardt, "4 Reasons Why Ohio Issue 3 Failed," *Cleveland.com*, November 5, 2015, www.cleveland.com.
109 Jackie Borchardt, "Ohio Voters Support Marijuana Legalization, Poll Finds," *Cleveland.com*, October 8, 2015, www.cleveland.com.
110 Jessie Balmert, "Marijuana Policy Project Drops Ohio Medical Marijuana Initiative," *Cincinnati Enquirer*, May 28, 2016, www.cincinnati.com.
111 Eric Sandy, "What You Need to Know about Ohio's Medical Marijuana Law, in Effect for Seven Months and Changing Every Day," *Cleveland Scene*, April 19, 2017, www.clevescene.com.
112 Balmert, "Marijuana Policy Project Drops Ohio Medical Marijuana Initiative."
113 Jackie Borchardt, "Gov. John Kasich Signs Medical Marijuana Bill into Law," *Cleveland.com*, June 8, 2016, www.cleveland.com.
114 Hannah, "The Politics of Passing and Implementing Medical Marijuana in Ohio."
115 Jackie Borchardt, "First Medical Marijuana Edibles for Sale in Ohio," *Cincinnati Enquirer*, May 14, 2019, www.cincinnati.com; Mollie Lair, "These 4 Ohio Dispensaries Will Start Selling Medical Marijuana Wednesday," *WLWT5*, January 15, 2019, www.wlwt.com.

116 Jessie Balmert, "7 Reasons Why Ohio Won't Be Selling Medical Marijuana This Year," *Cincinnati Enquirer*, September 4, 2018, www.cincinnati.com.
117 Jake Zuckerman, "WV Governor Signs Medical Marijuana into Law," *Charleston Gazette-Mail*, April 19, 2017, www.wvgazettemail.com.
118 Lacie Pierson, "WV House Fast-Tracks Medical Marijuana," *Herald-Dispatch*, March 31, 2017, www.herald-dispatch.com.
119 Andrea Lannom, "Lawmakers Reflect on Session Highlights," *Register-Herald*, April 9, 2017, www.register-herald.com.
120 Zuckerman, "WV Governor Signs Medical Marijuana into Law."
121 Zuckerman, "WV Governor Signs Medical Marijuana into Law"; Patrick M. Azcarate, Alysandra J. Zhang, Salomeh Keyhani, Stacey Steigerwald, Julie H. Ishida, and Beth E. Cohen, "Medical Reasons for Marijuana Use, Forms of Use, and Patient Perception of Physician Attitudes among the US Population," *Journal of General Internal Medicine* 35, no. 7 (2020), www.springer.com/journal/11606.
122 Erin Noon, "Eligible West Virginians Can Now Apply for Medical Cannabis," *WOWK-TV*, May 4, 2021, www.wowktv.com.
123 Dave Mistich, "U.S. Attorney Mike Stuart Holds Invite-Only Anti-Marijuana Event," *West Virginia Public Broadcasting*, December 13, 2018, www.wvpublic.org.
124 Jake Zuckerman, "With Feds in Mind, WV Treasurer Lawyers Up on Medical Marijuana," *Charleston Gazette-Mail*, September 23, 2019, www.wvgazettemail.com.
125 "West Virginia's Medical Cannabis Delays Test Patience of Marijuana Business Owners," *MJBizDaily*, December 17, 2021, https://mjbizdaily.com.
126 Steven Allen Adams, "Out-of-State Companies, Campaign Donors Make Up Majority of West Virginia's Medical Cannabis Growers," *Parkersburg News and Sentinel*, October 17, 2020, www.newsandsentinel.com.
127 Hemp is a cannabis sativa plant, and there is a federal statute that imposes specific restrictions on its THC content. The Code of Federal Regulations classifies it as follows: "The plant species *Cannabis sativa* L. and any part of that plant, including the seeds thereof and all derivatives, extracts, cannabinoids, isomers, acids, salts, and salts of isomers, whether growing or not, with a total delta-9 tetrahydrocannabinol concentration of not more than 0.3 percent on a dry weight basis" (7 CFR 990.1).
128 Adams, "Out-of-State Companies, Campaign Donors Make Up Majority of West Virginia's Medical Cannabis Growers."
129 Lexi Browning, "WV Medical Marijuana Market Still on Hold," *Daily Mail WV*, May 14, 2020, www.wvgazettemail.com/dailymailwv.
130 Azcarate et al., "Medical Reasons for Marijuana Use, Forms of Use, and Patient Perception of Physician Attitudes among the US Population."
131 Pennsylvania General Assembly, "2016 Act 16: Medical Marijuana Act—Enactment," April 17, 2016, www.legis.state.pa.us.
132 Ed Mahon, "Why Pennsylvania's Health Department Is Taking Spotlight PA to Court," *Spotlight PA*, May 10, 2022, www.spotlightpa.org.
133 Tim Silfies, "Pennsylvania's First Marijuana Dispensary Opens in Bethlehem," *WFMZ-TV*, October 1, 2019, www.wfmz.com.

134 Sam Wood, "Philadelphia Will Get Shops to Sell Pot," *Philadelphia Inquirer*, April 26, 2018.
135 Nick Evans, "Ohio Senators Mulling Major Revisions to Medical Marijuana System," *Ohio Capital Journal*, November 11, 2021, https://ohiocapitaljournal.com.
136 Janelle Patterson, "Marijuana Dispensary Sparks Concerns," *Marietta Times*, June 28, 2018, www.mariettatimes.com.
137 Chris Stewart, "Neighbors: Medical Marijuana Shops Will Attract Problems," *Dayton Daily News*, June 10, 2018, www.daytondailynews.com.
138 Sarah Volpenhein, "Medical Marijuana Sparks Debate at Special Council Meeting," *Marion Star*, October 31, 2017, www.marionstar.com.
139 Jeff Smith, "West Virginia's Long-Delayed Medical Marijuana Market Poised to Launch," *MJBizDaily*, December 17, 2021, https://mjbizdaily.com.
140 Laura Hancock, "Ohio Regulators Want 73 New Medical Marijuana Dispensary Licenses to Address Demand, More Double Current Number," *Cleveland Plain Dealer*, April 11, 2022, www.cleveland.com.
141 Americans for Safe Access, *2022 State of the States Report* (Washington, DC: ASA, 2023), www.safeaccessnow.org/sos.
142 Americans for Safe Access, *2022 State of the States*.
143 Americans for Safe Access, *2022 State of the States*.
144 Americans for Safe Access, "State of the States Scoring Rubric—2021," February 2022, https://www.safeaccessnow.org/rubric#equity.
145 Mike Pushkin, personal (virtual) interview by A. Lee Hannah, July 6, 2022.
146 Jacqueline Howard, "A 'Catch-22' of Medical Marijuana and Organ Transplants," *CNN*, April 3, 2017, www.cnn.com.
147 Hannah, "The Politics of Passing and Implementing Medical Marijuana in Ohio."
148 Brad McElhinny, "Governor Justice Signs Medical Marijuana Bill," *MetroNews*, April 19, 2017, https://wvmetronews.com.
149 Pushkin, personal interview.
150 Pushkin, personal interview.

CHAPTER 4. WHEN POLICY CREATES POLITICS

1 Paul Demko, "How One of the Reddest States Became the Nation's Hottest Weed Market," *Politico*, November 27, 2020, www.politico.com.
2 Demko, "How One of the Reddest States Became the Nation's Hottest Weed Market."
3 Paul Demko, "Inside the Rise—and Surprising Crackdown—of the Country's Hottest Weed Market," *Politico*, November 12, 2021, www.politico.com.
4 Demko, "Inside the Rise—and Surprising Crackdown—of the Country's Hottest Weed Market."
5 "Medical Marijuana Legalization Passes NC Senate with Bipartisan Support," *News & Observer*, June 2, 2022, www.newsobserver.com.
6 Suzanne Mettler and Mallory SoRelle, "Policy Feedback Theory," in *Theories of the Policy Process*, ed. Christopher M. Weible and Paul A. Sabatier (New York: Westview Press, 2018), 103–134.

7 Mettler and SoRelle, "Policy Feedback Theory."
8 James G. March and Johan P. Olsen, "The Logic of Appropriateness," in *The Oxford Handbook of Public Policy*, ed. Michael Moran, Martin Rein, and Robert E. Goodin (Oxford: Oxford University Press, 2006), 689–708.
9 Robert A. Dahl, *Who Governs?* (New Haven, CT: Yale University Press, 1961).
10 Jack L. Walker, "The Origins and Maintenance of Interest Groups in America," *American Political Science Review* 77, no. 2 (1983), www.cambridge.org/core.
11 Frederick R. Lynch, *One Nation under AARP: The Fight over Medicare, Social Security, and America's Future* (Berkeley: University of California Press, 2011).
12 B. Dan Wood, "Principals, Bureaucrats, and Responsiveness in Clean Air Enforcements," *American Political Science Review* 82, no. 1 (1988), www.jstor.org.
13 Mettler and SoRelle, "Policy Feedback Theory."
14 For perspectives on statutory immigration policy, see Jia Lynn Yang, *One Mighty and Irresistible Tide: The Epic Struggle over American Immigration, 1924–1965* (New York: W. W. Norton, 2020); Louis DeSipio and Rodolfo O. De La Garza, *U.S. Immigration in the Twenty-First Century* (New York: Westview Press, 2015). See also Ted Brader, Nicholas A. Valentino, and Elizabeth Suhay, "What Triggers Public Opposition to Immigration? Anxiety, Group Cues, and Immigration Threat," *American Journal of Political Science* 52, no. 4 (2008), https://onlinelibrary.wiley.com; Thomas C. Wilson, "Americans' Views on Immigration Policy: Testing the Role of Threatened Group Interests," *Sociological Perspectives* 44, no. 4 (2001), https://journals.sagepub.com.
15 Amanda Chicago Lewis, "California Legalized Weed Five Years Ago: Why Is the Illicit Market Still Thriving?" *The Guardian*, November 2, 2021, www.theguardian.com.
16 Deborah Stone, *Policy Paradox*, 3rd ed. (New York: W. W. Norton, 2012).
17 Robert A. Dahl, *How Democratic Is the American Constitution?* (New Haven, CT: Yale University Press, 2003).
18 Daniel J. Mallinson, "The Color of Mass Incarceration," in *Race in America: How a Pseudo-Scientific Concept Shaped Human Interaction*, ed. Patricia Reid-Merritt (Santa Barbara, CA: ABC-CLIO, 2017), 433–466.
19 J. O. E. Soss and Sanford F. Schram, "A Public Transformed? Welfare Reform as Policy Feedback," *American Political Science Review* 101, no. 1 (2007), www.cambridge.org/core/. Dionne Bensonsmith, "Jezebels, Matriarchs, and Welfare Queens: The Moynihan Report of 1965 and the Social Construction of African-American Women in Welfare Policy," *Deserving and Entitled: Social Constructions and Public Policy* (2005).
20 Suzanne Mettler, "Bringing the State Back In to Civic Engagement: Policy Feedback Effects of the G.I. Bill for World War II Veterans," *American Political Science Review* 96, no. 2 (2002), www.cambridge.org/core.
21 Margot Canaday, *The Straight State: Sexuality and Citizenship in Twentieth-Century America* (Princeton, NJ: Princeton University Press, 2009).

22 Amany Hulaihel, Or Gliksberg, Daniel Feingold, Silviu Brill, Ben H. Amit, Shaul Lev-ran, and Sharon R. Sznitman, "Medical Cannabis and Stigma: A Qualitative Study with Patients Living with Chronic Pain," *Journal of Clinical Nursing* 32, no. 7–8 (2023), https://onlinelibrary.wiley.com.
23 Cameron Duff and Patricia G. Erickson, "Cannabis, Risk and Normalisation: Evidence from a Canadian Study of Socially Integrated, Adult Cannabis Users," *Health, Risk & Society* 16, no. 3 (2014), www.tandfonline.com/; Shahida Anusha Siddiqui, Prachi Singh, Sipper Khan, Ito Fernando, Igor Spartakovich Baklanov, Tigran Garrievich Ambartsumov, and Salam A. Ibrahim, "Cultural, Social and Psychological Factors of the Conservative Consumer towards Legal Cannabis—A Review since 2013," *Sustainability* 14, no. 17 (2022), www.mdpi.com.
24 Anne Schneider and Helen Ingram, *Policy Design for Democracy* (Lawrence: University of Kansas Press, 1997).
25 Covadonga Meseguer, "Policy Learning, Policy Diffusion, and the Making of a New Order," *The ANNALS of the American Academy of Political and Social Science* 598 (2005); Covadonga Meseguer, "Rational Learning and Bounded Learning in the Diffusion of Policy Innovations," *Rationality and Society* 18, no. 1 (2006); Covadonga Meseguer, *Learning, Policy Making, and Market Reforms* (Cambridge: Cambridge University Press, 2009).
26 Herbert A. Simon, "A Behavioral Model of Rational Choice," *Quarterly Journal of Economics* 69, no. 1 (February 1, 1955), http://qje.oxfordjournals.org; Herbert A. Simon, *Models of Man: Social and Rational* (New York: Wiley, 1957).
27 Lawrence J. Grossback, Sean Nicholson-Crotty, and David A. M. Peterson, "Ideology and Learning in Policy Diffusion," *American Politics Research* 32, no. 5 (2004).
28 Grossback, Nicholson-Crotty, and Peterson, "Ideology and Learning in Policy Diffusion"; Daniel M. Butler, Craig Volden, Adam M. Dynes, and Boris Shor, "Ideology, Learning, and Policy Diffusion: Experimental Evidence," *American Journal of Political Science* 61, no. 1 (2017), https://onlinelibrary.wiley.com.
29 Rosalie Liccardo Pacula and Rosanna Smart, "Medical Marijuana and Marijuana Legalization," *Annual Review of Clinical Psychology* 13, no. 1 (2017), www.annualreviews.org.
30 Daniel J. Mallinson and A. Lee Hannah, "Policy and Political Learning: The Development of Medical Marijuana Policies in the States," *Publius: The Journal of Federalism* 50, no. 3 (2020).
31 Robert A. Mikos, "A Critical Appraisal of the Department of Justice's New Approach to Medical Marijuana," *Stanford Law & Policy Review* 22, no. 2 (2011), https://law.stanford.edu/stanford-law-policy-review-slpr/; David W. Ogden, "Investigations and Prosecutions in States Authorizing the Medical Use of Marijuana," Office of the Deputy Attorney General, memorandum, Washington, DC, 2009.
32 Arthur Robin Williams, Mark Olfson, June H. Kim, Silvia S. Martins, and Herbert D. Kleber, "Older, Less Regulated Medical Marijuana Programs Have Much

Greater Enrollment Rates than Newer 'Medicalized' Programs," *Health Affairs* 35, no. 3 (2016), www.healthaffairs.org.
33 James M. Cole, "Guidance Regarding Marijuana Enforcement," memorandum, Washington, DC, 2013.
34 John Schroyer, "The Famous Marijuana Memos: Q&A with Former DOJ Deputy Attorney General James Cole," *MJBizDaily*, July 27, 2016, https://mjbizdaily.com.
35 Schroyer, "The Famous Marijuana Memos: Q&A with Former DOJ Deputy Attorney General James Cole."
36 Sarah B. Klieger, Abraham Gutman, Leslie Allen, Rosalie Liccardo Pacula, Jennifer K. Ibrahim, and Scott Burris, "Mapping Medical Marijuana: State Laws Regulating Patients, Product Safety, Supply Chains and Dispensaries, 2017," *Addiction* 112, no. 12 (2017), https://onlinelibrary.wiley.com.
37 For example, see James E. Lange, Susette A. Moyers, and Julie M. Croff, "Responsible Cannabis Sales: A Narrative Review Considering Interventions for Dispensary Staff to Address Cannabis Harms," *Public Administration Quarterly* 47, no. 3 (2023), https://paq.spaef.org.
38 Ira Shefer, "Policy Transfer in City-to-City Cooperation: Implications for Urban Climate Governance Learning," *Journal of Environmental Policy & Planning* 21, no. 1 (2019), https://www.tandfonline.com; Wolfgang Haupt, "How Do Local Policy Makers Learn about Climate Change Adaptation Policies? Examining Study Visits as an Instrument of Policy Learning in the European Union," *Urban Affairs Review* 57, no. 6 (2021), https://journals.sagepub.com; Astrid Wood, "Learning through Policy Tourism: Circulating Bus Rapid Transit from South America to South Africa," *Environment and Planning A: Economy and Space* 46, no. 11 (2014), https://journals.sagepub.com; Liang Ma, "Site Visits, Policy Learning, and the Diffusion of Policy Innovation: Evidence from Public Bicycle Programs in China," *Journal of Chinese Political Science* 22, no. 4 (2017), https://link.springer.com.
39 PDAPS is a longitudinal dataset displaying medical marijuana laws in effect as of January 1, 2014, through February 1, 2017; see PDAPS, "Medical Marijuana Laws for Patients," Prescription Drug Abuse Policy System, accessed March 23, 2023, https://pdaps.org/datasets/medical-marijuana-patient-related-laws-1501600783.
40 For descriptions of the qualifying conditions authorized in each state, see NORML, "Medical Marijuana Laws," accessed September 7, 2023, https://norml.org/laws/medical-laws.
41 Kevin F. Boehnke, Saurav Gangopadhyay, Daniel J. Clauw, and Rebecca L. Haffajee, "Qualifying Conditions of Medical Cannabis License Holders in the United States," *Health Affairs* 38, no. 2 (2019), www.healthaffairs.org; Kevin F. Boehnke, Owen Dean, Rebecca L. Haffajee, and Avinash Hosanagar, "U.S. Trends in Registration for Medical Cannabis and Reasons for Use from 2016 to 2020: An Observational Study," *Annals of Internal Medicine* 175, no. 7 (2022), https://www.acpjournals.org.
42 M. B. Bridgeman and D. T. Abazia, "Medicinal Cannabis: History, Pharmacology, and Implications for the Acute Care Setting," *Pharmacy and Therapeutics* 42, no. 3 (March 2017).

43 Andrew Karch and Shanna Rose, *Responsive States: Federalism and American Public Policy* (Cambridge: Cambridge University Press, 2019).
44 Sveinung Sandberg, "The Importance of Culture for Cannabis Markets: Towards an Economic Sociology of Illegal Drug Markets," *British Journal of Criminology* 52, no. 6 (2012), https://academic.oup.com/bjc.
45 Patricia A. Cavazos-Rehg, Melissa J. Krauss, Shaina J. Sowles, and Laura J. Bierut, "Marijuana-Related Posts on Instagram," *Prevention Science: The Official Journal of the Society for Prevention Research* 17, no. 6 (2016), https://pubmed.ncbi.nlm.nih.gov.
46 Silje Anderdal Bakken and Sidsel Kirstine Harder, "From Dealing to Influencing: Online Marketing of Cannabis on Instagram," *Crime, Media, Culture* 19, no. 1 (2023), https://journals.sagepub.com.
47 Sandberg, "The Importance of Culture for Cannabis Markets: Towards an Economic Sociology of Illegal Drug Markets."
48 Anderdal Bakken and Kirstine Harder, "From Dealing to Influencing: Online Marketing of Cannabis on Instagram," 18.
49 Susan Dupej and Sanjay K. Nepal, "Tourism as an Agent of Cannabis Normalization: Perspectives from Canada," *Tourism Review International* 25, no. 4 (2021), www.ingentaconnect.com; Rachel F. Giraudo, "Cannabis Culture on Display: Deviant Heritage Comes Out of the Shadows," *Museum Worlds: Advances in Research* 8, no. 1 (2020), www.berghahnjournals.com.
50 Dupej and Nepal, "Tourism as an Agent of Cannabis Normalization: Perspectives from Canada," 353.
51 Kyle Jaeger, "California State Fair Announces Winners of First-Ever State-Sanctioned Cannabis Competition," *Marijuana Moment*, June 27, 2022, www.marijuanamoment.net.
52 Jaeger, "California State Fair Announces Winners of First-Ever State-Sanctioned Cannabis Competition."
53 Harrison J. VanDolah, Brent A. Bauer, and Karen F. Mauck, "Clinicians' Guide to Cannabidiol and Hemp Oils," *Mayo Clinic Proceedings* 94, no. 9 (2019); Nichola Black, Emily Stockings, Gabrielle Campbell, Lucy T. Tran, Dino Zagic, Wayne D. Hall, Michael Farrell, et al., "Cannabinoids for the Treatment of Mental Disorders and Symptoms of Mental Disorders: A Systematic Review and Meta-Analysis," *The Lancet Psychiatry* 6, no. 12 (2019).
54 Congressional Research Service, "Comparing Hemp Provisions in the 2014 and 2018 Farm Bills," *In Focus*, December 2, 2021, https://crsreports.congress.gov.
55 John Hudak, "The Farm Bill, Hemp Legalization and the Status of CBD: An Explainer," *Brookings Institution*, December 14, 2018, www.brookings.edu.
56 Danielle McCartney, Melissa J. Benson, Ben Desbrow, Christopher Irwin, Anastasia Suraev, and Iain S, McGregor, "Cannabidiol and Sports Performance: A Narrative Review of Relevant Evidence and Recommendations for Future Research," *Sports Medicine—Open* 6, no. 1 (2020), https://pubmed.ncbi.nlm.nih.gov.
57 Matej Mikulic, "Total U.S. Cannabidiol (CBD) Product Sales 2014–2022," *Statista*, July 27, 2022, 2022, https://www.statista.com/statistics/760498/total-us-cbd-sales.

58 Andrew Jacobs, "F.D.A. Seeks More Authority to Oversee CBD Products," *New York Times*, January 6, 2023; Hudak, "The Farm Bill, Hemp Legalization and the Status of CBD: An Explainer."
59 Jaclyn Diaz, "Gary Chambers' New Pot-Smoking Campaign Ad in Senate Race Goes Viral with Old Tactics," *NPR*, January 20, 2022, www.npr.org.
60 Kaitlin Lange, "Senate Democratic Candidate Tom McDermott Smokes Weed in Political Ad to Celebrate 4/20," *Indianapolis Star*, April 20, 2022, www.indystar.com.
61 Katharine Q. Seelye, "Barack Obama, Asked about Drug History, Admits He Inhaled," *New York Times*, October 24, 2006, www.nytimes.com.
62 Caitlin Byrd, "It Took SC Rep. Nancy Mace 25 Years to Share She Was Raped. She Never Expected This," *Post and Courier*, January 7, 2021, www.postandcourier.com; Will Yakowicz, "Republican Congresswoman Nancy Mace Is on a Mission to Legalize Cannabis—and Amazon Just Got behind Her," *Forbes*, January 25, 2022, www.forbes.com.
63 It is notable that not all states in figure 4.4 have comprehensive medical cannabis programs (e.g., Texas), but they do provide limited access to low-THC cannabis products and thus regulate that access.
64 Tiffany Kary, "Cannabis Banking Is Booming despite Federal Uncertainty," *Bloomberg*, January 18, 2022, www.bloomberg.com.
65 John Hudak and Christine Stenglein, "Public Opinion and America's Experimentation with Cannabis Reform," in *Marijuana Federalism: Uncle Sam and Mary Jane*, ed. Jonathan H. Adler (Washington, DC: Brookings Institution Press, 2020), 15–34.
66 Jeffrey Miron and Nicholas Anthony, "Cannabis Banking: A Clash between Federal and State Laws," *Cato Institute*, May 27, 2022, www.cato.org/blog.
67 Ken McCarthy, "Banks Set to Move in on Credit Unions' Cannabis Turf," *American Banker*, June 30, 2021, www.americanbanker.com; Christoph Henkel and Randall K. Johnson, "Why U.S. States Need Their Own Cannabis Industry Banks," 101 *Washington University Law Review Online* (2023), https://ssrn.com.
68 Richard Rothstein, *The Color of Law: A Forgotten History of How Our Government Segregated America* (New York: W. W. Norton, 2017); Michelle Alexander, *The New Jim Crow: Mass Incarceration in the Age of Colorblindness* (New York: The New Press, 2010); Kathleen Belew, *Bring the War Home: The White Power Movement and Paramilitary America* (Cambridge, MA: Harvard University Press, 2018).
69 Jeremy Berke and Yeji Jesse Lee, "Top Executives at the 14 Largest Cannabis Companies Are Overwhelmingly White Men, an Insider Analysis Shows," *Business Insider*, June 30, 2021, www.businessinsider.com; American Civil Liberties Union, "A Tale of Two Countries: Racially Targeted Arrests in the Era of Marijuana Reform Details Millions of Racially Targeted Arrests Made between 2010–2018," news release, April 20, 2020, www.aclu.org.
70 Jeff Smith, "Large Cannabis Operators Positioned to Dominate Potential Arizona Recreational Cannabis Market, Shut Out Small Businesses," *MJBizDaily*, December 17, 2021, https://mjbizdaily.com.

71 Dalton Conley, *Being Black, Living in the Red: Race, Wealth, and Social Policy in America* (Berkeley: University of California Press, 2010).
72 Berke and Lee, "Top Executives at the 14 Largest Cannabis Companies Are Overwhelmingly White Men, an Insider Analysis Shows."
73 Eli McVey, "Chart: Percentage of Cannabis Business Owners and Founders by Race," *MJBizDaily*, September 9, 2022, https://mjbizdaily.com/chart-19-cannabis-businesses-owned-founded-racial-minorities.
74 Shaleen Title, "Fair and Square: How to Effectively Incorporate Social Equity Into Cannabis Laws and Regulations," Drug Enforcement and Policy Center, December 6, 2021, https://papers.ssrn.com.
75 Nyron N. Crawford, "We'd Go Well Together: A Critical Race Analysis of Marijuana Legalization and Expungement in the United States," *Public Integrity* 23, no. 5 (2021), www.tandfonline.com.
76 Nyron N. Crawford, "Lost Boys, Invisible Men: Racialized Policy Feedback after Marijuana Reform," *Public Administration Quarterly* 47, no. 3 (2023), https://paq.spaef.org.
77 Jennifer A. Kingson, "Racial Equity Is Elusive in the Legal Weed Business," *Axios*, September 15, 2021, 2021, www.axios.com.
78 Meghan Thompson, "Data Reveals Lack of Minority Investors in Maryland Cannabis Industry," *Capital News Service*, May 26, 2020, https://cnsmaryland.org.
79 Alfred Lee Hannah, Daniel J. Mallinson, and Lauren Azevedo, "Maximizing Social Equity as a Pillar of Public Administration: An Examination of Cannabis Dispensary Licensing in Pennsylvania," *Public Administration Review* 83, no. 1 (2023), https://onlinelibrary.wiley.com.
80 Hannah, Mallinson, and Azevedo, "Maximizing Social Equity as a Pillar of Public Administration: An Examination of Cannabis Dispensary Licensing in Pennsylvania."
81 Kingson, "Racial Equity Is Elusive in the Legal Weed Business."
82 Kingson, "Racial Equity Is Elusive in the Legal Weed Business."
83 Title, "Fair and Square: How to Effectively Incorporate Social Equity Into Cannabis Laws and Regulations," 12.
84 Sam Wood, "Jefferson Set to Study Pot Effects," *Philadelphia Inquirer*, March 6, 2020.
85 Jeff Smith, "Company Tapped by DEA to Grow Marijuana for Research Files to List on Nasdaq," *Marijuana Business Daily*, March 29, 2022, https://mjbizdaily.com.
86 Sharon R. Sznitman and Anne Line Bretteville-Jensen, "Public Opinion and Medical Cannabis Policies: Examining the Role of Underlying Beliefs and National Medical Cannabis Policies," *Harm Reduction Journal* 12, no. 1 (2015), https://harmreductionjournal.biomedcentral.com.
87 Beau Kilmer and Robert J. MacCoun, "How Medical Marijuana Smoothed the Transition to Marijuana Legalization in the United States," *Annual Review of Law and Social Science* 13, no. 1 (2017), www.annualreviews.org.
88 It is important to recognize, though, that the claim that simply releasing all nonviolent drug offenders would eliminate mass incarceration is a myth. A full

80 percent of individuals in prison or jail in 2022 were incarcerated for something other than a drug offense. See Prison Policy Initiative, "Mass Incarceration: The Whole Pie 2022," news release, March 14, 2022, www.prisonpolicy.org.
89. Jacob Felson, Amy Adamczyk, and Christopher Thomas, "How and Why Have Attitudes about Cannabis Legalization Changed So Much?" *Social Science Research* 78 (2019), www.sciencedirect.com.
90. Vivian Chiu, Wayne Hall, Gary Chan, Leanne Hides, and Janni Leung, "A Systematic Review of Trends in US Attitudes toward Cannabis Legalization," *Substance Use & Misuse* 57, no. 7 (2022), https://www.tandfonline.com.
91. Rosalie Liccardo Pacula, David Powell, Paul Heaton, and Eric L. Sevigny, "Assessing the Effects of Medical Marijuana Laws on Marijuana Use: The Devil Is in the Details," *Journal of Policy Analysis and Management* 34, no. 1 (Winter 2015), www.ncbi.nlm.nih.gov; Rosanna Smart and Rosalie Liccardo Pacula, "Early Evidence of the Impact of cannabis legalization on Cannabis Use, Cannabis Use Disorder, and the Use of Other Substances: Findings from State Policy Evaluations," *American Journal of Drug and Alcohol Abuse* 45, no. 6 (2019), www.tandfonline.com; Christopher J. Hammond, Aldorian Chaney, Brian Hendrickson, and Pravesh Sharma, "Cannabis Use among U.S. Adolescents in the Era of Marijuana Legalization: A Review of Changing Use Patterns, Comorbidity, and Health Correlates," *International Review of Psychiatry* 32, no. 3 (2020), www.tandfonline.com; Maria Melchior, Aurélie Nakamura, Camille Bolze, Félix Hausfater, Fabienne El Khoury, Murielle Mary-Krause, and Marine Azevedo Da Silva, "Does Liberalisation of Cannabis Policy Influence Levels of Use in Adolescents and Young Adults? A Systematic Review and Meta-analysis," *BMJ Open* 9, no. 7 (2019), https://bmjopen.bmj.com; D. Mark Anderson, Benjamin Hansen, Daniel I. Rees, and Joseph J. Sabia, "Association of Marijuana Laws with Teen Marijuana Use: New Estimates from the Youth Risk Behavior Surveys," *JAMA Pediatrics* 173, no. 9 (2019), https://jamanetwork.com; Rebekah Levine Coley, Claudia Kruzik, Marco Ghiani, Naoka Carey, Summer Sherburne Hawkins, and Christopher F. Baum, "Recreational Marijuana Legalization and Adolescent Use of Marijuana, Tobacco, and Alcohol," *Journal of Adolescent Health* 69, no. 1 (2021), www.sciencedirect.com; Sarah B. Windle, Peter Socha, José Ignacio Nazif-Munoz, Sam Harper, and Arijit Nandi, "The Impact of Cannabis Decriminalization and Legalization on Road Safety Outcomes: A Systematic Review," *American Journal of Preventive Medicine* 63, no. 6 (2022), www.sciencedirect.com.
92. Sylia Wilson and Soo Hyun Rhee, "Causal Effects of Cannabis Legalization on Parents, Parenting, and Children: A Systematic Review," *Preventive Medicine* 156 (2022), www.sciencedirect.com; Barrett Wallace Montgomery, Meaghan H. Roberts, Claire E. Margerison, and James C. Anthony, "Estimating the Effects of Legalizing Recreational Cannabis on Newly Incident Cannabis Use," *PLOS ONE* 17, no. 7 (2022), https://journals.plos.org/plosone/; Megan A. O'Grady, Marissa G. Iverson, Adekemi O. Suleiman, and Taeho Greg Rhee, "Is Legalization of Recreational Cannabis Associated with Levels of Use and Cannabis Use Disorder

among Youth in the United States? A Rapid Systematic Review," *European Child & Adolescent Psychiatry* (2022), https://link.springer.com; Charles M. Farmer, Samuel S. Monfort, and Amber N. Woods, "Changes in Traffic Crash Rates after Legalization of Marijuana: Results by Crash Severity," *Journal of Studies on Alcohol and Drugs* 83, no. 4 (2022), www.jsad.com.

93 Jesse Hinckley, Devika Bhatia, Jarrod Ellingson, Karla Molinero, and Christian Hopfer, "The Impact of Recreational Cannabis Legalization on Youth: The Colorado Experience," *European Child & Adolescent Psychiatry* (2022), https://link.springer.com/; Nicole V. Tolan, Tolumofe Terebo, Peter R. Chai, Timothy B. Erickson, Bryan D. Hayes, Sacha N. Uljon, Athena K. Petrides, et al., "Impact of Marijuana Legalization on Cannabis-Related Visits to the Emergency Department," *Clinical Toxicology* 60, no. 5 (2022), www.tandfonline.com; Andrea H. Weinberger, Katarzyna Wyka, and Renee D. Goodwin, "Impact of Cannabis Legalization in the United States on Trends in Cannabis Use and Daily Cannabis Use among Individuals Who Smoke Cigarettes," *Drug and Alcohol Dependence* 238 (2022), www.sciencedirect.com; Christopher Wheldon, Ryan J. Watson, Casey Cunningham, and Jessica N. Fish, "State Marijuana Laws and Marijuana Use among Sexual and Gender Minority Youth in the United States," *LGBT Health* 10, no. 2 (2023), www.liebertpub.com.

94 Ashley C. Bradford and W. David Bradford, "Medical Marijuana Laws Reduce Prescription Medication Use in Medicare Part D," *Health Affairs* 35, no. 7 (2016), www.healthaffairs.org; Ashley C. Bradford, W. David Bradford, Amanda Abraham, and Grace Bagwell Adams, "Association between US State Medical Cannabis Laws and Opioid Prescribing in the Medicare Part D Population," *JAMA Internal Medicine* 178, no. 5 (2018), https://jamanetwork.com/; Marcus A. Bachhuber, Brendan Saloner, Chinazo O. Cunningham, and Colleen L. Barry, "Medical Cannabis Laws and Opioid Analgesic Overdose Mortality in the United States, 1999–2010," *JAMA Internal Medicine* 174, no. 10 (2014), https://jamanetwork.com/; Yuyan Shi, "Medical Marijuana Policies and Hospitalizations Related to Marijuana and Opioid Pain Reliever," *Drug and Alcohol Dependence* 173 (2017), www.sciencedirect.com/science; Hefei Wen and Jason M. Hockenberry, "Association of Medical and Adult-Use Marijuana Laws with Opioid Prescribing for Medicaid Enrollees," *JAMA Internal Medicine* 178, no. 5 (2018), https://jamanetwork.com/; G. Benedict, A. Sabbagh, and T. Conermann, "Medical Cannabis Used as an Alternative Treatment for Chronic Pain Demonstrates Reduction in Chronic Opioid Use—A Prospective Study," *Pain Physician* 25, no. 1 (January 2022); Neil K. Mathur and Christopher J. Ruhm, "Marijuana Legalization and Opioid Deaths," *Journal of Health Economics* 88 (2023), www.sciencedirect.com; Archie Bleyer, Brian Barnes, and Kenneth Finn, "United States Marijuana Legalization and Opioid Mortality Epidemic during 2010–2020 and Pandemic Implications," *Journal of the National Medical Association* 114, no. 4 (2022).

95 Kilmer and MacCoun, "How Medical Marijuana Smoothed the Transition to Marijuana Legalization in the United States," 181.

96 "Marijuana Industry Will Add Nearly $100 Billion to US Economy in 2022," *MJBizDaily*, April 11, 2022, https://mjbizdaily.com.
97 Barcott and Whitney, *Jobs Report 2022*.
98 Barcott and Whitney, *Jobs Report 2022*.
99 The Weedmaps billboard campaign, also known as the #weedfacts campaign, is detailed at "Learn the Facts, Drive the Movement," accessed April 10, 2023, https://weedmaps.com/weedfacts.
100 S. Lancione, K. Wade, S. B. Windle, K. B. Filion, B. D. Thombs, and M. J. Eisenberg, "Non-Medical Cannabis in North America: An Overview of Regulatory Approaches," *Public Health* 178 (2020), www.sciencedirect.com; David M. Yaskewich, "Local Prohibitions on Marijuana: Factors Associated with Bans on Medical and Recreational Businesses," *Contemporary Drug Problems* 49, no. 4 (2022), https://journals.sagepub.com/; Jeffrey Moyer and Sungu-Eryilmaz, "Understanding Local Control in the Wake of State Adult-Use Cannabis Liberalization," *Public Administration Quarterly* 47, no. 3 (2023), https://paq.spaef.org.
101 Daniel J. Mallinson, A. Lee Hannah, and Gideon Cunningham, "The Consequences of Fickle Federal Policy: Administrative Hurdles for State Cannabis Policies," *State and Local Government Review* 52, no. 4 (2020), https://journals.sagepub.com.
102 Jonathan H. Adler, ed., *Marijuana Federalism: Uncle Sam and Mary Jane* (Washington, DC: Brookings Institution Press, 2020).
103 Americans for Safe Access, "Legalization of Cannabis for Recreational Use," n.d., accessed July 8, 2022, https://www.safeaccessnow.org/legalization_of_cannabis_for_recreational_use.
104 Graeme Zielinski, "Activist Robert C. Randall Dies," *Washington Post*, June 8, 2001, www.washingtonpost.com.
105 Justin Franz, "Medical Marijuana Users Brace for Shortages as Montana's Recreational Market Opens," *Kaiser Health News*, January 5, 2022, https://khn.org/news/article.
106 Americans for Safe Access, *Medical Marijuana Access in the United States: A Patient-Focused Analysis of the Patchwork of State Laws*, (Washington, DC: ASA, 2017), https://american-safe-access.s3.amazonaws.com/sos2017/ASA_state_of_state_report_2017_14_online.pdf.
107 Joseph O'Sullivan, "Patients Fear Medical Pot May Not Fare Well with New Rules," *Seattle Times*, April 25, 2016, www.seattletimes.com.
108 Washington State Liquor and Cannabis Board, "Preparations in Place for July 1 Alignment of Medical and Recreational Marijuana Systems," news release, 2016, https://lcb.wa.gov/pressreleases/alignment-med-and-rec-mj-systems.
109 Omar Sacirbey, "WA Readies for Bumpy Ride as State's Medical, Rec Markets Merge," *MJBizDaily*, December 17, 2021, https://mjbizdaily.com.
110 "WA Legislature Must Act on High-Potency Cannabis," *Seattle Times*, February 9, 2023, www.seattletimes.com.
111 Brad Racino, "NY's Medical Marijuana Program Suffering as State Focuses on a Recreational Market," *Syracuse.com*, June 8, 2022, www.syracuse.com.

112 Racino, "NY's Medical Marijuana Program Suffering as State Focuses on a Recreational Market."
113 Racino, "NY's Medical Marijuana Program Suffering as State Focuses on a Recreational Market."
114 Stephon Johnson, "Gray Market Thrives Even as Licensed Weed Takes Root in Greenwich Village," *The City*, February 3, 2023, www.thecity.nyc.
115 "E. Coli, Heavy Metals, Copyright Infringement, and 100 Percent Failure Rate," New York Medical Cannabis Industry Association, New Jersey Cannabis Trade Association, and Connecticut Medical Cannabis Council, November 2022, https://leafly-cms-production.imgix.net/wp-content/uploads/2022/11/30124236/Leafly-NYC-Illicit-Cannabis-Market.pdf.
116 "Why Are Illinois Medical Marijuana Dispensaries Limiting Their Sales?" *CBS News Chicago*, November 26, 2019, www.cbsnews.com/chicago.
117 Erik Sofranko, "New Illinois Cannabis Law Presents Challenges for Medical Patients," *CU-Citizen Access*, June 2, 2020, https://cu-citizenaccess.org.
118 Sarah Schulte, "Medical Marijuana Shortages in Illinois Reported at Dispensaries since Legalization," *ABC 7 Eyewitness News*, January 20, 2020, https://abc7chicago.com.
119 Sofranko, "New Illinois Cannabis Law Presents Challenges for Medical Patients."
120 Schulte, "Medical Marijuana Shortages in Illinois Reported at Dispensaries since Legalization."
121 Robert McCoppin, "Rough 2022 for Illinois Marijuana Industry Leads to Higher Hopes for the New Year," *Chicago Tribune*, January 1, 2023, www.chicagotribune.com.
122 Jordan Nathaniel Fenster, "With Concerns about Medical Cannabis Supply Shortage, CT Lawmakers Look to Create Ombudsman Job," *CT Insider*, February 21, 2023, www.ctinsider.com.
123 Fenster, "With Concerns about Medical Cannabis Supply Shortage, CT Lawmakers Look to Create Ombudsman Job."
124 David Abbott, "Arizona Recreational Marijuana Sales Hit New Record, Medical Sales Slip Again," *Tucson Sentinel*, January 11, 2023, www.tucsonsentinel.com.
125 Tony Lange, Michigan's Medical Market Prognosis," *Cannabis Business Times*, January 2023, www.cannabisbusinesstimes.com.
126 Lange, "Michigan's Medical Market Prognosis."
127 Lange, "Michigan's Medical Market Prognosis."
128 "Some Arkansas Marijuana Activists Oppose Legalization Measure on November Ballot," *Marijuana Moment*, August 17, 2022, www.marijuanamoment.net.
129 Kyle Jaeger, "Lawmakers Must 'Step Up' and Address Federal-State Marijuana Conflict, Trucking Executive Tells Congress amid Labor Shortage," *Marijuana Moment*, February 6, 2023, www.marijuanamoment.net.
130 Parisa Kavousi, Taylor Giamo, Gwen Arnold, Mateo Alliende, Elisabeth Huynh, Jaclyn Lea, Rachel Lucine, et al., "What Do We Know about Opportunities and Challenges for Localities from Cannabis Legalization?" *Review of Policy Research*

39, no. 2 (2022), https://onlinelibrary.wiley.com; Keith Taylor, Nathan Goodman, Parisa Kavousi, Taylor Giamo, Gwen Arnold, and Zoe Plakias, "Economic Governance of Cannabis: The Implications of Polycentric Governance in Mendocino County," *Public Administration Quarterly* 47, no. 3 (2023), https://paq.spaef.org.
131 Adrianne Glenn, "False Representations: Media Portrayal of Marijuana," *The Pitt News*, April 19, 2015, https://pittnews.com; Partnership to End Addiction, "Marijuana Increasingly Depicted on Television," February 2015, https://drugfree.org.
132 Lisa Respers France, "Jim Belushi Believes Pot Would Have Saved His Brother John," *CNN*, August 20, 2020, www.cnn.com.
133 Jeff Tracy, "Where It Stands: Weed Policies by U.S. Sports League," *Axios*, October 20, 2021, www.axios.com.
134 Tom Haberstroh and Monte Poole, "Marijuana and the NBA: Erasing the Stigma and Healing the League," *NBC Sports Philadelphia*, February 27, 2020, www.nbcsportsphiladelphia.com.
135 Jabari Young, "Former NBA Forward Al Harrington Wants to Make 100 Black Individuals Millionaires through the Cannabis Business," *CNBC*, June 15, 2020, www.cnbc.com.
136 Partnership to End Addiction, "Marijuana Increasingly Depicted on Television."

CHAPTER 5. LABORATORIES IN LIMBO
 1 Natalie Fertig, "Budget Deal Is Latest Sign of Democrats' Empty Weed Promises," *Politico*, March 13, 2022.
 2 Joseph R. Biden Jr., "A Proclamation on Granting Pardon for the Offense of Simple Possession of Marijuana," The White House, October 6, 2022.
 3 Kyle Jaeger, "Biden Signs Marijuana Research Bill, a Historic First for Federal Cannabis Reform," *Marijuana Moment*, December 2, 2022, www.marijuanamoment.net.
 4 Kyle Jaeger, "Kansas Lawmakers Plan to Work on Medical Marijuana over Summer as 2022 Session Ends," *Marijuana Moment*, May 23, 2022, www.marijuanamoment.net.
 5 Daniel J. Mallinson, "Policy Innovation Adoption across the Diffusion Life Course," *Policy Studies Journal* 49, no. 2 (2021), https://onlinelibrary.wiley.com.
 6 Burrel Vann Jr., "Direct Democracy and the Adoption of Recreational Marijuana Legalization in the United States, 2012–2019," *International Journal of Drug Policy* 102 (2022), www.sciencedirect.com.
 7 Graeme Boushey, *Policy Diffusion Dynamics in America* (New York: Cambridge University Press, 2010).
 8 Daniel J. Mallinson, "Building a Better Speed Trap: Measuring Policy Adoption Speed in the American States," *State Politics & Policy Quarterly* 16, no. 1 (March 2016), https://journals.sagepub.com; Todd Makse and Craig Volden, "The Role of Policy Attributes in the Diffusion of Innovations," *Journal of Politics* 73, no. 1 (2011); Everett M. Rogers, *Diffusion of Innovations*, 5th ed. (New York: Free Press, 2003).

9. German Lopez, "Meet the Man Trying to Halt Marijuana Legalization," *Vox*, March 24, 2016, www.vox.com.
10. A. Lee Hannah and Daniel J. Mallinson, "Why It Will Be Difficult for Jeff Sessions to Put the Genie Back in the Bottle on Marijuana Policy," *London School of Economics, United States Politics and Policy* (blog), January 9, 2018, https://blogs.lse.ac.uk/usappblog.
11. Juhohn Lee, "America Has Spent over a Trillion Dollars Fighting the War on Drugs. 50 Years Later, Drug Use in the U.S. Is Climbing Again," *CNBC*, June 17, 2021, www.cnbc.com.
12. Michael Lind, "Obama and the Dawn of the Fourth Republic," *Salon*, November 7, 2008, www.salon.com; Ross Douthat, "The Obama Realignment," *New York Times*, November 7, 2012, https://archive.nytimes.com/campaignstops.blogs.nytimes.com/2012/11/07/douthat-the-obama-realignment.
13. Don Gonyea, "Why Republicans Are Out of Step with Young Voters," *NPR*, March 1, 2013, www.npr.org; Pew Research Center, "GOP Seen as Principled, but Out of Touch and Too Extreme," February 26, 2013, www.pewresearch.org.
14. David Gilbert, "Porn, Weed, and Single Moms: Everything the GOP Blames for School Shootings," *Vice*, June 8, 2022, www.vice.com.
15. Ben Blanchet, "Tucker Carlson Points Finger at Women and Weed for Latest Mass Shooting," *HuffPost*, July 6, 2022, www.huffpost.com.
16. Lester Black, "How Falling Pot Prices Killed a 3rd Generation Family Farm in California," *SF Gate*, December 14, 2022, www.sfgate.com.
17. Amanda Chicago Lewis, "California Legalized Weed Five Years Ago: Why Is the Illicit Market Still Thriving?" *The Guardian*, November 2, 2021, www.theguardian.com.
18. "Amid Explosion of Illegal Marijuana Production, Oregon Looks to Toughening Laws," *PBS News Hour*, December 8, 2022, www.pbs.org/newshour.
19. Alison Saldanha, "Armed Robberies at WA Pot Shops Hit Decade High," *Seattle Times*, December 26, 2022, www.seattletimes.com.
20. Dylan Goforth, Clifton Adcock, and Reese Gorman, "Oklahoma Didn't Say 'No' to Recreational Pot—It Said 'Hell No,'" *The Frontier*, March 8, 2023, www.readfrontier.org.
21. Goforth et al., "Oklahoma Didn't Say 'No' to Recreational Pot—It Said 'Hell No.'"
22. Sean Murphy, "Oklahoma Voters Reject Legalizing Recreational Marijuana," Associated Press, March 7, 2023, https://apnews.com.
23. International Narcotics Control Board, *Annual Report 2022* (Vienna: United Nations, 2023), https://unis.unvienna.org/unis/en/events/2023/incb_2022.html.
24. Charles R. Shipan and Craig Volden, "Bottom-Up Federalism: The Diffusion of Antismoking Policies from U.S. Cities to States," *American Journal of Political Science* 50, no. 4 (2006), www.jstor.org.
25. Drug Enforcement Agency, "Drug Scheduling," July 10, 2018, www.dea.gov/drug-information/drug-scheduling.

26 Omar Sacirbey, "Pros and Cons of Moving Marijuana from Schedule 1 on the List of Controlled Substances," *MJBizDaily*, March 1, 2022, https://mjbizdaily.com.
27 John Hudak and Grace Wallack. "How to Reschedule Marijuana, and Why It's Unlikely Anytime Soon," *Brookings Institution*, February 13, 2015, www.brookings.edu.
28 "How to End Marijuana Prohibition with Regard to the Controlled Substances Act," *NORML*, accessed March 24, 2023, https://norml.org/marijuana/fact-sheets.
29 Kyle Jaeger, "Bipartisan Group of 29 Congressional Lawmakers Pushes Biden to Back Marijuana Legalization," *Marijuana Moment*, December 22, 2022, www.marijuanamoment.net.
30 Shaleen Title and Matt Stoller, "Cannabis Legalization Must Address Monopoly Dangers," Parabola Center, September 21, 2022, www.parabolacenter.com.
31 Shaleen Title, "How to Ruin Marijuana Legalization: Put Big Alcohol and Tobacco Corporations in Charge," *Marijuana Moment*, November 17, 2022, www.marijuanamoment.net.
32 "The MORE Act," Marijuana Policy Project, accessed March 24, 2023, www.mpp.org/policy/federal/the-more-act.
33 Marijuana Opportunity Reinvestment and Expungement Act, H.R. 3617, 117th Cong. (2021–2022), www.congress.gov/bill/117th-congress/house-bill/3617.
34 Natalie Fertig, "House Passes Marijuana Legalization Bill (Again), but with No Clear Path Forward," *Politico*, April 1, 2022, www.politico.com.
35 "GOP Cannabis Caucus Leader Explains Why He Opposes Marijuana Legalization Bill Getting House Vote," *Marijuana Moment*, April 1, 2022, www.marijuanamoment.net.
36 SAFE Banking Act of 2021, H.R. 1996, 117th Cong. (2021–2022), www.congress.gov/bill/117th-congress/house-bill/1996/text.
37 Aris Folley and Karl Evers-Hillstrom, "Momentum Builds in Senate for Major Cannabis Bill," *The Hill*, May 4, 2022, https://thehill.com.
38 Dario Sabaghi, "Biden Signs Medical Marijuana Research Bill," *Forbes*, December 3, 2022, www.forbes.com.
39 Kyle Jaeger, "Top Federal Drug Agency Seeks New Suppliers of Marijuana for Research," *Marijuana Moment*, May 23, 2022, www.marijuanamoment.net.
40 Daniel J. Mallinson and Francisco Puello, "Veterans and Medical Cannabis: A Perfect Federalism Storm," *Public Administration Quarterly* 47, no. 3 (2023).
41 Natalie Fertig and Gavin Bade, "An Inconvenient Truth (about Weed)," *Politico*, August 10, 2021, www.politico.com.
42 Black, "How Falling Pot Prices Killed a 3rd Generation Family Farm in California."
43 Andrew Bahl, "With Legislative Session Dwindling, Odds of Legalizing Medical Marijuana Remain Uncertain," *Topeka Capital-Journal*, April 20, 2022, www.cjonline.com.
44 Jann S. Wenner, "The Day After: Obama on His Legacy, Trump's Win and the Path Forward," *Rolling Stone*, November 29, 2016, www.rollingstone.com.

45 Jacob Sullum, "On His Way Out the Door, Obama Suggests Marijuana Should Be Legal," *Reason*, November 30, 2016, https://reason.com; Chris Roberts, "Barack Obama's Marijuana Legacy: Thanks for Nothing," *High Times*, November 30, 2016, https://hightimes.com.
46 "Medical Marijuana Patient Numbers," Marijuana Policy Project, accessed July 8, 2022, www.mpp.org.

APPENDIX A

1 A. Lee Hannah and Daniel J. Mallinson, "Defiant Innovation: The Adoption of Medical Marijuana Laws in the American States," *Policy Studies Journal* 46, no. 2 (2018), https://onlinelibrary.wiley.com.

APPENDIX B

1 Sarah B. Klieger, Abraham Gutman, Leslie Allen, Rosalie Liccardo Pacula, Jennifer K. Ibrahim, and Scott Burris, "Mapping Medical Marijuana: State Laws Regulating Patients, Product Safety, Supply Chains and Dispensaries, 2017," *Addiction* 112, no. 12 (2017), https://onlinelibrary.wiley.com.
2 Mohsen Tavakol and Reg Dennick, "Making Sense of Cronbach's Alpha," *International Journal of Medical Education* 2 (2011), https://doi.org/10.5116%2Fijme.4dfb.8dfd.

INDEX

ABC. *See* media
adult-use marijuana (aka recreational), 1, 5, 7–8, 15–16, 21, 30, 36, 41, 44, 47–52, 54, 60, 66–67, 80–81, 84, 95, 98, 104, 116, 119, 122–125, 131–146, 150–157, 160–163, 195n88; adoption of recreational program, 125, 148–152; policy implementation, 94; recreational impact on medical, 136–144
advocacy coalition, 89
Advocacy Coalition Framework (ACF), 12
Afghanistan (war in), 40–41
agenda setting, 10, 14, 23–26, 46, 49, 50, 52, 119, 148; framing, 13, 14, 26, 29–32, 37, 41, 46, 52, 103, 149; Multiple Streams Framework (MSF), 10, 23–32, 52, 149
Agriculture Improvement Act of 2018 (aka the farm bill), 96, 130
AIDS: approved conditions, 29, 40, 126, 175–176; media coverage of, 40–42, 47; patients, 17, 27–29, 33, 159
Alaska, 1, 65
Amendment 2 (Missouri), 53–54
Americans for Safe Access (ASA), 47, 89, 139; state policy ratings, 110–114. *See also* interest group
Anslinger, Harry, 6–7
Anti-Drug Abuse Act of 1986, 23
anti-marijuana, 18, 19, 154
Arizona, 1, 4, 8, 94, 127; adoption of medical program, 63–64; impact of recreational program, 142–143
Arkansas, 1, 54, 144, 155
attorney. *See* U.S. attorney

attorney general, 34, 93, 95, 158, 163; Bill Barr, 97; Dan Lungren, 63–64; James Cole (deputy), 124; Jeff Sessions, 2, 96–98; John Ashcroft, 65; Josh Hawley, 54; Merrick Garland, 97; Patrick Morrisey, 106; Janet Reno, 63
attorneys general, 61, 162

banking, 44, 97, 115, 119, 132–133, 136, 150, 156; industry, 106; legislation, 156, 161, 163; regulations, 136; reforms, 148; SAFE Banking Act, 161–162; services, 107
Belushi, Jim, 145
Biden, Joe, 4, 61, 62, 76, 77, 97, 172, 173; executive order expunging marijuana offenses, 81, 147; rescheduling, 156–157
Black (African American), 18, 122, 145; Black, Indigenous, (and) People of Color (BIPOC), 50; codes, 6–7; social equity, 49, 133–134
black market, 118
Boggs Act (1951), 7, 23
Bourne, Peter, 21–22
Brandeis, Louis, 2–3, 60, 80. *See also* U.S. Supreme Court
Brownie Mary. *See* Rathbun, Mary
bureaucracy: barriers of, 157; capacity of, 89; crisis of, 6; efficiencies of, 131
Bush, George H. W., 1, 35, 63
Bush, George W., 35, 63, 172–173; Department of Justice, 65–66; impact on implementation, 123–124; response to *Raich*, 93–94

223

California, 28, 32, 101, 123, 142, 151, 154, 165; adoption of medical program, 1, 4, 8, 13, 62–65; attorney general, 64; cannabis culture in, 130–131; early cannabis use in, 5–7; federal pressure on, 1, 93–95; governor, 62, 64; impact on other states, 45–48; Pete Wilson (governor of), 62; senator, 94; University of, 27

cancer, 20, 29, 33, 40, 42, 75, 103, 105, 145, 175–176

cannabidiol (CBD), 99, 130, 145, 163

Carter, Jimmy, 1, 63; and decriminalization, 21–22

CBS. *See* media

CBS Morning News. *See* media

Chambers, Gary, 50, 130–131

Cheech and Chong. *See* popular depictions of marijuana

Christie, Chris, 48, 83–84, 89. *See also* New Jersey

clinical research, 132, 135–136, 147, 156–157; federal government and, 92, 156–158, 163; Medical Marijuana and Cannabidiol Research Expansion Act, 147, 162–163 (*see also* Congress); medical efficacy, 40–41, 101, 134–135, 185nn60–61

Clinton, Bill, 29, 34–35, 37, 76, 93, 131; Department of Justice, 93; impact on implementation, 93, 123–124; opposition to Prop 215, 1, 63–65

Cole Memorandum (2011), 95–98, 124

Cole Memorandum (2013), 95–98, 124

Colorado, 7, 47–48, 67, 69, 125–126, 140, 145, 151; adult-use recreational, 67–69, 125–126, 140, 151; implementation of medical program, 95–96; River, 4

Congress, 21, 24, 26, 44, 60, 61, 68, 90, 144, 147–148; act of, 6; action of, 36–37, 147; activity of, 61; delegation of, 117; gridlock of, 80; hearing of, 6; leadership of, 160; media attention, 36–39;

polarization of, 80; policy proposals, 156–163; response to first medical adoptions, 65; response to *Raich*, 94–97

Congressional Cannabis Caucus, 159–160

Controlled Substances Act (CSA) of 1970, 4, 8, 13, 18–19, 46, 60, 92, 93, 149, 153, 157–161; scheduling, 4, 8, 18–20, 47, 50, 60, 64–65, 79, 81, 92, 147–148, 155–160, 165

Corzine, Jon, 83. *See also* New Jersey

data, 30, 61, 90, 107–108, 135; availability, 116; collection, 15, 107; management system, 141; opinion, 72; sets, 55, 111, 126, 171–172, 175, 210n39

decision making, 112, 114, 120

decision-making agenda, 10–11, 23, 52, 149

defiant innovation, 3–4, 14, 60, 62–63, 68, 80–81

DeSantis, Ron, 90. *See also* Florida

deschedule. *See* Controlled Substances Act (CSA) of 1970

discrimination, 6, 114, 127, 176

dispensaries, 15, 49, 64, 102, 104, 106, 118–119, 135; expansion of, 83–84, 108–114; impact of recreational policies on, 138–143; regulation of, 94–95, 98, 100, 175

District of Columbia, 1, 4, 8, 65, 69

Dogoloff, Lee, 22

Drug Enforcement Administration (DEA), 47, 92–93, 135, 147, 157–158, 163, 165

Drug Policy Alliance (DPA), 67. *See also* interest group

early adopter, 3, 15, 63–66, 78

early-adopter states, 3, 15, 73, 129, 152

ecological capacity, 62, 75, 79, 81, 86, 173; fiscal, 90–91; political, 90–91; situational, 90–91

Eisenhower, Dwight, 7

Environmental Protection Agency (EPA), 121

INDEX | 225

epilepsy, 36, 40, 42, 50, 176
equity. *See* social equity

Fallin, Mary, 68, 117–118. *See also* Oklahoma
Farm Bill. *See* Agriculture Improvement Act of 2018
Federal Bureau of Narcotics (FBN), 6
federalism, 13, 25, 33, 36–37, 39; coercive, 56, 97–98; federal-state relations, 156; fiscal, 86; mandate resistance, 61–62; role in policy diffusion, 58–60, 81–82
feedback channel: citizenship, 12, 121–122, 129–130; governance, 121, 130–131, 146; negative, 121; new problems, 120, 125–126; positive, 121–129, 136, 144, 150; power, 120, 129–130, 145, 149
Florida, 72, 90, 129; Ron DeSantis (governor of), 90
Folmer, Mike. *See* Pennsylvania
Food and Drug Administration (FDA), 27, 64–65, 100, 130, 157–158, 161, 163
Ford, Gerald, 1, 63
Fourteenth Amendment, 131
framing. *See* agenda setting

Gallup polling. *See* public opinion
gateway theory, 6, 20, 94, 155
Goggin, Malcolm, 60, 84, 86
Gonzales v. Raich, 36–37, 70, 93; *Raich*, 70, 80
gray market, 94, 121, 130, 141, 154, 157

Hansen, Jay, 19
Harrington, Al, 145
healthcare, 48, 54, 92, 99
hemp, 6–7, 80, 96, 106, 130
heroin, 1, 4, 8, 18, 63, 157

illicit market, 118, 140, 151, 154–155
Illinois, 54, 72–73, 127, 140–141
immigrants, 18; Mexican, 5–7; undocumented, 81

implementation theory, 12, 81, 85–91, 102, 116, 150
Institutional Analysis and Development Framework (IAD), 12
interest group, 25, 49, 115; Americans for Safe Access (ASA), 47, 89, 94, 102, 110, 112–114, 139; Marijuana Policy Project (MPP), 46–47, 67, 89, 104, 149; NORML, 19, 22, 27, 46, 89, 143
Iraq (War in), 40–41

Justice, Jim. *See* West Virginia
"Just Say No" campaign, 23, 45, 74, 153

Kansas, 164; Laura Kelly (governor of), 149
Kentucky, 79

laboratories of democracy, 70, 80, 91, 147–148, 165; federalism and diffusion, 58–60; origins of, 2–3
League of Nations, 8
legislative oversight, 88
LGBTQ rights, 41, 62, 122, 153, 165; same-sex marriage or marriage equality, 41, 122, 165; transgender rights, 62, 122
logic of: appropriateness, 120; consequentiality, 120
Louisiana, 6, 50, 130
Lowi, Theodore, 41
Lungren, Dan. *See* attorney general
lysergic acid diethylamide (LSD), 4, 8, 18–19, 63, 157

Mace, Nancy, 50–51, 160–161
Marihuana: A Signal of Misunderstanding. *See* Shafer Commission
Marihuana Tax Act (1937), 7
Marijuana Business Daily, 134
Marijuana Opportunity Reinvestment and Expungement (MORE) Act, 140
Marijuana Policy Project (MPP). *See* interest group
McCaffrey, Barry, 1, 29, 33, 63

MDMA (ecstasy), 8
media: ABC, 32–33; CBS, 32–33; *CBS Morning News*, 33; NBC, 32–33; *NBC News at Sunrise*, 33; *New York Times*, 7, 21, 28, 32, 37–42, 45
medical marijuana, 27, 83, 93–94, 106; acceptance (also support) of, 29, 34, 41, 74; discussions of, 137; evidence for use, 137; growing pains, 142; industry, 97; licenses for growing, 107; list of conditions, 41; permits for, 109; pressure over, 150
Medical Marijuana Advisory Board (MMAB). *See* Pennsylvania
medical research. *See* clinical research
Michigan, 54, 136, 142–143
Mississippi, 30, 72–73, 163; Tate Reeves (governor of), 30; Supreme Court, 72
Missouri, 1, 78, 155; adoption of medical program, 48, 53–54
Monson, Diane, 93
morality policy, 41, 43
Multiple Streams Framework (MSF). *See* agenda setting
Murphy, Phil, 84. *See also* New Jersey

Narcotics Control Act (1956), 7, 23
National Institute on Drug Abuse (NIDA), 33, 162
National Organization for the Reform of Marijuana Laws (NORML), 19, 22, 27, 46, 89, 143. *See also* interest group; Stroup, Keith
NBC News at Sunrise. See media
Nebraska, 67; Eric Holcomb (governor of), 62; Pete Ricketts (governor of), 30
New Jersey, 48–49, 69, 83–84, 137, 140; Chris Christie (governor of), 48, 83, 89; Jon Corzine (governor of), 83; Phil Murphy (governor of), 84
New York, 48–49, 129, 140–141; adoption of medical program, 48–49; impact of recreational program, 140–141
New York Times. See media

Ninth Circuit Court of Appeals, 93
Nixon, Richard, 46, 121; Controlled Substances Act (CSA), 8, 18–21; response to Shafer Commission, 19–21
North Carolina, 48, 118

Obama, Barack, 3, 35, 61–62, 67, 131, 150, 153; and Department of Justice, 85, 95, 124; impact on implementation, 85–86, 95–98, 124–125; policy adoption under, 73–77, 172–173; views on state adoptions, 164–166
Ogden Memo, 95, 124
Ohio, 14, 29–30, 45, 85–86, 88, 129, 150; John Kasich (governor of), 67, 104, 115; and Kenny Yuko, 29–30; policy adoption, 63, 66–67, 73, 79, 103–104; policy design, 98, 100–103; policy feedback and evaluation, 110–115; policy implementation, 107–111
Ojeda, Richard, 105
Oklahoma, 1, 54, 63, 79, 155; adoption of medical program, 66–68; backlash to medical program, 117–118; Kevin Stitt (governor of), 117–118; Mary Fallin (governor of), 68, 117; *New State Ice Co. v. Liebmann*, 2
opioid, 40–41, 43–44, 92, 105, 137, 145; epidemic, 40, 96, 137; media coverage, 40–41, 43–44; opioid-use disorder, 92; substitution, 137
Oregon, 1, 20, 65–66, 133, 155

parents' movement, 23, 153
Pennsylvania, 14–15, 19, 45, 88, 98, 161, 163; Medical Marijuana Advisory Board (MMAB), 103, 108; Mike Folmer, 50–51, 103; Mike Regan, 103; policy adoption, 50–51, 84–85, 98; policy design, 100–103, 105; policy feedback and evaluation, 110–115, 134–135; policy implementation, 107–111; Tom Wolf (governor of), 103, 115
Peron, Dennis, 28, 63

physician recommendation, 92, 101, 108
policy: adoption, 12, 14, 52, 54–55, 68, 74, 79, 82, 88, 116, 148, 156, 173; advocate, 46; agenda, 37; arena, 46, 72; alternatives, 46; bundles, 87; community, 46, 50; congruence, 72–73; context, 55; cycle, 148, 150; debate, 15, 31; design (or development), 11–12, 14–15, 45, 47, 54, 82, 85–90, 102, 107, 110, 123, 129, 150; drift, 87; diffusion, 3, 11, 13, 15, 52, 54–55, 57–60, 70, 74, 80–82, 85, 89, 91, 123, 149, 152, 156; drug, 4, 9, 88, 133; effect, 87 (or outcome, 61, 107); entrepreneur, 10, 15, 26, 41, 46, 50–51, 88–89, 166; experiment, 3, 118; expert, 34; evaluation, 12, 148; federal, 36, 61–62, 79–80, 86, 92, 136, 157; feedback (negative or positive), 15, 36, 120–121, 124–126, 136, 148; framing, 14; goal, 52, 87–88; ideas, 24–25, 46; implementation, 12, 15, 45, 54, 60–61, 82, 85–86, 88–91, 94, 107, 110, 114, 116, 148, 150; images, 32; information, 11; landscape, 4; learning, 13, 15, 56, 119, 123 (or lessons, 15, 76), 125–126; marijuana (or cannabis), 4–9, 13, 15, 32, 36, 43–44, 49–50, 55, 60, 69, 79–80, 96–98, 119–120, 123–124, 133, 136, 139, 144, 149, 156–159, 162–164; medical marijuana (or cannabis), 2–4, 27, 72, 83–84, 95, 124, 147–149; mood, 49; morality, 41–45; Policy Feedback Theory (PFT), 12, 119; policymaker, 14–16, 32, 40, 46, 54, 56, 90, 120–121, 123, 151; policymaking, 9, 11–12, 14, 24–26, 31, 41, 51, 88, 91, 119, 132, 136, 150; preferences, 30; problem, 26, 29–30, 46, 120; process, 4, 9–13, 16, 85, 88, 119–120, 123, 148–150; proposals, 24–25; regime, 3, 120, 149; salience, 91; scholars (or researchers), 3, 13, 87); solutions, 25–26, 149; state, 37–38, 92, 129; stream, 46–51; target, 40; theory, 12; tools, 87; typologies, 41; venue, 33; windows, 10, 26

popular depictions of marijuana, 29–30, 145; *Bones*, 145; *Cheech and Chong*, 1, 29–30, 145; *Dazed and Confused*, 145; *Half Baked*, 145; *Modern Family*, 145; *That 70s Show*, 145
post-traumatic stress disorder (PTSD), 40–41, 48, 103, 126
Preparing Regulators Effectively for a Post-Prohibition Adult-Use Regulated Environment (PREPARE) Act, 163
Prescription Drug Abuse Policy System (PDAPS), 126–129, 175–176, 210n39
principal-agent problems, 62
Proposition 215, 63–65
public opinion, 2, 6, 14–15, 18, 41–45, 66–67, 72, 80, 153
Punctuated Equilibrium Theory (PET), 10–11
Pushkin, Mike. *See* West Virginia

race, 6, 73, 133; presidential, 67; to the bottom, 57, 164; to the top, 57
Raich, Angel, 93
Randall, Robert, 27–29, 47, 139
Rathbun, Mary (Brownie Mary), 28, 47
Reagan, Nancy, 23, 47
Reagan, Ronald, 3, 23, 153
REAL ID Act (2005), 4, 61
recreational marijuana. *See* adult-use marijuana
Reefer Madness (1936), 6, 154
Reeves, Tate, 30. *See also* Mississippi
Regan, Mike. *See* Pennsylvania
renewable portfolio standards (RPS), 56
Reno, Janet, 63. *See also* attorney general
research. *See* clinical research
Ricketts, Pete, 30. *See also* Nebraska
Rohrabacher–Farr Amendment, 95–96
rulemaking, 115, 158

SAFE Banking Act. *See* banking
scheduling. *See* Controlled Substances Act (CSA) of 1970

Section 280E, 97, 157
seed-to-sale (n, adj), 97, 99, 139, 163
Senate Bill 119 (New Jersey), 83
Sessions, Jeff, 2, 96–98. *See also* attorney general
Shafer, Raymond, 19
Shafer Commission, 19–20; National Commission on Marihuana and Drug Abuse (1972, not alt. spelling)
Single Convention on Narcotic Drugs (1961), 8
social construction theory, 11–12, 40
social contagion, 56–57
Social-Ecological Framework (SES), 12
social equity, 100, 103, 112–114; policy feedback, 119–120; state reforms, 48–49, 133–136; federal reforms, 150–151, 159–161
South Dakota, Supreme Court, 136
Standing Akimbo, LLC v. United States, 69–70
startup, 134
Stitt, Kevin, 117–118. *See also* Oklahoma
Strengthening the Tenth Amendment through Entrusting States (STATES) Act, 161
Stroup, Keith, 19, 22, 27. *See also* National Organization for the Reform of Marijuana Laws (NORML)

tetrahydrocannabinol (THC), 103, 212n63
Thomas, Clarence. *See* U.S. Supreme Court
Thompson, Rick, 143
Traumatic Brain Injury (TBI), 41, 48
Trump, Donald, 2, 4, 35, 81, 106, 164; Department of Justice, 96–98; federalism, 61–62; policy adoption under, 74–77, 172–173

Uniform Controlled Substances Act (1970), 8, 20
United Nations (UN). *See* Single Convention on Narcotic Drugs (1961)

U.S. attorney, 93–94, 97, 116, 124; Mike Stuart, 106
U.S. Supreme Court, 72, 93, 153; and Clarence Thomas, 69–70, 80; and Louis Brandeis, 2–3, 60, 80; in media coverage, 33, 36–37, 39
Utah, 54, 73

Vermont, 8, 66; adoption of medical program, 66
veterans, 30, 40–41, 103, 105, 122, 126, 136; advocacy by, 48, 105, 126, 149; as beneficiaries of revenue, 53–54; federalism issues raised by, 146, 161, 163; medical conditions and, 40–41, 48
Vietnam (War in), 19
Viets, Dan, 53–54. *See also* Missouri

Walters, John. *See* White House Office of National Drug Control Policy
War on Drugs, 2, 16, 23, 27–28, 81, 153, 165–166; costs, 153; demonization of marijuana, 7–8; equity programs, 133–135, 148, 151; exclusion from industry, 133; origins of, 7–9, 23, 27; and legalization of adult-use recreational programs, 137; mass incarceration, 122; public opinion, 28, 137; racial disparities in policing, 27–28, 45, 49, 134
Washington (state), 1, 65, 125, 140; implementation of medical program, 94, 140
West Virginia, 14–15, 45, 85–86, 88, 98, 150; Jim Justice (governor of), 15, 105, 114–115; Mike Pushkin, 114; policy adoption, 104–107; policy design, 101–102, 105–107; policy feedback and evaluation, 110–115; policy implementation, 107–111; Rusty Williams, 105; Mike Woefel, 105
White House Office of National Drug Control Policy, 66

Xenophobia, 5

ABOUT THE AUTHORS

Daniel J. Mallinson is Associate Professor of Public Policy and Administration at Penn State Harrisburg. He has published research in journals including *Public Administration Review*, *Policy Studies Journal*, *Policy & Politics*, *Evidence & Policy*, *Public Administration Quarterly*, *State Politics & Policy Quarterly*, and the *Journal of Political Science Education*. Mallinson received the 2021 Lowi Prize from the Public Policy Section of the American Political Science Association and his PhD in political science from Penn State in 2015.

A. Lee Hannah is Professor of Political Science in the School of Social Sciences and International Studies at Wright State University in Dayton, Ohio. He has published articles in journals including *Science*, *Public Administration Review*, *Policy Studies Journal*, and *Publius*. Hannah earned his PhD in political science from Penn State in 2015.

www.ingramcontent.com/pod-product-compliance
Lightning Source LLC
Chambersburg PA
CBHW020405080526
44584CB00014B/1185